Five Weeks in the Land

Five Weeks in the Land

Bruce Ritchie

RESOURCE *Publications* · Eugene, Oregon

FIVE WEEKS IN THE LAND

Resource Publications
An Imprint of Wipf and Stock Publishers
199 W. 8th Ave., Suite 3
Eugene, OR 97401

www.wipfandstock.com

PAPERBACK ISBN: 978-1-6667-1457-9
HARDCOVER ISBN: 978-1-6667-1458-6
EBOOK ISBN: 978-1-6667-1459-3

08/27/21

This *Journal* is dedicated to all who took part in the Shoresh Study Tour in October 1996, including lecturers and guides, especially Bob Mullins, David Pileggi, and Joseph Francovic, but most of all to James, my room-mate.

Contents

Interlude

Over Jordan

Beyond Aqaba

Postscript

The Journal

THIS JOURNAL WAS WRITTEN up immediately on returning from the Middle East. I was required to submit a Study Leave Report to the Church of Scotland and decided to present it in this form. I had kept detailed notes during the five weeks of the Study Tour and Bike Ride, often writing out these in fuller form in the evenings. Prior to publication, the *Journal*, unaltered since 1996, was edited for mainly stylistic reasons, but no new material was added. David Pileggi read through a draft, and suggested corrections. James Spanner and Robin Brodie also cast their eye over the text. However, for any errors which remain I am solely responsible.

The North

— *Day 1—Arrival* —

Tuesday 8th October

FIFTY-ONE PEOPLE WERE SHOT dead in the West Bank two weeks before we flew into Israel this afternoon. Benjamin Netanyahu's new government had decided to go ahead with the opening of a new entrance to the Western Wall tunnels in Jerusalem, sparking off protests and riots leading to bloodshed. The whole issue is ultra-sensitive in the fragile relationship between Jews and Arabs. Two years ago, hope was high as Yitzak Rabin and Shimon Peres led Israel into the Oslo Peace Agreements. But, last November, Rabin was assassinated. That happened on the same night as my wife Grace and I flew into Israel to take part in a sponsored Bike Ride for the Nazareth Hospital. Netanyahu is now in office. Hamas have started a bombing campaign. Everything is changed.

The smell of hot tarmac, and the touch of soft air pierced by searing heat, hit me as I stepped onto the runway at Ben Gurion Airport. Some sensory experiences travel across the miles, and the aroma of a Jerusalem street-market occasionally hits me even in Scotland when walking past shops selling spices and olives. But the sunlight, heat, sights, and sounds at Ben Gurion spoke uniquely of Israel. It said: this is a different country, a different place, a different climate, a different people. For the next four weeks twelve of us are on Study Leave under the auspices of Shoresh, an offshoot of the Anglican Church in Israel. On Week Five, I will join one hundred Bike Riders cycling through Jordan to Aqaba, on this year's sponsored fund-raising event for the hospital.

Stella Carmel

We loaded our luggage into a minibus and travelled north from Tel Aviv, accompanied by our Shoresh guide, Bob Mullins, who had come to meet us. On the way Bob pointed out the three massive towers of a huge electricity generating plant, producing power from coal. These three towers on the Mediterranean coast are reminiscent of the three towers of Herod's palace in first-century Jerusalem. Now, as then, dominating structures symbolize power. Perhaps different forms of power for different times, but raw power nevertheless, which directly or indirectly fuels the ability to control the land.

After two hours the sunshine changed to driving rain as we neared Mount Carmel, the large massif east of Haifa, which rises 1,700 feet above sea level, and extends for over twenty miles. The name Carmel means 'vineyard of God', and in biblical times, as now, Mount Carmel was a hugely fertile plateau. It was there that Elijah undermined the credibility of the prophets of Ba'al when fire came from heaven to burn up his sacrifice while they were powerless to do the same. Today the Carmel hills are populated by numerous villages, most of them Druze communities. Bob took up the bus microphone.

"The Jews welcome the presence of the Druze in Israel," he commented, "because the Druze hate the Syrians, and it is the Syrians who control Lebanon. The young Druze go into the Israeli army with enthusiasm, and they fight like the Ghurkas of the British army, preferring cold steel to firearms. Some Druze are in southern Lebanon at this moment on active duty."

"Bob, is everyone in Israel drafted?"

"No, Israeli Jews are automatically drafted for National Service. Israeli Arabs, however, can individually choose whether to be drafted or not; but the Druze are automatically in the draft because, when the State of Israel was formed in 1948, they chose to be so. Make no mistake, the Druze are among the keenest fighters in the whole army."

I was surprised by Bob using the term 'Israeli Arabs.' "Bob, surely Arabs object to being called Israelis?"

"No. Arabs are not a homogeneous people," Bob replied. "There are Bedouin Arabs, Palestinian Arabs, Druze Arabs. Many of them have long accepted the existence of Israel and are willing to be part of it, voting in elections, serving in the army, and so on."

"But not the Palestinian Arabs?"

"No, not the Palestinian Arabs. Definitely not the Palestinians."

THE BUS DROVE ON through heavy traffic and heavier rain until we arrived at Stella Carmel, which is an Anglican Christian guest house and conference center. After dinner we convened as a Study Group for the first time and met David Pileggi, Director of Shoresh in Israel. As David spoke, a lizard scuttled across the floor. Conversation stopped. David saw our apprehension,

"It's OK Shoresh. It's only a gecko." The lizard disappeared through a crack in the wall.

"Okay Shoresh. Here you are. We have you for a whole month. Now, why have you come here? And what are you looking for on this Sabbatical?" 'Shoresh' is David's shorthand term for our group. It means *root* in Hebrew, and Shoresh Tours aim at finding the *roots* of Christian faith in their Jewish setting.

Expectations

As a group, we are on this Study Tour for a variety of reasons. Tony Hurle has the Shoresh Offices in his parish in St. Albans. Marion and Clive Porthouse from Tunbridge Wells want to learn more about the New Testament and its Jewish origins. Rosie Meikle has led pilgrimage groups to the Holy Land, but wants to study in more depth on her own. Dee Roberts is a layworker and her church has given her a sabbatical: Dee has already been in Israel since August. Alison and David Veness from St. Albans are in the same diocese as Tony and, like him, are in Israel for the first time. Alison is looking forward to 'walking in the steps of Jesus.' David feels tired and is looking for spiritual strengthening. Sharon McAuslane, a doctor from Ayr in Scotland, was on last year's Bike Ride and is keen to deepen her understanding of her faith. James Spanner, another Anglican vicar, is to be my room-mate for the month, and the Shoresh tour was recommended by Michele Guinness whom he met back in England. David and Anne Broomfield feel that the Study Tour is a unique opportunity to deepen their spiritual understanding, "in a fascinating way" as Anne put it. As for myself, under the Church of Scotland Study Leave scheme, I have accumulated enough weeks over the last few years to be able to come on this extended course, anticipating that it will enrich my own work as a parish minister in the town of Crieff in Perthshire.

Our main teachers are to be David Pileggi, Bob Mullins, and Joseph Francovic. David Pileggi is a big American with a thick mop of short, curly, black hair. Bob Mullins, another American, has been working on the Tel Bet She'an excavations since 1988. Bob is to be our archaeological guide and lecturer when we are out in the field and away from Jerusalem. Joseph Francovic is also American and specializes in Rabbinic Judaism. Joseph's task is to help us read the New Testament through first-century Jewish eyes rather than through twentieth-century western ones. His main teaching input will come in Jerusalem itself.

Joseph's wife, Janet, joined us for the evening. She has lived in Israel for two and a half years, and is an artist currently producing a series of drawings and black and white photographs for publication. Though David, Bob, and Joseph are the study-course teaching powerhouse, from time to time one-off lecturers are to be drafted in.

David summed up. "OK Shoresh. You want fresh insights into the Bible. You want to get away from reading scripture through Western eyes. You want new hermeneutical tools. You want to meet local Christians. And you want to understand the contemporary political and religious situation in Israel. Have I got it right?"

"Yes."

"Well, tell us if you want things changed. Don't wait until the end of the course and then say you wanted something different. We'll do our best. OK?" All of us were happy with that.

David continued, "Now Shoresh. There are some practical things to be aware of. First, drink water! If you wait until you feel thirsty, then that is too late. Second, our bus-drivers don't make much of a living, and, though the course fees cover official tips for the drivers, occasionally they'll take you to shops or restaurants run by relatives. This is just part of life. Now, Shoresh, there is no need to buy. Third, remember that in the Middle East being *flexible* is not enough. You have to be *fluid*! Arrangements are always being changed. Fourth, Israel has one of the world's highest ultra violet levels. So sun-hats and sun-cream are a must."

"By the way, did you know that in the Middle East a cat used to be considered as valuable as a doctor?"

We shook our heads and looked blank.

"Yea. In the long hot summers, and before fridges became available, one of the best ways of checking whether meat was still safe to eat or not was to offer it to the cat. If the cat refused the meat it was off. If the cat started to eat, it was safe! OK that's all."

Joseph broke in, "Say, did I see someone with a golf club?"

"Me," I said. I had to own up. The golf club had attracted attention all the way from Edinburgh. On the aeroplane it was banished to the cargo hold because it was classified as an offensive weapon and banned from the aircraft cabin. At Tel Aviv, as we waited for our luggage, my golf club reappeared, lying in solitary splendour on the carousel, gazed at by wondering and curious eyes before I whipped it away.

"Why on earth have you brought a golf club?"

"Well, it's a long story. Back home my friend Bob and I play golf together, and when we were talking about my sabbatical out here, one thing led to another. The outcome was that Bob challenged me to hit a golf ball off Mount Sinai."

"Mount Sinai? But the Shoresh course doesn't go to Mount Sinai!"

"No, but I go there after the Study Leave. In November I'm joining a Bike Ride down through Jordan. At the end of that there's a short expedition to Sinai. Five weeks from now."

"I see," Joseph said, though he still looked bemused.

Introductions over. Instructions handed out. We dispersed. Ready for the first expedition tomorrow.

— Day 2 — Akko —

Wednesday 9th October

THIS MORNING WE AWAKENED to the noises of a building site. The din of pneumatic drills, the thump of hammers, the rasp of saws, the sound of workers shouting to each other, came from outside our window. A worship center is being built at Stella Carmel and relays of volunteers are over from the USA to work on the church under supervision. Each day the volunteers start work at 6.00 am and stop at 3.00 pm. Most of them are from Times Square Church in New York, though not all are US citizens. At breakfast I met Cotina from Trinidad. When we arrived yesterday the group were relaxing at the coast near Haifa, about twenty miles away. One of them, Ian, jogged to the beach, intending to travel back with the rest.

"Unfortunately," Cotina told me, "no one saw Ian, and when we arrived back at Stella Carmel we were without him. So we sent a taxi back to collect Ian; but meanwhile, realising that we'd already left, he chartered his own taxi which was just as well since the taxi driver we sent had no idea what Ian looked like. Where that taxi driver got to we have no idea. He hasn't been seen again!"

"But twenty miles! Ian jogged twenty miles to the beach?"

"Yeah, he's a triathlete. After helping out here he's going on to Paris to compete in an international triathlon."

The construction group from Times Square Church are young, high-spirited, dedicated, and fun-loving. Last night when returning in the taxi none of them could remember the name Stella Carmel, and were telling the driver, "Stella Maris! Stella Maris!" Finally, they remembered it was Stella Carmel they were looking for. Then someone saw a sign, and yelled, "That's it! Route 70! I saw that yesterday! Its route 70!" "Oh no it ain't!" said another, "That's not route 70. That's the speed limit! Every road says 70!"

One of the American women had both her arms covered with tattoos. She told me she had been a real hell-raiser before conversion. The turning-point came when her grandmother spoke to her directly. "You're on your way to hell, young miss! You backsliding gal!" That made her sit up and think about what she was doing with her life and her faith. She then made a recommitment to God and has not turned back since.

IT IS IMPOSSIBLE TO be in Israel without engaging in political conversation. And already, at the breakfast table, the question of the existence of Israel as a homeland for the Jews was raised. According to Geoff, an Australian, the British take much of the blame.

"Look, the problem at the root of the whole situation in Israel today is the thinking that lay behind the Balfour Declaration by the British."

"What do you mean?"

"Well," argued Geoff, "The philosophy behind the Balfour Declaration was, 'A Land with no people, for a People with no land.' Unfortunately, that totally overlooked the fact that there were people here already, the Arabs. OK, at that time the Arabs in Palestine were mainly a nomadic people and the land looked deserted. At least to European eyes it looked deserted compared with Britain, or France, or Germany. But it wasn't really empty. So when you put yourself in the shoes of an Arab what happened was totally unjust. People in countries far away decided that their land would be taken over by the Jews. Now, how would you feel if people elsewhere decided that the USA, or England, or Scotland, would be taken over by other people? And how would you feel if international treaties were signed, and arrangements were made for that to happen, without consulting the indigenous people? You would be pretty angry!"

Not everyone was comfortable with Geoff's argument, and Vince was prepared to contest the issue.

"Well, maybe. But, look Geoff, the Bible says that in the latter days Israel will be restored to its own land. Now, that prophecy is obviously being fulfilled. Therefore, all that has happened, such as the creation of the State of Israel, *must* be part of God's plan."

Geoff shook his head. After devouring a spoonful of cereal, he came back to his point.

"Not necessarily. OK it might be God's plan to restore Israel to the land in the fullness of time. But not by these means. Surely not. The Bible says God is a God of justice, and what that means to me is that God will not use unjust means to achieve his objectives. A just God will not use unjust means."

Geoff took another mouthful before continuing. "OK prophecy says that the Jews are to return, but perhaps Israel was to come back slowly and gradually as was happening before things were accelerated by the Zionists and the creation of the State of Israel. Perhaps the impetus leading to the creation of the State of Israel was a 'forcing' of events by misguided Christians looking for the 'end times'? Remember, the Zionists who upped the pace on returning to Israel were largely secular Jews. The religious Jews didn't want to 'force' God's hand. Perhaps the people have been restored to the land out of God's time? Perhaps that's why they have been beset by problems ever since?"

Geoff presented his case strongly and cogently. This was obviously a well plowed furrow for him. Vince did not agree.

"Look Geoff, you've got to admit that the salvation of Israel against all the odds in the Six-Day War of '67, and against all the odds in the Yom Kippur War of '73 proves that God is behind the State of Israel being established. You can't deny it was a miracle that Israel survived these wars. And, as for the Zionists being secular, well, God has often used secular, unbelieving people to achieve his purposes. Like King Cyrus in the Old Testament. And, since the Jews returned the land has blossomed in a way it never did with the Arabs."

Geoff shook his head and buttered his toast with great energy.

"No. That's unfair on the Arabs. People always make this point. They keep saying that before the Jews returned the land was wasted. But remember, it wasn't the Arabs who were in control then, it was the Turks. And it was the Turks who ruined the land, not the Arabs. Moreover, if a people choose to have a nomadic lifestyle rather than a settled agricultural one, is that a sin? That doesn't make them an inferior people. That doesn't disqualify them from belonging to the land they live in!"

Vince held to his line of argument. "Look Geoff, for two thousand years the Jews have been persecuted wherever they went. The world owes them a home."

"Maybe it does," responded Geoff, "but it would have been a lot better if due regard had been taken of the people already living here. That's the problem. It's not the Jewish people's fault! The Jews have been kicked about for two thousand years. They need a home. No, the blame for the mess lies with dreamy, dopey politicians who set things up the wrong way and gave everyone a poisoned chalice."

Geoff drank his coffee. He then made his final point,

"Anyway, a commentary on the rights or wrongs of history doesn't do anything for today's problems. We have to deal with reality. The Jews are here. The Palestinians are here. Whether God's timing has been forced or not, this is how it is. God improvises within the liberty he gives human beings. The question is not, 'What happened in the past?' The question is, 'What happens next?'"

The Northern Border

After breakfast our field-trip today was to the coast, north of Haifa, which was the Phoenician seaboard in biblical times. The Phoenicians are important for biblical studies not only because they bequeathed an alphabet, but because they were traders and a sea-faring people and so had an advanced, internationalist culture which impacted profoundly on all the peoples around.

Today was the first day of our course and we were full of anticipation. Bob Mullins our field guide, plus the twelve of us, plus Joseph and Janet, bundled into the GB Tours minibus. Bob made a point of making the driver feel part of our group.

"Good morning folks, let me introduce you to our driver who is called Kareem, and comes from Nazareth."

A chorus of cheerful 'Good mornings!' came from the group, and Kareem turned round to give a broad smile and cheery wave. He is an Arab Catholic Christian, and his bus sports an array of window stickers featuring the Church of the Annunciation in Nazareth and the Church of the Holy Sepulchre in Jerusalem. Bob told us that, after driving us to various places during the day, Kareem would return each night to Nazareth, which is one hour's journey from Stella Carmel. Kareem is a quiet, polite, mannerly man.

Clive chatted to him. "Kareem, do people in Israel have a siesta at lunchtime? It's so hot already."

"No, there is no siesta. People start work at about 6.00 am and work for eight or nine hours and then go home."

The road north to the Lebanese border crossed and re-crossed a single-track railway, built by the Turks as a line from Cairo to Beirut. The railway continued in use through the British Mandate, but recently, with no diplomatic relations between Israel and Lebanon, it has been interrupted at the Israeli-Lebanese border. If relationships were to be restored between the three countries of Egypt, Israel, and Lebanon, the railway could reopen in its entirety.

On the way we saw an old Roman aqueduct which had been repaired by the Turks in the fifteenth century to bring water to Akko. I had a question for Bob

"Bob, pardon me for asking what must be a simple question, but is Akko the same as the Acre of the Crusaders?"

"Yeah, sure, same place."

The bus finally stopped at Rosh Hanikra where road and international boundary meet above steep cliffs which plunge down to the Mediterranean. At the Lebanese border the Galilean hills go right to the water. North and south of this point there is a fertile plain, so the hills which meet the sea with their high, steep, white, limestone cliffs, make a natural frontier between the two nations. Rosh Hanikra is a closed border post and absolutely no photography is allowed near any of the military installations or the border gates themselves. Israel treats the southern part of Lebanon as a security zone, with Israeli soldiers and Hezbollah guerrillas playing a deadly game of watching, tracking, day after day.

We took the cable car down the cliffs to see the caves. Centuries of salt water wave action has eroded the soft white limestone to form a network of caves and tunnels. This erosion has also revealed fragments of flint scattered through the rock. After visiting the caves, I met a young Israeli soldier on the lower path.

"Hello. Good morning."

He replied politely and in good English, "Good morning."

"I'm a visitor from the UK. Have you been there?"

"No, I have never been outside Israel."

He was a pleasant young man, and happy to be photographed. His guard duty was for one hour and his relief guard arrived as we talked. The incoming guard brought a fishing rod along with his machine-gun, and I contemplated that this particular guard station must be one of the most eagerly sought after for soldiers on active service. Any marauding Hezbollah would be considered a serious annoyance to a pleasant day's fishing.

WE LEFT THE BORDER-POINT at mid-day as the heat of the sun became overpowering. Kareem took us south to Akko where we were to have lunch, and in the bus Bob told us more about the Phoenicians, especially with regard to their alphabet:

"The first writing that we know about from anywhere is from Mesopotamia in about 3,200BC. Shortly after this, signs of writing appeared in Egypt. Both writing systems were based on the concept of a different symbol for each different object or different action, and so both systems had hundreds and hundreds of different symbols. Now, round about 1,500BC, someone in Phoenicia realized that their language (Canaanite) only had 22 *sounds*, and so, if symbols were made for *sounds*, rather than for *things*, then only 22 symbols would be needed rather than the hundreds of different pictures for different objects. So marks were made for sounds rather than objects. This was a gigantic step forward."

Bob further explained that the first symbol used for their alphabet was the symbol previously used for an ox, but now it referred to a sound. Their second symbol was the one previously used to denote a house, and so on. Greek traders to Phoenicia were influenced by this development and took the idea to Greece where the stylized Phoenician symbols were adapted into the basis of the alphabet we have today, sometimes with the symbols turned through ninety degrees. The Hebrew alphabet was also developed from Phoenician. As Bob talked we took notes and looked out at the fertile, yet cluttered countryside we were passing through. Back home we are so used to tidy fields with tidy hedges and tidy fences that the open-plan nature of life in Israel seems incomplete.

Bob continued. "Now folks, one of the consequences of having an alphabet system was the democratization of reading and writing. You see, in the complex Mesopotamian and Egyptian systems only a few people could read or write, because only specialists could know all the hundreds and hundreds of different symbols used for objects. And so, for example, although the Laws of Hammurabi were inscribed in stone in the city center for all to see, a professional scribe was required to read them for ordinary people. In contrast, the new phonetic alphabet system was more egalitarian. It was easier for more people to learn the couple of dozen symbols used for sounds. And so, in the Israel of the Old Testament, it may well be that a high proportion of the populace could read the Hebrew script. Even grave robbers could read."

"How do you know that Bob?" queried Tony.

"Well," Bob replied, "there is an inscription in an ancient tomb in Jerusalem which reads 'There is no gold or silver here, only the remains of so and so with his concubine. Do not disturb.' Look, notices like that were only worthwhile if even thieves and robbers could read. An alphabet system made that possible for more people."

Akko

We arrived in Akko for lunch. Mid-day meal for me today was Coca-Cola and falafel. I view these as safe for my stomach. As we looked around, I noticed the high number of military personnel. And yet, although in Britain, we live in a country which has unarmed police it is remarkable how soon we got used to seeing Israeli soldiers walking about with submachine guns slung over their shoulders.

"There are severe penalties for Israeli soldiers who are in uniform without their gun." Bob told us. "One day, I stopped to give a young Israeli a lift. Before the soldier got into the car he cried out, 'Oh no! My gun!' The fellow was a new recruit and had left his gun in the barrack room. He ran back to get it but unfortunately he had already been spotted by the unit commander. The result was two years in jail."

Israel is a nation prepared to be attacked at any moment. All soldiers are always on duty. No exceptions. No excuses.

As we munched our falafels an old, battered, white Mercedes taxi drew up. All taxis seem to be old, battered, white Mercedes. This one disgorged a child, a mother, and a father. The father was railing loudly against the child for some reason, with the public verbal onslaught continuing as father crossed the street, with mother and child following ten yards behind and keeping tactfully quiet. The megaphonic father and his silent family then disappeared into the shadows of a side street.

After lunch, we wandered round the Old City looking at the many stalls set out in the street. I bought some postcards from an elderly man and engaged him in conversation.

"Thank you for the cards."

"Where are you from, my friend?" he said in perfect English.

"I am from Scotland. Have you been there?"

"Oh yes! I served in the British Army," he replied. "I was in the British Army for four years in the 1940s, and I have been to Scotland many times. I have many friends near Edinburgh."

"Never!"

"Yes, we were attached to a Scottish Regiment."

"Well, well. It's good to meet you. I'm Bruce, what's your name?"

"My name is Chaim. Where in Scotland does Bruce live?"

"In a small town called Crieff, north of Edinburgh."

"Yes, I have been to Crieff with my friends many times. I was at the Cultybraggan camp and often cycled into Crieff on a day off. But I am not so well now. I have had four heart bypasses, and I do not travel anymore."

Chaim showed me the scars on his legs where veins had been taken for the operations. He told me that his pension from the British Army helped pay for the medical costs. It was remarkable to find this man in faraway Akko who was so familiar with home.

Next to Chaim's postcard stand was the entrance to the old Mosque of Akko. We went in past two gatekeepers who checked that visitors were modestly dressed. They gave skirts to the women wearing trousers, and skirts to two French soldiers who had wandered into the grounds in shorts. "You know," said Bob, "It must be confusing for visitors, trying to remember the correct protocol in holy places in Israel. In churches the custom is to remove your hat. In synagogues you put on a hat. In mosques you take off your shoes."

"By the way folks," Bob continued. "In Islam there are three basic rules concerning correct prayer posture. First, you face Mecca. Second, you kneel on a raised platform—a mat is sufficient to constitute a raised platform: hence the Muslim prayer carpets. Third, when you bow in prayer your forehead must be able to touch the ground, and so your hat cannot have a brim. That's why skull-cap head-coverings with no rim are so popular with men."

A large number of cats wandered about the courtyard of the mosque which was quiet and empty apart from us; the two French soldiers having left. The original mosque was destroyed by Napoleon in 1799 in a fit of pique after he was unable to take Akko despite a sixty-day siege. When Napoleon realized failure was inevitable he ordered all remaining ammunition to be taken inside the mosque, and then blew it to smithereens. In due course the mosque was rebuilt and took the name of Akko's most notorious ruler, the eighteenth-century Ahmed Pasha, known as Al-Jazzar, 'The Butcher.'

Bob told us Al-Jazzar's history and that he ruled by fear, particularly relishing cutting off the hands and gouging out the eyes of his victims. All his staff, even the most loyal, had some part of their body mutilated. Apparently, Al-Jazzar frequently dressed up as a common man and visited the bazaars of Acre. Any trader caught cheating was dealt with ruthlessly. In the second half of the eighteenth century it was Ahmed Pasha who was responsible for building the walls of present-day Akko, and it was these which had withstood all that Napoleon could throw at them. Bob then took us beneath the Al-Jazzar Mosque to see the remains of an old Crusader Cathedral whose vaults are now water reservoirs.

LEAVING THE MOSQUE, WE moved to the ruins of the Crusader Castle of Akko, with its bloody history. During the British Mandate the British imprisoned Zionist agitators in the old Turkish Prison which was formed out of the Castle. In 1946 some of them tried to escape by tunnelling. They broke through their prison floor, but then encountered impassable rubble and had to abandon the attempt. In fact, the rubble was filling massive Crusader halls, whose existence below the prison had been forgotten for hundreds of years. These vast halls have now been excavated, and, from their floor level, we looked up and could see, high above us, marks in the arched stone ceilings where the prisoners broke through in 1946.

In 1947 the Jewish prisoners were more successful. Dynamite was smuggled into the prison, and a hole blown in the side of the jail. Bob related that it was morning when this happened, and women were bathing in the adjacent Turkish baths. At the sound of the massive explosion the women panicked and fled for safety, some with towels, but most with nothing at all. The local people in the bazaar, already stunned by the roar of the explosion and plume of smoke, watched open-mouthed as naked women ran through the street, followed by two hundred Arab prisoners who also escaped in the melee, followed by fifty Zionist prisoners, followed by the British Police blowing their whistles and shouting "Stop! Stop!"

At Akko Crusader Castle there was an audio-visual presentation, followed by a tour with a young, bright, cheerful French guide from Toulouse. She pointed out the bats hanging from the roof, "Voila! You can see that bats love dark, humid places!" We then entered the former Crusader hospital.

"Mes amis! In the time of the Crusaders many pilgrims to the Holy Land needed hospital treatment as soon as they arrived. Sometimes because of the long, arduous trip from Europe. Sometimes because they had been attacked on the way."

The banqueting hall of the Crusader Castle had been recently excavated, and our guide speculated on who may have feasted in it.

"Mes amis! We know that Marco Polo passed through Acre on his way to China, and, given his importance, he probably breakfasted in this same banqueting hall. Now, mes amis, in this hall we see stone carvings of the lily which is found in the Holy Land. See, there they are above us."

We looked up and saw lily shapes carved in the stonework of the ceiling. Our guide continued with great enthusiasm,

"Mes amis, when King Louis came to Acre he was so fascinated by the beauty of the lily that he had it adopted as the symbol for France. This is why in France we have the Fleur-de-Lys as our national symbol. And of course it is the same representation which appears on the modern Israeli shekel."

She then led us through a long, low, dark passageway, which was dug by the Crusaders as an underground tunnel from the northern sector of the city to its southern sector. The Crusaders used it as an escape route when the castle was besieged and over-run by the Muslim armies. But not all of them made it to safety. Of those captured, the men were butchered and the women sent to harems. Those who escaped to the southern port of Acre sailed back to Europe.

The Crusaders are an embarrassment to Christendom. Though there had been Muslim provocation over generations, many Crusaders were fuelled by the superstition that if they recaptured the Holy Places they would gain merit before God. And their bloody cruelty is a blot on the landscape of Christian history. A few individual crusader kings, nobles, and foot-soldiers had deep piety and personal courage, and genuinely thought they were doing the right thing. But, collectively, they were a disaster, fighting totally unnecessary campaigns to reclaim Holy Places, and doing so through blood, slaughter, torture, and brutality. The kingdom of God is not established by the sword but by the Holy Spirit.

Haifa

Leaving Akko, we motored south to Haifa. We noticed that everywhere the land is rocky and bare. Bob explained that the barrenness is partly due to the Crusaders, who not only indulged in slaughtering the populace, but also decimated the environment. The bed-rock in Israel is all near the surface, with little top-soil. The Crusaders, plus the Turks who followed them, cut down thousands upon thousands of trees without a thought to replanting, losing so much top-soil. The Crusaders used wood for building. The Turks used wood to fire Turkish baths, build railway lines, and construct more buildings. Before the Crusader and Turkish occupations, the maritime plains of northern Israel were wooded, lush, and fertile. Modern Israel is trying to reforest the land as the first stage towards creating a stable soil base for the future. Bob drew our attention to the palm trees growing by the roadside.

"Now folks, in Israel the date-palm is traditionally known as the Tree of Life because every part of it is useful. The dates can be eaten. The leaves can be used for roofing (or at least they used to be). And the trunk provides wood. Some Jews think that the date-palm was the Tree of Life in the Garden of Eden, which is a far cry from the apple tree in our books of Bible illustrations."

Bob then pointed out clumps of eucalyptus. He told us that eucalyptus trees grow all over Israel, even though they are not native to the country. What happened was that the Jezreel and Hula valleys were traditionally swampy areas with mosquitoes and malaria until, in modern times, the Hula valley was drained, a process partly made possible through Australian Jews bringing eucalyptus trees into Israel and planting them where the ground was marshy. The trees have now spread widely.

"Some scholars say that Capernaum, just south of the Hula valley, was particularly vulnerable to malaria," added Bob. "And they speculate that Simon Peter's mother-in-law was in fact suffering from malaria when Jesus healed her. At that time malaria was fatal. The text says that she was 'sick with a fever', and the fever could well have been malaria."

The road from Akko to Haifa skirted round the north-west corner of the Mount Carmel range. Since Carmel is the first mountain at the Mediterranean coast then rain clouds, which form over the sea, break on its higher slopes, giving Carmel the reputation in Old Testament times as the mountain which brings the storm. That was why the prophets of Ba'al saw Mount Carmel as a holy site, since the pagan deity Ba'al was a fertility god who rode on thunder clouds with bolts of lightning in his hands. The Old Testament kings, David and Solomon, whose power bases were further south, forged trading links with King Hiram of Tyre. However, alongside any economic benefits which these trade agreements brought, came concomitant dangers through contact with paganism. Consequently, paganism made severe inroads into the culture of Israel especially in the north.

"Jezebel," said Bob, "was Ahab's Queen. But she was from a pagan people. And it has to be admitted that Jezebel was an effective proselytizer for her faith. You see, polytheism was an attractive option for the Israelite people because they often felt that their austere, monotheistic religion was lacking color. The God of Israel was a single Deity, whereas Jezebel offered many gods. The God of Israel gave the Ten Commandments, whereas the gods of polytheism promised sexual and agricultural fertility. Jezebel's gods offered exciting, colorful, immoral ceremonies and celebrations. Jezebel's gods gave you a choice. You could choose your favorite god rather than be restricted to only one with no alternatives! And so, on the northern border of Israel, far from the seat of religious and political power, it was easy for the people to drift."

WE ENTERED THE OUTSKIRTS of Haifa and Bob switched to the contemporary situation. "Now folks, in Haifa Jew and Arab get on well. But Haifa is not the same as Jerusalem. Because Jerusalem is a Holy City for three faiths, it has unique tensions. A popular saying is: Haifa is the City of Work; Tel Aviv is the City of Pleasure; and Jerusalem is the City of Religious Study. Did you know that Muslim sermons are monitored by the Israeli authorities to gauge the mood of the people? OK, Haifa is relatively trouble free and has a long tradition of tolerance. But it's not like that elsewhere."

We stopped at a panoramic viewpoint overlooking the sea-front. Below us, the Mediterranean sparkled blue in late afternoon sunshine, and fat oil-tankers lay at anchor off the harbour from which, centuries ago, the Apostle Paul sailed on his missionary journeys. The viewpoint was thronged with tourists from all over the world, and an enterprising trumpeter was making a good living playing for each group. He scanned the groups, made an educated assessment where the people came from, and played accordingly. He played really well, with loads of expression in his music. Italian arias, such as 'O Solo Mio', were followed by 'The Battle Hymn of the Republic', 'The Marseillaise', 'Grandfather's Clock', and even 'God save the Queen'! I tried to get a good angle for a photograph.

"Are you a Protestant?" he asked.

"Yes."

So he played several verses of 'Amazing Grace'. He truly earned the shekels I threw into his trumpet case as payment for the music and the photograph. A musician with real talent.

Joseph and the Rabbis

Back at Stella Carmel, we got to know each other better over the evening meal. Rosie Meikle is a vicar's wife from Surrey, though she herself is Irish.

"I used to live in Scotland," she said.

"Oh, whereabouts?"

"In the late 1960s I went to Hawick in the Scottish borders to teach at Craigmount Girls' School. It was at Minto near the village of Denholm. I ended up marrying the Episcopal curate at Hawick."

"You know Rosie," I said, "I was brought up at Jedburgh, just ten miles from Hawick. We went to Hawick High School for the senior years of our schooling, and we passed through Denholm every day. Then, when I was a student, I got a summer job planting fir trees in the grounds of the old Craigmount school!"

"The school is closed now, isn't it?"

"Yes, by the early 1970s it was abandoned. It's been pulled down since."

AFTER THE MEAL BOB gave a lecture about the physical geography of the Holy Land, relating it to Scripture. When he was finished most of the group drifted off to their rooms, but Tony, James, Rosie, and I stayed on to chat with Bob and Joseph.

"I have big problems teaching evangelical Christians how to read scripture through Rabbinic eyes," said Joseph. "But I strongly believe that the Mishnah shows us how Rabbis such as Jesus taught and understood themselves. And it is impossible to get into Jesus' mind-set unless the Rabbinic writings of that time are studied."

"You know," he continued, "conservative evangelicals concentrate so much on the literal text that they miss the method of interpreting the text which existed at the time. Now, let me give you an example of Rabbinic exegesis. In Ecclesiastes 10 verse 18, we have the text *'Through sloth the roof sinks in, and through indolence the house leaks.'* Now, what we have to realize is that the Rabbis were committed to finding deep meaning in the text. In particular, everything was related to the Sinai experience where God met His people and gave the Torah. So how did they interpret this verse in the light of these principles?"

"Well, first, they said, 'The word 'sloth' means 'laziness' but laziness in what?' Well, in the Sinai desert the people argued nearly all the time. They argued with each other. They argued with God. They argued with

Moses. On this basis the Rabbis concluded that 'laziness' means 'laziness in arguing.' Now, if you are lazy about arguing, you must be agreeing with each other. So to be lazy in arguing meant that the people were of one mind, and had unity."

"Second, what did the text mean by the phrase 'the roof sinks in'? Well, if the roof sinks in, the beam-layer has to come to the house. Who is the beam-layer? He is the Lord. So, putting these two things together, the conclusion the Rabbis came to was that the verse meant: *When God's people stop arguing and have unity, the Lord will come down to them.* This, of course, is what the Rabbis say happened at Sinai. And this is why, in the New Testament, Luke emphasises that at Pentecost the people were in unity, and therefore the Spirit of God came down amongst the people."

This type of textual interpretation took a bit of swallowing. And we were not at all sure about Joseph's approach. James spoke up.

"But Joseph, that interpretation is the opposite to the plain meaning of the text! To get to your conclusions you have to know what your goal is before you set out!"

"No, no," replied Joseph. "The point is that the Rabbis didn't see things like that. And we have to get into *their* mind-set. You see, for them everything related to Torah. All biblical texts were regarded as multi-faceted jewels shedding new light on Torah. You turn the text round. You turn it upside down. You look at it in different ways. The point is that the New Testament writers had this background as well. That's how they thought."

We were still not convinced, and Tony intervened. "But, Joseph, that's just using texts as illustrations of truths you know already from elsewhere."

"Not really Tony. Again, the Rabbinic mind-set is all-important. The texts all come under the rigour of shedding light on Torah. Now, you can see why conservative evangelicals find this an alien world. But this is the world of the New Testament. You see, the Rabbis never worried about Scriptural consistency. If they found an apparent inconsistency they re-joiced because it gave more scope for interpretation! More interpretation means more Torah! And more Torah means more blessing!"

We puzzled over this radically different approach.

"My faith is rooted in the encounter with God," said Joseph. "This is what Scripture is all about. Encounter. This is why I find renewal groups the most receptive to reading scripture through middle-eastern eyes, be-cause renewal groups have a high view of scripture *allied* with emphasis on an encounter experience. You see, if our theology, or if our method of interpreting the Bible, is not doing justice to God, then either we have to change our theology or we have to change our interpretative method. We can't change God."

Joseph went on to expound why he believed that all Churches should train their ministers in Israel. Israel is the only place where students can come to terms with the Rabbinic background to the New Testament. "Look, the Mormons already do major training in Israel. If they can do it, why can't the mainstream Churches? But the problem behind training pastors in Israel is not financial, it is ideological and theological. It raises the whole Jewish question. It raises so many questions about the relationship of the Church to Israel through the centuries. So it doesn't happen. But things are changing."

—Day 3—Mount Carmel—

Thursday 10th October

WE ROSE AGAIN TO the noise of construction workers building the new worship center, and at breakfast I met Andrea and Claudia who are part of the volunteer group from Times Square Church in New York. Andrea is bright, bouncy, and cheerfully talkative.

"Gee Bruce! We had a real busy day yesterday. It was real hard!"

"Andrea, how did you find out about this project? And why are nearly all of your volunteers female?"

"Well Bruce, some months ago the need for help at Stella Carmel was announced in our church, and people were encouraged to sign up. And then, at the church service on the Sunday before we left to come over to Israel our Pastor asked all the volunteers to stand up. The congregation was amazed to see that nearly all of us were women! Our Pastor spoke real direct to the congregation. 'Folks' he said, 'Look at our volunteers! These women, they gonna be buildin', they gonna be diggin', they gonna be bricklayin' an' pick-axin'. Where are you men! Come on men! Can only women do the work?' Well, you know Bruce, today we got a fax from the USA saying that five more men have signed up for the next group! Praise the Lord!"

The design of the worship center is to be symbolic of Elijah's triumph. The floor will be green like the grass of Mount Carmel. There will be twelve stones like the twelve stones Elijah set up during the contest with the prophets of Ba'al. And light will come from the roof, reminiscent of the fire coming down from heaven. The function of the worship center is to be a meeting place and a refuge, or safe haven, for Messianic Jews and Arab Christians. Over one hundred and fifty already come each

Shabbat. At present they meet in the Stella Carmel dining-room and use every possible ante-room and corridor for teaching groups.

AFTER BREAKFAST I WENT over to the site. James, from New York, was busy sawing wood to make battens for the foundations. His sleeveless, red-checked shirt revealed heavily tattooed arms. His luxuriant long hair was brushed back like a 1950s' rock and roll fan. He looked up and smiled with a broad grin. He shouted over to me, "Hi! Praise the Lord! What a glorious morning!"

Coming from Britain with its generous helping of grey clouds, grey skies, and grey weather, I agreed enthusiastically.

"I'm going to the UK in December, Bruce! And that's due to the Lord providing!"

"In what way James?"

"Well Bruce, when I came over to Israel to work as a volunteer I was given a six-month visa. That was OK. But the rules have changed since I arrived, and all visas are now limited to three months. Well, before the change of rules I had already been praying about the possibility of going to England, and, you know Bruce, the day after I had been praying real hard about this, it all worked out."

"Oh? How?"

"Well Bruce, one of my workmates here is called Gary. And Gary had been phoning his parents back in England, and he told me that his folks insisted that I come and stay with them for Christmas. Now, it was just after they invited me for Christmas that the Israeli government changed the regulations about visas. So I would have had to be out of the country for two weeks anyway, before returning to work here for another three months. The Lord has been really good to me!"

"Will you see more of the UK or are you staying with Gary's folks all the time?"

"Bruce, I'm goin' up to Scotland as well."

"Oh, whereabouts James?"

"I dunno. Say Bruce, have you met the Stella Carmel manager, John Stevenson?"

"Not yet."

"Well, John has a sister in Scotland. I'm gonna' to stay with her family for a while."

The Place of Burning

Today our field-trip was to the monastery on Mount Carmel at a site known as 'The Place of Burning' since it commemorates the triumph of Elijah over the prophets of Ba'al. We went by bus most of the way, but stopped a mile short of the monastery in order that we could walk over the undulating plateau and get the feel of the land. The sun blazed down as we picked our way across the summit terrain, which was covered with rocks, stones, bushes, olive-trees, and prickly-pear. Bob, our ever informative guide, filled us in with background information.

"Folks, the native born Israeli describes himself as a prickly pear plant: hard, tough, and spikey on the outside; but soft and tasty inside! Now, the prickly pear was introduced from South America in the sixteenth century. At that time the Arabs still dwelt in or around the ruins of the biblical towns and villages, and the prickly pear was planted wherever they lived. So this means that any place where there are clumps of prickly pear there is also a high probability that it may have been the site of a village in biblical times."

Below the numerous clumps of bushes and piles of rocks and stones the distinctive red soil of Mount Carmel was clearly evident. The redness of the soil gives the name, *Terra Rosa*.

"See all these stones, folks." said Bob, "They are everywhere. Well, the farmers on Mount Carmel deliberately don't gather stones from the fields. This is because the dew condenses on the stones each morning, and the moisture runs down into the soil. In the absence of rain for months on end dew is vital for growth."

"An old legend says that, after Elijah's victory over the prophets of Ba'al and Ashtoreth, Elijah was walking over the fields of Mount Carmel when he saw three melons. Elijah asked the farmer if he could eat one, but the farmer said 'No!' Elijah said, 'May your melons be turned to stone!' And that, according to legend, is why Mount Carmel is covered with so many stones!"

A shepherd, herding his sheep and goats, beckoned us as we walked by. Although he spoke little English he was cheery, friendly, and keen to communicate. His name was Yusuf, and he emphasized proudly that he was a Druze. Yusuf encouraged us to photograph him. He was an excellent subject with his sun-tanned face, his red-chequered Arab scarf over his head, and strong character written deep into his features. After we took the photographs Yusuf politely suggested that we might give him five shekels. Unfortunately, quite genuinely we had no money because our hand-baggage was on the minibus which had gone on ahead. We apologized to Yusuf, and he smilingly and toothlessly accepted this reverse.

Arriving at the monastery we sat in the shade of some olive trees as Bob led us in a high-level Bible study on Elijah which was both academic and devotional. The Monastery of Muhraqah is famous as the traditional site of the victory of Elijah over the false prophets, and is situated on a spot traditionally thought to have been where he offered his sacrifice to God. This is at the north-east corner of the Mount Carmel range, overlooking the plain of Esdraelon.

The dramatic events of Elijah's ministry took place in the time of Queen Jezebel, daughter of the King of Tyre. It was she who introduced Ba'al worship into the northern kingdom after her marriage to Ahab, King of Israel. Elijah resisted the apostasy, and persuaded King Ahab to assemble both the people and the prophets of Ba'al on Mount Carmel where he challenged them to a contest. The prophets of Ba'al failed to invoke fire from heaven to burn up their offering, whereas Elijah had astounding success. After his triumph, Elijah had the false prophets seized and taken down to the river Kishon for execution.

"But Mount Carmel is a pretty big place," said Anne. "You told us that it extends for twenty miles. So how do we know this is where it happened? Or is it just a place chosen at random?"

"Well," replied Bob, "various features favor this site as being the place. OK, 100 percent certainty is impossible, but three crucial pieces of evidence point here. First, even in drought conditions a permanent spring of water exists just below the ridge on which the monastery is built, and a source of water is essential for any site fulfilling the conditions described in the Elijah story. Second, the Mediterranean Sea is in view, and again this is crucial because Elijah's servant looked out to sea and saw a cloud 'no bigger than a man's hand.' Third, the Kishon brook where the Ba'al prophets were executed is nearby at the foot of the ridge, and can be easily seen from the roof of the monastery. We cannot find another location on Mount Carmel which fulfils these conditions, so the probability that this is the place where Jezebel's priests were routed is pretty high."

"Jezebel was a real powerful woman. Make no mistake about that. And the people were terrified of her. Even after his great triumph Elijah was still frightened enough to flee to Mount Sinai a couple of hundred miles away."

Joseph broke in. "Did you know that the writers of the Hebrew Bible changed her name?" We shook our heads.

"Yep. They changed her name in order to get revenge. Her original name was Jeze-BUL which means 'where is the Ba'al?', but they changed it to Jeze-BEL which means 'Where is the rubbish?'!"

Bob consulted his thick folder of notes which he carried everywhere, and told us that the site of the present chapel, with its high statue of Elijah, was formerly occupied by an oratory which fell into ruin.

"Folks, Mount Carmel was a religious mountain for the peoples of the area even before the Israelites invaded the land. It was a sacred place in the Canaanite era. During Canaanite times, it was common for people to gather and worship in places where there were groves of trees, because groves were considered to be holy places. However, if you lived in a city and had no groves of trees available, a pole could be used to symbolize a tree. This is how Ashtorah-Poles originated, and these poles evolved in significance to become powerful symbols of pagan religious practice."

LUNCH TODAY WAS AT a roadside cafe a couple of miles from the monastery. Adjacent to the cafe a trader had set up a craft stall.

"All these things made by my family." he told us proudly.

We were amazed: "Really? Everything? By your family?"

"Yes indeed, my family. My family make all of these things."

We then discovered that by 'family' he meant all the Druze Arabs. All Druze belong to one family, the Druze family. We have to learn what words mean in this culture.

Dalyat El Carmel

After lunch we went to the Druze village of Dalyat El Carmel, which is typical of many other Arab towns in Galilee. It has busy streets and concrete buildings, with many of the houses sporting steel reinforcing rods sticking up from their roofs, ready for the next storey to be added when needed and when money is available. Goods and wares were stacked on the pavement outside the shops, and there was a general air of relaxed, quiet disorder. The Druze are a friendly people who feel comfortable in Israel. I spoke to a man with a thick, greying, handle-bar moustache, who was dressed in a white shirt and white gown, and sitting on a white plastic chair outside his shop. He was eager for conversation and opened his hands in an expressive welcoming gesture as he talked.

"My name is Halabi and I own all of this." With a sweep of his arm he indicated the whole side of the street which included several shops.

"I am, what do you say, retired? And now my oldest son runs the businesses."

A young boy came along and sat on a chair beside him.

"This is my grandson. When he grows up he will have the business."

I photographed Halabi and his grandson as they sat side by side in matching white chairs on the veranda of his property. Halabi seems to be a common name in Dalyat El Carmel. There were two brass name-plates, on either side of the main street, mentioning two Dr. Halabis, both dental surgeons. Some of us wandered into the town's camera shop which was well stocked with modern film, and which also had a selection of second-hand classic cameras of thirty and forty years ago gathering dust in the window.

The Druze have a distinctive style of clothing. The women wear a white headpiece and a black dress. The men wear white head-dresses and often sport handle-bar moustaches like the one Mr. Halabi had. Bob told us about their religious philosophy.

"Folks, the Druze believe in reincarnation."

"Like the Hindus?"

"No, not in the same way. The Druze believe that their reincarnation will always be as a person, not as another creature as in Hinduism. An outsider cannot be converted to become a Druze, but a Druze can choose to be a secular or religious. If a man becomes a religious Druze, he enters a system of secret teaching which introduces him to the Druze mystery religion and advances him through different levels. All Druze religious knowledge is contained in six volumes of writings. These are closely guarded and total secrecy is observed regarding their content. When a man reaches one of the higher levels, he wears a turban. In fact, religious Druze have distinct clothing, but non-initiated Druze do not wear any special gear."

"Bob, where did the Druze come from?"

"The Druze sect originated in Egypt in the eleventh century as a reform movement in Islam, but when they were persecuted they fled north, and in particular to remote areas which were normally found high in the hills. Today Mount Carmel is as far south as the Druze live."

After leaving Dalyat El Carmel Kareem took the bus on a road which wound down from the Mount Carmel plateau to the Jezreel Valley. On the way we saw the rusty wreckage of an oil derrick lying in an abandoned quarry, and wondered what that was doing there.

Bob grinned. "Well folks, some years ago a Mr. Hill, a Texas Oil tycoon, was reading his Bible when he came across a text in Deuteronomy chapter three which says '*And the tribe of Asher will bathe their feet in oil.*' Mr. Hill concluded this meant that huge oil reserves lay under the land allocated to Asher, one of the twelve tribes when Israel conquered the land. So Mr. Hill came over here and spent years drilling for oil around Mount Carmel until he gave up."

"And was this the area given to Asher?"

"No, not at all. You see Mr. Hill was mistaken on three counts. First, the tribe of Asher did not live here; they were given land further north. Second, the oil referred to in Deuteronomy was olive oil, not heavy hydrocarbons. And third, the text in Deuteronomy simply means that the tribe of Asher will be blessed in a land of plenty. Now, to his credit, Mr. Hill's motives were unselfish. He believed that when he discovered oil in Israel then the oil could be given freely to the nations round about and bring universal peace, blessing and harmony between Jews and Arabs!"

All that now remains of Mr. Hill's misguided, if possibly well-intentioned, enterprise is a rusty derrick on Mount Carmel's lower slopes.

Beit Shearim

Late in the afternoon we visited Beit Shearim. This was a holy burial place for the Rabbis, and because everything Rabbinic is Joseph's territory, he took his turn at tuition, filling us in on Beit Shearim's significance. Joseph started with a question.

"Folks, what's the most significant date for Jews after Jesus' death?"

"70AD?"

"Why that date?"

"Because in 70AD the Jewish Revolt failed and the Jerusalem temple was destroyed?"

"You know," said Joseph, "what I find is that students nearly always focus on the events of 70AD. But the real blow to Judaism was not in the year 70, but in the failure of the Bar Kokhba revolt of 132 to 135. It was after that revolt that the Emperor Hadrian outlawed Judaism and did all in his power to wipe every trace of their religion and culture from the face of the earth. OK, the ban was lifted after Hadrian's death, but a fundamental dispersion had taken place, a process only reversed in the last one hundred years. And it was as part of this dispersion that the Rabbis moved from Judaea to Galilee, with Beit Shearim becoming their burial place."

"Were all of them buried here?"

"No, just the most important."

The Beit Shearim graveyard is on the slopes of a wooded hill, with a village above. Catacombs tunnel into the hillside, and, at the extreme rear of the main chamber of one catacomb is an ancient representation of the Temple Menorah. Bob became really excited about this: "Folks, very few Menorah representations like these exist from pre-Byzantine times. One is on a wall in Jerusalem. One is on Hadrian's arch in Rome. There is this one here in Beit Shearim. And very few others."

All the tombs are cut into the rock, and, surprisingly, some of the artwork features animals. Sharon was puzzled,

"Why do we have this type of art work here?" she said. "I thought that real-life art was forbidden in Judaism because of the Second Commandment?"

"Hey," said Joseph, "that's a good question! Representational art in Judaism! How can that be? Well, two reasons can be given for the appearance of some real-life art at Beit Shearim. The first possibility is that there was a liberalization of culture. The second possibility is that the Second Commandment was seen as having the specific purpose of guarding against pagan influences. And so, if it were felt that threats from pagan cultures were less intense in a closed Rabbinic community then it was not a live issue. But I don't know the reason. These are simply two possibilities."

"I favor the second," said Bob. "In the Mishnaic and Talmudic periods, Jewry was unconcerned with idolatry. Idolatry was not seen as a real threat, and so the Rabbis adopted a more liberal approach to the use of ornamental symbols."

As we wandered round the catacombs an attendant came to close the doors. Most of the catacombs are approached through a wide courtyard and feature heavy stone doors which are exact replicas in stone of wooden doors, complete with representations of hinges, iron clasps, and door-knockers carved into the stone. In spite of their great weight the perfectly balanced doors turn smoothly on their hinges. An information board lists some of the inscriptions which are found in the tombs. One is: *'Anyone who shall open this burial, upon whomsoever is inside, shall die of an evil end.'* (written in Aramaic). Another is: *'Good luck in your resurrection'* (written in Greek). Cats abounded everywhere.

The Messianic Community

Tonight was our last night at Stella Carmel, and John Stevenson, its director, met us after supper to talk about his work. John is an ordained minister in the Anglican Church, and he and his wife Jane have come to Stella Carmel on a four-year contract. There are five full-time members of staff under them. John told us that CMJ (*The Church's Mission Among Jewish People*) bought Stella Carmel thirty years ago.

"You must be wondering," John said, "how our impoverished organization could afford to buy a place like this. Well, it was going cheap because a murder had taken place in the house when it was a private residence. The cook had murdered the owner, and the owner's widow was at a loss to know what to do because no one wanted to buy a house which had been the scene of a killing! CMJ had no such fears, and bought it at a ridiculously low price."

John sees the main purpose of Stella Carmel as enabling the Messianic community to grow, and described to us what he meant by this.

"CMJ gives 'protection' for Messianic Jews who otherwise have an extremely hard time," he explained. "Messianic believers suffer extremes of prejudice. Often they cannot get jobs. Or they may lose their current jobs because of their faith. Officially there is complete religious tolerance in Israel. But the reality on the ground is quite different."

Marion asked, "If that is so, then why is Stella Carmel allowed to exist?"

"Well," John responded, "our presence here predates the State of Israel, so we have a right to be here. Of course, we also bring foreign money into Israel, which the government likes. But let me tell you something very wonderful. One of the amazing things that happens here is that, on Shabbat, Arab believers in Jesus come to worship with Jewish believers in Jesus. In fact, the assistant pastor at Stella Carmel is an Arab Christian. And so we see Stella as a place of meeting and reconciliation."

"Are there many Jewish Christian believers?"

"No. Unlike exaggerated claims made in the West by some Christian publications, the number of Messianic believers in Israel is extremely small. They are tender plants in a hostile environment. They need a lot of nurture, a lot of care, and this is what Stella Carmel is all about."

"Is there a Christian work in Haifa?"

"Oh yes," replied John. "There is a Drug Centre in Haifa called 'The House of Victory', and it has strong links with the David Wilkerson Teen Challenge Centres in New York. Some of the Americans went to Haifa yesterday afternoon and to a service at the Drug Centre."

This evening I wore my kilt. People keep asking which tartan it is. Shamefully, I have to confess that I don't know. I borrowed it from my friend Bob and, before leaving home, I tried to find out what the tartan is but without success. One of the young Americans who led devotions this morning met me in the corridor and said, "Gee! It's smart! It's really smart!"

—Day 4—Nazareth—

Friday 11th October

TRAVELLING BY BUS IN Israel creates an ideal opportunity to observe the vibrancy of this busy, industrious, young nation. Huge pipelines are being laid. Giant earthmoving machines are commonplace. Building construction is everywhere. Massive roadbuilding is underway. Wide highways are being created. The Jewish people have a shared dramatic history which has molded them into what they are today. The memory of ethnic persecution through Diaspora, Pogrom, and Holocaust, plus the immediate dangers of the present time make the Israeli populace fiercely patriotic. Everywhere, young men and women are seen doing their National Service, which experience intensifies a shared philosophy amidst the disparities of their natural argumentative culture. Within the framework of the scaffolding of this Jewish State, lives the indigenous Arab population with their own thoughts, their own history, their own culture, and their own philosophy, hopes, dreams, viewpoint, and attitude.

Sepphoris

This morning we were taken to Sepphoris, near Nazareth. This was Herod Antipas' provincial capital in Galilee. On its hillside were masses of prickly pear plants. Bob pointed to the far side of the valley where we saw houses and buildings clustered on the far slopes.

"Look, you can see Nazareth over there. Nazareth is only three, maybe three and a half miles, from Sepphoris. So, in fact, Jesus grew up right next door to Herod Antipas' seat of power. Nazareth was not 'out in the sticks' as some authors have written. OK, in the time of Jesus,

Nazareth was small, maybe only a population of about four hundred, but Sepphoris' proximity, plus the nearby busy trade-routes of the Galilee, meant that Nazarenes met numerous foreigners, and were well aware of the contemporary political climate."

Joseph came in on the discussion, explaining that Sepphoris was the main center for Rabbinic learning immediately after the Bar Kokhba rebellion. He also corrected the pronunciation. "'Sepphoris' is the Greek pronunciation, but the Hebrew says 'Tzippori' which means 'bird', because for a traveller the town of Sepphoris looked like a bird on a hill." Joseph stressed it was at Sepphoris where the Mishnah went through its final editing, with the Mishnah providing rich insights into the mind-set of people like Jesus and Paul.

"What's the Mishnah, Joseph?"

"Sorry, I should have explained. The Mishnah is the written account of the Oral tradition."

"Is there an English translation?"

"Sure, Danby's translation is still highly acclaimed by Jewish scholars despite it being quite old now." Joseph held up his copy of Danby's Mishnah.

"Remember folks, what I said yesterday. For Judaism, the heaviest blow was not the fall of the Temple in 70AD, but the failure of the Bar Kokhba counter-revolt of 135 to 137. Now, yesterday we stressed the effect of Hadrian's anti-Jewish edicts after the rebellion, but there was another reason why the failure of that uprising was so traumatic."

"Remember, the Temple had fallen before. It fell at the end of the first Temple period when the Babylonians wrecked it; and yet the nation had risen again after seventy years of the Babylonian exile. So when the Second Temple fell in 70AD, the people believed that history would repeat itself, and that the Lord would restore His people after seventy years. But when the revolt of 132 to 135 was routed, these hopes turned to dust. This was why the people were totally shattered. Psychologically, this was a far heavier blow than the events of AD 70, because the restoration did not happen when it was expected."

"So the Rabbis came here after the Bar Kokhba Revolt?"

"Well, after 70AD the center of Jewish learning moved from Jerusalem to Yarne, which is present day Tel Aviv. Then from Yarne they moved to Lower Galilee, which is this area. But after 135 the Emperor Hadrian outlawed Judaism and it became punishable by death to practice the faith. Make no mistake, the years under Hadrian were years of terrible

suffering for Jews. However, following Hadrian came Antonius who re-
pealed Hadrian's draconian measures, and Antonius was known as the
'beloved' by Jewish people. Once again Judaism could flourish publicly in
places like Sepphoris and Tiberias. Rabbi Judah the Prince was the domi-
nant figure at this time. However, even during the period of Hadrian's
laws rabbis still functioned in quiet areas like this away from Jerusalem.
It all depended on the attitude of the local Roman official."

"Was Sepphoris central for a long time?"

"Sepphoris flourished as the Rabbinic center in the second and third
centuries AD. Gradually, the center of learning moved to Beit Shearim
where it lasted from 200 to 400AD. Sepphoris, therefore, is particularly
important for the study of Jesus."

"Look folks," Joseph emphasized, "Jesus' thought was not Greek
thought. Jesus was not of the school of Aristotle. Like all native Jews,
Jesus did not use abstract concepts. Jesus was of the school of the Sages
who used parables, pictures, and puns."

"Sages?"

"Yes, sages. They were only widely called 'rabbis' as a collective term
after 70AD. We should really call Jewish teachers of Jesus' day 'sages.'"

The excavated ruins of Sepphoris reveal a lower and an upper city. A
large square building dominates the hill, which was built by the Crusaders as a watchtower, using stones from the Roman period buildings. At
the end of the Ottoman period the Bedouin ruler of the Galilee, Dahr
El-Omar, rebuilt the tower for use as a schoolhouse and it was renovated
again during the British Mandate. It then served as the village schoolhouse until 1948, when the village was flattened during the Israeli War of
Independence.

After Joseph's talk, I wandered around on my own until a man with
a gun appeared.

"What group are you with?"

"A Study Group from Britain."

"Where are they?"

"In the building with our guide."

"You are not with them?"

"No, I wanted to take some photographs."

He said no more. But neither did he go away. He loitered nearby and
watched me suspiciously. On the principle that it is unwise to displease a
man with a gun, I rejoined the others.

The construction of the residential area of Sepphoris began during the Hasmonean period in the century before Jesus' birth, and Sepphoris continued as an up-market place to stay until the end of the Byzantine period. But before Jesus started his public ministry Herod Antipas moved his regional capital from Sepphoris (in the Galilean hills,) to Tiberias (by the Sea of Galilee.) This was for several reasons. First, Tiberias was warmer all year round. Second, it had hot thermal springs. Third, it was a new city with a Graeco-Roman outlook and Graeco-Roman habits. Yet, despite losing the presence of Herod's court, Sepphoris remained a desirable place to stay.

EARLY EXCAVATIONS AT SEPPHORIS uncovered a paved street flanked by houses, and beneath these houses and courtyards have been discovered water cisterns and storage rooms. Mikvah ritual baths and beautiful artwork have also reappeared, all evidence of the luxurious lifestyle of the Jewish population which lived in the area at the time. On one corner of the site a villa has been reconstructed around an original floor mosaic which features Dionysius, the Roman god of wine and pleasure. The central panel of the mosaic shows a drinking competition between Hercules and Dionysius. Bob pointed out that a three-sided (triclinium) seating arrangement was in place around the mosaic.

"Folks, the triclinium here is very obvious. What is interesting is that no archaeological excavations in the old Jewish quarter of Jerusalem have ever revealed a triclinium. None at all. This is why I reckon that, at the Last Supper in Jerusalem, Jesus and the disciples reclined at several small round tables and did not form a triclinium arrangement for the meal."

This surprised us, but Joseph agreed with Bob. Joseph pointed out that much New Testament scholarship has accepted the Roman triclinium model. In Joseph's view, that is simply another example of scholars reading New Testament culture through Latin, Western eyes. Bob and Joseph may be correct. But, if so, they are in direct disagreement with Jim Fleming who runs the Biblical Resources Centre at Tantur outside Jerusalem. Fleming has written books and issued videos on the context of New Testament images and strongly favors the triclinium arrangement for the Last Supper.

"Bob," I interrupted, "last year, at the close of the Bike Ride, our group attended one of Jim Fleming's Passover meals, and what he said about the seating arrangement of Jesus and the disciples at a triclinium seemed to fit in with various New Testament verses."

Bob smiled. "Yeah, I know Jim Fleming well. And I think that he does a great job, and I don't want to undermine any of his work. But there is no archaeological evidence for his assumption. You have to reckon with the absence of archaeological evidence for his theory on this particular issue. The trouble is that Jim has made so many videos based on his interpretation that it's hard for him to change his presentation."

We admired the mosaic with its provocative and teasing pictures: then Bob pointed to a cubicle at the far corner of the room.

"You know what that is over there?"

"No."

"That is a Byzantine era toilet! Do you know the definition of a rich man in the Byzantine era?"

"No idea."

"A rich man was defined as one who was rich enough to build a toilet right next to the dining-room! That was THE status symbol!"

Nazareth

We left Sepphoris and motored to Nazareth. Everywhere there was building work and construction. In Nazareth itself, massive traffic jams slowed us to a crawl. We moved at a snail's pace through the streets. Yet, somehow, one of the many old, battered, white Mercedes cars cut through the gridlock: it was taking a bride to her wedding and by some means it wove in and out of the lines of traffic. The bride was on the front seat in radiant white with a beaming, giggling smile. Her car found gaps where none existed, and then disappeared at great speed up a Nazareth side-street, hopefully getting her to the church on time.

Our bus was hardly moving. The owner of a fruit stall watched us for a time; then he wandered over and handed half a pomegranate through the open bus window to Rosie. He returned with two more pomegranates for Dee and Anne. These were handed round the bus and tasted delicious.

The sun blazed down as our crawl into Nazareth continued. I could see the Nazareth Hospital up on the hill. I could see the Gabriel Hotel where the Bike Riders stayed for the first night of the Rides in 1994 and 1995. The mosque behind the Gabriel Hotel which woke us up at 4.30 am with the call to prayer came into sight, and other landmarks hove into view. Children were walking back from school, with small haversacks on their back or carrying colored briefcases. Four older girls, in blue jeans and cream blouses with their school crest on the pocket, walked past, talking and laughing as schoolgirls do everywhere.

Eventually we reached the center of town and, leaving the bus, we strolled to the church which is built over Mary's Well. Although the spring of water which feeds the well was interfered with in the last century, this church marks the spot where Nazareth's original water supply came from, and so there is an extremely high probability that Mary, along with other Nazareth women, obtained water for her household each day at this spot. This afternoon the crypt of the church was crowded with Italian pilgrims filling bottles and cups with water from the well. According to legend, a man or woman who drinks water from Mary's Well will live long and be blessed.

Lunch in Nazareth consisted of falafel, bananas, and bread from a nearby shop. I then walked through the back streets to the Church of the Annunciation. One shop front had the superscription 'The Arab Bureau for Human Rights.' In a side-alley children were playing.

The Church of the Annunciation is too vast to get a decent photograph, so I wandered up to a little church which is built over the traditional site of Joseph's house. A service was taking place in its sanctuary, so I stood at the back and watched. Six people sat in the pews. All in different rows. Four white-robed clergy sat behind the altar, and a fifth white-robed clergyman gave a tired homily in English. His subject was 'humility', focusing on the example of Joseph who took the minor role in the Mary and Joseph story. While he spoke his four brethren sat with heads wearily resting on their hands, and with eyes gazing at the ground or closed altogether. When the speaker sat down there was a prolonged empty silence before one of the other clergy staggered to his feet, and started another homily whilst leaning heavily on the lectern. The congregation of six sat patiently in the pews. Each in their own space. I listened for a few more minutes and then left. Not a demonstration of vibrant Christianity.

Meandering back towards where the bus was parked, I heard a shout. "Bruce! Over here!"

It was Sharon. She had been to buy an English newspaper and the shopkeeper had asked if she was from the UK. She told him that was so, and that she was in fact Scottish.

"Ah! Scottish! The EMMS Hospital. Very, very good. I had double hernia done there. All doctors, all nurses, very, very good."

"The Bike Ride raises money for the hospital each year, "explained Sharon. "I was involved in it last year."

Back at the bus, we sat on a low wall near Mary's Well alongside an old Arab and tried to converse with him. He did not speak any English, but a passer-by helped out. The old fellow was called Ali, but even with the aid of an interpreter he was a poor conversationalist. Still, when I offered him a shekel in exchange for taking his photograph he agreed enthusiastically. The passer-by was more communicative, and told us that he had a brother who is a male-nurse at the Nazareth Hospital. He also knew Dr. Basil who gave the 1994 Bike Riders a guided tour of all the facilities.

Kibbutz Malkiya

Mid-afternoon, we left Nazareth to travel to our new accommodation at Kibbutz Malkiya in the far north of Israel on the Lebanese border. Out of Nazareth the bus followed much of the first day of the Bike Ride route which we cycled in 1994 and 1995, though the miles were so much shorter by bus. We passed a tel which Joshua made his administrative capital in the north after his conquest of Canaan. Before then, only a few miles out from Nazareth, we passed through Kfar Cana, and Sharon and I noticed the Municipal Offices where the Bike Riders were welcomed in 1995 on the morning of Yitzak Rabin's funeral, and where stunned and sobbing Arab town-councillors shared their feelings of grief with us. Just past the Municipal Offices was a garage, where today we saw a young boy rolling a tyre into the work-place. The tyre gathered momentum, rolled away from the boy, bounced behind a car, and crashed into the shoulder of a garage-hand who was sitting on a chair reading his newspaper. The last I saw of the incident from our bus was the man on his feet, shaking his fist and shouting in Arabic at the miscreant.

On the journey Bob filled in details about northern Galilee. When the Hula marshes, north of the Sea of Galilee, were drained, there was an ecological disaster. Several species were seen no more, including many migrating birds which had had regular stopovers in the marshes from time immemorial. They stopped coming altogether. However, not all the drained marshland proved profitable agriculturally, and so the government decided to allow some of the land to revert to its natural state. Already some of the birds had returned. Bob also told us about the local geology.

"The northern Galilean hills are not only higher than the southern ones, but are characterized by black rock. This is because ancient volcanoes on the Golan spewed lava, not only over the Golan (making it a relatively level plateau), but on the western side of the River Jordan covering the native limestone. This created a layer of dark rock."

Bob told us to watch out for the three volcanic plugs which are clearly visible, and explained that underneath the black rock is the original white limestone. Many old buildings in the Galilee, such as the walls of Tiberias, are constructed from black rock, quite different from the white walls of Akko or Jerusalem.

OUR KIBBUTZ TONIGHT, AND for three nights altogether, is Kibbutz Malkiya. After journeying for two hours we saw the barbed wire and electronic fencing which marks the Lebanese frontier. Our driver had not realized the exact location of Kibbutz Malkiya, and was pretty startled to find himself right on the Lebanese border. He had an animated conversation with Bob in Hebrew, pointing with his finger to the land beyond the barbed wire. The bus climbed up to Malkiya on a steep and sharply winding road, with Mount Hermon in full view through the coach windows, before slipping into Malkiya through its massive yellow painted steel gates which were opened by an armed guard. We disembarked and waited for Rabbi Johnny who was due to meet us. As we unloaded our luggage my single golf club continued to get strange looks.

It seems that the most influential man on the Kibbutz is Natan Hacker. Natan was a lawyer in Chicago before coming to Israel twenty years ago, and he gave us an orientation talk on the philosophy of the Kibbutz.

"Some people think we are communists," said Natan, "but nothing could be further from the truth. Last century, when Jews were accused of being extreme socialists they pointed to the Bible text which says that 'every man will sit under his *own* vine, and his *own* fig.' The Jews said 'Look, the Bible says 'his OWN vine, his OWN fig tree' not 'the people's vine or the people's fig tree!'"

Natan grinned as he made his point.

"We are in fact a community of cooperative capitalists!" he continued. "Our kibbutz has its own credit cards. It has its own Smart Cards which deal with purchases in the kibbutz supermarket, with car-hire, and with personal petrol usage. When I fill the car with petrol my smart card tells the kibbutz computer which car it is, and who is driving. The petrol cost is then credited to the allowances which the kibbutz gives me. We are more than self-sufficient. In fact, we export. Our kibbutz industries export toys. We are involved in international advertising. We produce fruit at a profit for Israel. And so we thrive as a 'capitalist' Kibbutz!"

Natan then moved to his favorite theme.

"Today all of us—yourselves included—live in a global village. We plug into a global society. For example, I do a lot of work on the Internet, and I can access any library in the world which is on-line. It is now easier for me to access information in the main library in Chicago than it was when I lived there. In these days I had to leave home, get on the bus, check-in at the library, fill in a form, all before getting the book. Now, I sit at my desk, press a few keys, and it's all on screen. Nowhere is remote in today's world of the Internet. So it is more important than ever that we have a real peace, because no nation or society can live in isolation from others."

Natan took pains to emphasize the good relationships the kibbutz has with the ordinary people of South Lebanon. He told us that there are people working on the kibbutz who get day-passes into Israel from South Lebanon. Only the previous week, a bus-load of women arrived. They came from all backgrounds. Some were fundamentalists totally wrapped in clothing from head to foot. Others were mini-skirted modern girls. All were friendly. But when a camera was produced they screamed 'No! No! No!'

"Do you know why they reacted like that?" Natan asked.

"Religious scruples?"

"No. They were afraid that the pictures might get to Beirut, and that they would be identified, and then suffer at the hands of Hezbollah for fraternising with Israelis. You see, we have no real peace. Israel has no peace with its neighbors. Yes, there are peace treaties with Egypt and Jordan. But it is not real peace. When real peace comes all the countries in the area can share resources, skills, water. For everyone's benefit. That is our dream."

KIBBUTZ MALKIYA WAS FOUNDED in 1949 but dwindled to forty or so members by the early 1970s. There are now four hundred, including children, and it is clearly a go-ahead kibbutz. On Shabbat evening all kibbutz members eat in the dining hall, and Natan and Rabbi Johnny have established a center for religious pluralism. Natan believes that if economic equality with Israel can be established among the nations surrounding Israel, then Israel will be less of a target. Natan is a deep thinking humanist who believes that if people are dealt with fairly, and removed from poverty, then most political impasses will no longer be relevant.

After the meal we had coffee downstairs. From the terrace we looked over the Hula valley. Above us the night sky was inky black with stars twinkling brightly. Below us were the lights of townships all over the Hula. In 1973, during the Yom Kippur war, the fighting on the Golan was seen from the kibbutz, and fighter planes roared overhead. In 1948/49 the final battle of the Israeli War of Independence was fought at Kibbutz Malkiya, and a memorial to the fallen is on its eastern edge.

Rabbi Johnny rejoined us and we had coffee together. "In Israel," said Johnny, "Instant coffee is invariably *Nescafe*. And when it was introduced twenty years ago, it caused great amusement because in Hebrew the word 'Nes' means 'miracle'. So it was known as 'Nes-Cafe', or 'miracle coffee.'"

I spoke up. "Does this mean that the Loch *Ness* monster is the 'miracle monster'?"

"Probably!" he laughed.

Kibbutz Malkiya is a 'liberal' kibbutz, although in Judaism words are applied differently to our normal usage. For example, 'Conservative' and 'Reformed' groups are both relatively liberal, and it is the 'Orthodox' group which we would call conservative. Accordingly, in the kibbutz synagogue, where we had the welcome talk from Natan, we did not have to wear a head covering; and in the dining-hall we noticed that the young girls on the kibbutz wore modern and revealing dresses.

The Jewish people of modern Israel are an enigma. They argue continually with each other. At the same time, as we have already noted, they have strong, common, shared experiences to draw on, such as National Service, work on the land, defence of the nation, and a unique history. All of these factors are drivers in the corporate psyche of a young nation determined to plough ahead. These characteristics, allied with a natural energy and ingenuity make a formidable force. It raises a big question. How can any politician, apart from someone with the stature of a Yitzak Rabin, make them choose a different way than that of absolute, uncompromising, unchanging belligerence?

TO CLOSE THE DAY Clive told us some of his jokes and stories. Clive is an ex-RAF man, and he and Marion have already built up a formidable reputation among us for being totally prepared for absolutely anything. There are able instantly to produce clothes-pegs, coffee, an iron, sewing equipment, clothes-lines, washing powder, medicine, etc., etc., from the depths of their luggage.

After we left the others, James said to me, "You know Bruce, Natan has the right surname for someone so immersed in computers and the Internet as he is."

"Oh? What?"

"Hacker!"

— Day 5 — Malkiya —

Saturday 12th October

AFTER BREAKFAST RABBI JOHNNY took us on a tour of the kibbutz. He told us that when the Temple was destroyed in 70AD, a group of priests came north to the Galilee and started a community on the spot where Kibbutz Malkiya now stands. As we wandered through the grounds we noticed that between many of the houses were clumps of pomegranate trees. Johnny explained: "There is an old Jewish saying: 'May your blessings be multiplied as the seed of the pomegranate.'" Here and there, beside the houses and administrative offices of the kibbutz, we saw low lying concrete roofs with air-vents emerging from them.

"These are the Air-Raid shelters," Johnny said. "They were first used in earnest during the *Grapes-of-Wrath* Israeli offensive against the Hezbollah in southern Lebanon earlier this year. The Closed Circuit Television gave precise information as to where each bomb blast took place. For example, it might say 'The latest bomb blast was half a kilometer outside the perimeter fence.'"

"Did that not increase panic, knowing the details!?"

"No. The opposite in fact. Precise accurate information decreases panic. People cannot cope with not knowing what's happening. It's lack of knowledge which creates panic."

"Did everyone stay on in the kibbutz?"

"Well, during the *Grapes-of-Wrath* war, the adults stayed on to tend the orchards, whilst the children went to another kibbutz, further away from the Lebanese border, until the dangerous days passed."

"Were there casualties here?"

"No. But a neighboring kibbutz lost one hundred apartments when a shell made a direct hit. But there was no Israeli loss of life in the *Grapes-of-Wrath* offensive." Johnny hesitated and then continued. "Unfortunately, some Israeli missiles hit a United Nations refugee camp in southern Lebanon with considerable loss of life. That distressed us so much."

"What about the Gulf War? Did that affect you up here in the north?"

"Oh yes. During the Gulf War, and at the height of the Scud missile attacks on Israel, we sat in sealed rooms with our gas-masks on watching the war on CNN. For us the action took place on TV! But it wasn't a phoney war! There was real fear and uncertainty."

WE CAME TO THE edge of the kibbutz where old and disused watchtowers were dotted along the perimeter fence. These watchtowers are now redundant because electronic surveillance and satellite information have replaced men and women with binoculars. But Kibbutz Malkiya has an assured place of honor in the history of the State of Israel, being part of the Front Line defence for the nation during the War of Independence in 1948.

Johnny pointed to the Lebanese border. "If the electronic fence on the Israel/Lebanon border is activated the Army will be at the spot within four minutes, and our kibbutz will be alerted immediately. The gates seal shut automatically. And all individuals must take rehearsed precautions until the all-clear is given."

"Does this happen often?"

"Oh yes. It can happen several times a week. No chances are taken. No one jokes about security in Israel."

When the kibbutz was founded earlier this century, top soil had to be imported because the original soil had been eroded and washed away. Across the military border we saw the fields of the Lebanese farmers, and Johnny reminded us that agriculture was the original industry of all kibbutzim. Latterly kibbutzim have diversified; and now, as well as raising and selling one million chickens a year, Kibbutz Malkiya manufactures educational toys and is involved in advertising and packaging.

There is a kibbutz children's zoo where the children are taught to look after the animals and develop a respect for living things. The zoo is both for the children's pleasure and a tool to train their sense of responsibility. They are expected to run it, maintain it, and look after it. We admired a magnificent tawny owl which stared at us with its unblinking yellow eyes.

"Notice that the aviary has no net over it," said Johnny. "The birds are to be free, like the people of the kibbutz are to be free. The kibbutz also has a riding-school specialising in teaching trail riding."

JOHNNY THEN GAVE US some insights into personal relationships in modern Israel. On several days in the past week we had seen bridal parties, both in Haifa and Nazareth. Johnny explained that Jewish marriages often take place on a Tuesday because, in the creation narrative of the first chapter of Genesis, a double blessing is mentioned on the third day of creation (Tuesday) and so that day is considered lucky.

"Regulations governing marriage are quite complicated in Israel," he said. "To begin with, the State recognizes marriages as valid which have taken place in another country. Second, religious marriages carried out by authorized Rabbis are also valid. Third, marriages carried out in Israel by licensed religious officers of other faiths between people of these faiths are recognized as valid. However, if a Jew wants a non-religious marriage that is impossible in Israel, even though the State is 'officially' a non-religious State. So what happens is that most couples live together, and then go over to Cyprus to have their marriage registered under Cypriot law. When they return to Israel their marriage is automatically validated because it was a valid marriage under the law of another country! This situation originates from the early days of Zionist Israel in which members of pioneer kibbutzim threw aside traditional conventions."

"One of the reasons why Israel in general, and kibbutzim in particular, are secular is due to Zionism. In the late nineteenth and early twentieth century, the Zionists were proactive in their determination to return to the 'homeland', whereas the Orthodox Religious Jews believed strongly that they should simply 'wait on God' and not force the Divine plan. The Zionists rejected this passive attitude and came to Israel to 'reclaim' the land. Thus the early kibbutzim were, in the nature of things, non-religious."

DURING OUR TOUR, WE overheard Johnny speaking animatedly to Bob. Johnny wanted Bob to examine a tel near Malkiya, with the possibility of it being excavated. Bob knew the tel, promised to have a look at it, but indicated there could be problems caused by the ultra-Orthodox. We asked Bob to explain why.

"Well, on two grounds really. First, the ultra-Orthodox believe that the Old Testament leaders Deborah and Barak are buried in the Tel, therefore it is a sacred burial place. Second, the Roman temple which was later constructed on the site was used as a synagogue at one stage of its existence. So again, that makes it a sacred site."

Bob explained more. "You see, the views of the ultra-Orthodox concerning burial grounds might yet totally paralyse archaeology in Israel. In the Knesset the minority governments need cross-party support, so a lot of horse-trading goes on with small parties. So the ultra-Orthodox have a powerful position, despite having only a small number of Knesset members. It's quite ironic. Originally the ultra-Orthodox were against the formation of the State of Israel, but now that it has happened they are its most fervent supporters!"

Bob shook his head in despair. "The ultra-Orthodox are totally irrational. For example, they frequently oppose excavations on the grounds that Jewish graves are being disturbed, even when there is obvious proof that the graves are Muslim. For example, the graves might be facing Mecca and so on. But the ultra-Orthodox default position is to define all graves to be 100 percent Jewish. And because they have become the balancing party in the ruling coalition they get their way so often."

"To change the subject," Bob continued, "the new Israeli missile system, revealed on TV this week, is called 'Barak' after the same guy who is probably buried down the hill here, three thousand years ago!"

The House of Assembly

The kibbutz synagogue is called Beit Knesset or 'House of Assembly.' Today was Saturday (Shabbat) and Johnny led us in a study of the Torah portion for this week of the year. It was the creation narrative in Genesis chapter One, concentrating on the theme of Light. Johnny wanted to know about the New Testament understanding of Light, and the theology lying behind it. He is a gentle, humble, sincere man, and genuinely enjoyed the Bible study with us.

Johnny also explained various aspects of synagogue worship. He put on his prayer shawl. He took out the Torah Scroll. And he recited today's Torah portion in Hebrew, always taking care never to touch the sacred text with his finger, but indicating each word with the short pointer called a 'yam', as he chanted from the Genesis text. It was a beautiful experience. We gathered close around him, and listened as this good man read the scriptures with us.

One thing puzzled us. We wondered when the kibbutz was going to have its Shabbat worship, since Johnny was clearly spending the whole morning with our group. Perhaps someone else was taking it today. When we asked what we thought were innocent questions, Johnny answered with clear disappointment in his voice.

"When does the kibbutz meet for Shabbat worship?"

"We don't have a service. The only time the kibbutz comes to the synagogue is on Yom Kippur. I wish it were more often, but not many people say they would come."

Johnny smiled through his hurt.

We asked more questions. "Do the boys on the kibbutz go through a Bar-Mitzvah?"

"Only 10 percent of the boys go through a religious Bar-Mitzvah. The other 90 percent do a secular version of a 'Bar-Mitzvah year.' This focuses on family roots and identity, without the religious component. I am the only one on the kibbutz who prays regularly."

No wonder Johnny is enjoying our company. He is spiritually starved. It was sad to see him disconsolate when our questions inadvertently touched this area of his life. Because the people of the kibbutz don't bother about the synagogue, groups like ours give him his only religious fellowship. Natan encourages Johnny. But my feeling is that Natan's support does not come from a strong piety, but from a generous humanist tolerance of all things which people feel deeply about. Johnny needs the encouragement of someone who shares his faith on a devotional level. The discussion Johnny had with us on the Torah section must have been one of his rare opportunities for group Bible study and fellowship. On Thursdays he has started a Pluralism Group with the local priest, the local imam, and himself. Natan encourages that as well.

Watching and Guarding

This afternoon there was free time to wander and explore the kibbutz. Rosie, Sharon, Clive, Marion, and I went for a stroll outside its gates and along the main road which follows the route of the Border. After we returned, I walked back down to the main entrance. On the massive, imposing, steel gate is a tiny notice saying 'Welcome to Kibbutz Malkiya,' and the contrast between the enormous, forbidding, yellow barrier, and that small, neat, notice of welcome is a delightful mismatch.

The guard at the sentry-post was listening to pop music on his radio when I spoke to him.

"Could you please open the gate so that I can go outside and take a picture?"

"Yes certainly."

He pressed a button, and with the whirr of electric motors the massive gate slid back smoothly on its rollers making a gap big enough for me to squeeze through and go outside. I took a couple of pictures and then re-entered.

"Thank you very much," I said to the young soldier. "I'm Bruce from the UK. What's your name?"

"Slava. I came to Israel from Minsk in Belarus six years ago."

"Have you always been in the army since coming to Israel?"

"No. Just for the last three years. This is my National Service."

"Are you always on sentry duty, Slava?"

"Oh no. I serve in the Air Force as a mechanic with Phantom jets, and I am only here on guard duty at the kibbutz for six days. Then I go back to my base. Not tomorrow, but the next day."

I pointed to the hills over the barbed wire.

"That is Lebanon," I said. "Is this not a dangerous area to work in?"

"Yes, that is why I'm here, because that is Lebanon." He shrugged his shoulders, and looked over to the Lebanese border. "It's not too bad. Everyone has to do their duty. It's OK."

I thanked him for his help and walked back up to the chalets. He put the radio on and listened to his pop-music as he opened and closed the gates for each vehicle coming and going.

BOB TOLD US THAT there was English speaking news on Israeli TV at six o'clock, so we tuned in and watched. Israel controls the Lebanese border zone for eight miles into southern Lebanon, and, on the English speaking news, we were told of Hezbollah rocket attacks on villages in south Lebanon last night. We discussed this over the evening meal.

David commented, "Anne and I heard 'booms' over the border before we got to sleep last night; we wondered if it might be guns."

"They have it rough over there," said Johnny. "The local south Lebanese people, who come and work on our kibbutz, suffer terribly from Hezbollah."

Development and Progress

Natan joined us. He talked about the farming principles of the kibbutz in contrast with the methods used by farmers of southern Lebanon whose fields we had seen earlier in the day. And he slapped his hand on the table in exasperation.

"These Lebanese farmers have not advanced their methods one iota, despite watching with their own eyes the success of kibbutz style farming for years now. They do not irrigate properly. Their fields are still small strips. And the fields are continually sub-divided amongst family members, precluding any proper machine use! How can you farm like that, four years away from the twenty-first century!"

Natan shook his head in despair. "You know, they arrive at their fields in Mercedes cars, and yet plough using donkeys! They harvest using the scythe as in biblical times. I am so frustrated by the slow progress of the Lebanese because it perpetuates the economic imbalance which is a major factor in middle-eastern tension."

"What do you mean Natan?"

"What I mean is that equalized prosperity among the nations of the area will bring peace. I am convinced of that. Equalized prosperity will bring peace! It will! Instability does not come from Absolute Poverty, but from Relative Poverty. You see, surrounding nations see Israel as a rich country relative to themselves, and that creates envy. What Israelis have to do is to help the other countries become efficient and prosperous themselves. That will help bring real peace. But strip farming will never get there! Part of the point of creating the kibbutz system in Israel was to get away from the middle-eastern custom of tiny land divisions. and to give agriculture a big-scale, economically profitable basis."

As Natan pursued his theme, Tony opened his camera to put in a new film. To his horror he saw that the old film had not caught on the sprockets and had never wound on. Poor Tony. He has lost all his first week's photos! The camera belongs to a friend of his, and is an excellent Canon T90. Unfortunately, it can be tricky to become adept with new equipment, and accidents happen. But Tony was philosophical about it all, and we offered to give him duplicates from our collections.

After supper, Tony, James, and I were chatting and drinking coffee in our chalet when the noise of helicopter gun-ships going north sounded overhead. All air traffic in this area is military. What might be afoot? And is Natan right in his conviction that economic imbalance is the key issue?

— Day 6—Jish —

Sunday 13th October

TODAY HAS BEEN A major experience. Kareem came all the way from Nazareth to Malkiya with his bus so that we could have an early departure. We then set off on a winding road which took us through the hill country to the town of Jish. It was good to see Kareem again, and he overheard Sharon and I talking about the Nazareth Hospital.

"You know the Hospital?" he asked.

"Oh yes."

"My brother, he works in the X-Ray department of the Hospital. We are so grateful to the English hospital."

"Oh Kareem! It's the *Scottish* Hospital!"

This provoked light-hearted banter with the other members of the Study Group, all of whom come from south of the Scotland/England border, except Rosie who is Irish.

NATAN GAVE A RUNNING commentary as the journey progressed, and, after some miles, when we came round a sharp bend in the road, we were shocked when he told us what had happened at that spot. He said, "In 1970 a school bus was ambushed and all the Jewish school-children, plus their teachers and the bus-driver, were shot by Arab terrorists. The bodies of the children and their teachers were left lying in blood as the gunmen escaped back across the border into Lebanon. What was so cynical and evil was that the terrorists had allowed other traffic through before stopping the bus. Their actions were deliberate and cold-blooded."

History is rarely one-sided. Half a mile further on, Natan pointed out the ruins of a village called Bar'am, on our left-hand side, and told us the story behind that as well.

"In 1948, on the very next day after the State of Israel was declared, the surrounding Arab nations invaded Israel. It happened immediately. The Arab people of this village of Bar'am, all of whom in fact were friendly to Israel, were asked by the Israeli army to evacuate for their own safety. After two weeks they were to be allowed back. However, the villagers have never been allowed back from that day to this. Two weeks has become fifty years. Every Israeli government makes promises to the people. Nothing has happened."

"Then, in the late 1950s the Israeli air-force bombed the empty village for 'practice', but with the obvious political aim of making the people of Bar'am—now living in exile in Jish—give up their claim. But the people have not given up their claim. The Bar'amites were friendly to Israel. They did what they were asked to do. They co-operated. They have never resorted to any terrorist actions against the State. They have been patient, long-suffering, and peaceful. And the result? They have been ignored. I am myself an Israeli, and I am ashamed of how the people of Bar'am have been treated. The people still use the ruined church in Bar'am for weddings and funerals. But you will meet them yourselves."

James queried, "Natan, if the Bar'amites have always sought a peaceful settlement, then, quite apart from the justice or injustice of the situation, would it not be advantageous for the government to demonstrate that peace is rewarded, otherwise terrorists are correct when they claim that only the gun changes things?"

"Exactly! Exactly! But try getting politicians to see that!"

The bus massacre, and the Bar'am expulsions were two stories, two events, two histories, each with pain and suffering and contributing to the building of mistrust. They encapsulate the problems of this nation.

The Maronites of Jish

Jish is a typical town in Israel, and the main thoroughfare was cluttered with mechanical diggers and bulldozers powering backwards and forwards because the street is being torn up for relaying pipes. Overarching the town was a glorious blue sky. Brilliant sunshine blazed down. The heat was stifling. Noting this in my *Journal* makes me wonder how often will I need to record the heat of the sun? Coming from the UK and more used to cold north winds than thirty-plus degree temperatures, it is hard to avoid mentioning it day after day. Slowly, however, the oven is making our bodies adjust.

Halfway up the main street of Jish is the new Maronite church. This is a magnificent building, and its construction has been an outstanding achievement by the villagers. Natan—who appears to have contacts with the movers and shakers of every community of the area, both Jewish and Arab—introduced us to the local priest.

"Folks, this is Father Elias Elias—so good they named him twice!"

Everyone laughed. Father Elias Chacour is a stocky, strongly built man, who studied for the priesthood in Paris for six years, and who is the author of a much-read book about Bar'am, entitled *Blood Brothers,* which has been translated into over twenty languages. Father Elias was smiling, charming and welcoming.

"My English, it is not too good," he said. "My French, it is better: but welcome to Jish. Welcome to our church. We, the people of Jish, have built this lovely church ourselves. It has been a labour of love, and you are welcome with us this morning."

"The church," interjected Natan, "has been paid for and built by the ordinary people of Jish. It is a tremendous achievement, and the official opening will be Christmas Eve." He turned to Father Elias, "Am I right? Is that correct Father? Christmas Eve?"

"Yes. At least, that is the official opening ceremony. But our church was dedicated a few weeks ago and several Arab members of the Knesset came to the dedication. We were pleased about that. Very pleased."

"Jish is 70 percent Christian, and 30 percent Muslim," added Natan. "The only historic Jewish presence in the town is the tomb of an ancient Rabbi, and occasionally a Jew will come to light a candle there. The Christian community consists of Roman Catholics, Greek Catholics, and Maronites. So there are three churches in town with a population of two thousand five hundred people."

Father Elias explained further. "The Maronite Church is based mainly in Lebanon, and our Maronite community in Israel is waiting for a new Bishop who will come from Lebanon."

"My friend, you should have been the new bishop!" said Natan.

Father Elias smiled. "No, no, but it is true that several of our church members feel that one of the six priests serving in Israel should have been made Bishop. Nonetheless, we are looking forward to meeting our new Bishop."

THE CHURCH IS NO small chapel. It is massive. And it gleamed in the morning sunlight. We climbed its broad white steps into the sanctuary where the congregation were already singing. No one held prayer books, hymn books, or any liturgical aids. Everyone knew the words of worship. On the far side of the sanctuary a choir led the worship. It is difficult to describe the singing. If I were to say that it was an 'Arabic Wail' then that would be the closest description I can find, but the word 'wail' suggests something discordant. In fact, the singing was fantastically beautiful. Yet it was truly an Arabic Wail, but sounding as a crescendo of praise and as a wondrous offering of sound and song rising from the whole congregation, drawing every man, every woman, every child, into the experience of worship. The main singer was a young woman who had her baby in her arms. She stood in the front row of the choir, dressed in everyday clothes, keeping her baby soothed by swaying her body from side to side, as she sang with power and clarity. Her voice was strong. It filled the church. And the rest of the choir and congregation followed her lead.

When we entered the church Father Elias had still to come in. As the people sang and waited for their priest many of the older folk stood, though most of the congregation were seated. Some men wore Arab head-dress. Some were bare headed. When Father Elias arrived all the people sat down. Throughout the service we stood or sat according to what the people were doing around us.

Two boys with large candles preceded the priest wherever he went in the sanctuary. A young girl read the scriptures. The service was in Arabic, but Father Elias gave part of his homily in English purely for our sakes. He preached on prayer, emphasising that prayer is both *speaking words* to God, and *living lives* for God. Holy Communion was celebrated, and all our Study Group plus Kareem our driver went forward to receive communion. It was only when we were returning to our pews that we noticed that few of the large congregation had taken the sacrament.

Father Elias then took a picture of the Madonna and Child, held it above his head, and carried it around the church. He went up and down each aisle accompanied by a crowd of children, plus mothers with babes in arms, plus grandmothers and young teenagers. Whilst this was going on, and as Father Elias displayed the icon above his head, the choir sang, and the voice of the young mother who led the singing rose above every other sound. It was an incredible experience. There is a special veneration of the Virgin Mary in Jish, and a lady had come with her new baby to the church for a prayer of blessing. She was coming forty days after the child's birth, following the Old Testament example of Hannah bringing the infant Samuel to the Temple. The Maronite Church observes infant baptism, but baptism is additional to these prayers of dedication and blessing, and would be celebrated on a later date.

FOLLOWING THE SERVICE, WE met twelve of the senior men and women of the church for Coca-Cola and biscuits. The gathering was in a downstairs hall and, after the biscuits and drinks were handed out on trays, we talked together. The church cost three million dollars which was raised over sixteen years by a community of believers who are not wealthy in any way. There are only seven thousand Maronites in the whole of the Holy Land, mostly in Haifa, and nearly all of those in Haifa come originally from Jish.

I spoke to the man beside me. "We enjoyed the service this morning, but I am puzzled so few people took communion. Did you take communion?"

"No, not today."

"Can I ask why?"

"Today I breakfasted too close to the service, and I did not want to take a holy thing into my mouth until more time had passed from the meal."

I was still perplexed as to why hardly anyone, out of a large congregation did not take communion. Not all of them could have miscalculated breakfast time. The man beside me was friendly and eager to chat.

"Our communion service is in the language of our Lord."

"Oh? Really?"

"Yes indeed. Our Lord spoke the Aramaic language; and in the Mass, when our priest says our Lord's words 'This is my body, this is my blood', he speaks the very words Jesus would have used. The Aramaic."

He then gesticulated and attracted the attention of another man across the room. "George! George! Our Lord's Prayer! You say the words in his language!" George recited the Lord's Prayer in Aramaic for us, then told us about life in Jish.

George had open-heart surgery in recent years. Prior to that he was a teacher, and so he focused on education. George explained that there are two schools in Jish. The Elementary School takes children from first to eighth grade, and the Secondary School goes from ninth to twelfth grade. The best pupils go on to University. He also told us that Jish has an active local council.

"You will have seen that our main street is being dug up." We had noticed! "And the men are working hard to complete it in a month's time. If only the government would give the Arab villages more money, we could do things more quickly."

Natan came in on the conversation. "Now George, you know that the Arab villages get plenty of money from the Israeli government! You get the same amount as the Jewish villages! It's just that in the Arab villages things take ages to get done!"

George smiled. "Our relationship with Israeli settlements is very, very good. Our friend Natan is such a help to all of us. In many ways what he says is correct. We are slower. But the Israelis, they are quick, very quick."

The church people in Jish obviously have a high regard for Natan who is a natural bridge-builder between communities. Father Elias spoke about the relationship between the churches and other faiths in the town.

"Jews, Christians, Muslims all have the same Father, but the Jews and Muslims reject brother Jesus. That is the difference. Now, the beginning of our church was in the fourth century when it was started by a monk from Syria called Saint Marum. That is why we are called Maronites. We have good relationships with other Christian churches. Some Roman Catholic nuns have a small school next to the church for children under four years old, and the nuns come to our services as well."

WE SOON CAME TO the Bar'am issue, and it became clear that was why the local people were meeting us. Bar'am villagers settled in Jish after 1948, and many of the prominent people in the Jish church were Bar'amites. Father Elias spoke again.

"We met President Hertzog in Jerusalem, and I gave him a judgment of Solomon. I said to him that the people of Bar'am want to go back alive and not dead to their village. Could he please make this happen? I said to President Hertzog that the people of Bar'am are not bitter, but they feel great pain."

A lady called Emily, a retired school-teacher, spoke up. "You see, the loss of Bar'am also meant the loss of land, and that affects our young people. We are refugees in Jish from Kfar Bar'am, and we have our own land no longer. It was confiscated when the town was destroyed, even though our people were on Israel's side. Because we lost the land at Bar'am there is now too little land for our families, and so not all of our young people in Jish can make a living in our community. Therefore, our young people must train at University for a profession. But competition for University places is severe, and often the young people have to go overseas. I was born at Kfar Bar'am. It is my home. I want to go back."

Emily's sentiments were echoed around the room.

Another man, Philip, came into the discussion. "The people in Jish, like me, who have lived in Bar'am still feel like refugees, because we remember everything about our village." Philip then paused, before adding, "But not all our children are so keen on returning. That is sad."

Natan spoke again. "You see, it's not just the village *per se*. Bar'am has twelve thousand acres associated with it. The people need their land back. There is no strategic military reason for Israel to deny them their land today, so why can't the land be handed back? They ask me, and I have to say I don't know. I can't see a reason. They have asked the government for a portion of their land, but have been refused. Some government officials say the problem is security. But, four points. First, successive governments have conceded the argument in principle. Second, Israel is strong enough to fight all the Arab countries. Third, there are many other Arab villages on Israel's borders and *they* are allowed to stay. Fourth, the people of Bar'am are Israeli citizens, they are not like the people in the West Bank or Gaza."

Philip interrupted. "Yes, Yes. We pay taxes. We vote in elections. We are loyal to the State of Israel. We are Israelis. There is much hurt and pain over such betrayal, and over broken promises by people we were supporting in 1948."

The feelings of injustice ran deep.

Tony asked a question, "Given that nearly all Israeli Arabs supported the Peace Process, what do you think of Netanyahu's new government?"

There was silence. George thought for a moment. Choosing words carefully, he said, "This government could be a good government—at least after America trains our new Prime Minister to be more moderate! Not yet. But it will be."

George's sentiment may have been an expression more of hope than of reality. But it was sobering to see how these people take everything seriously. Politics, like security, is not an area for jokes or for superficial comments. The people *have* to believe that the government *can* become a good government for them, otherwise there is no hope. In Jish, life is serious. Politics is about death or survival, not the western preoccupation with the standard of living. In Britain we can afford the luxury of shrugging our shoulders about the government if we do not like it, because life is secure whoever is in power. Not so in Jish, where people must look for glimmers of faith in their leaders, because everything depends on them.

Natan spoke again, addressing George. "But returning to Bar'am is not simply a return to an old house, George. It won't be the same as 1948."

George nodded, "Yes. We know that. But it will be the return of a community. In this country people have real roots. This is not the West where people move from town to town without a second thought. The return to Bar'am would be a return to the type of society as it was at the times of our fathers and grandfathers in terms of 'belonging together.' That is the point Natan."

Emily added, "We want to live with the people of our own village, in our own community. We know that we are welcome in Jish. We have wonderful friends in Jish. But Bar'am has our houses, our land, our orchards, our streets, our gardens, our homes."

Natan came in again. "You know that I work with you on the committee to try and persuade the government to let you back. But it will not be the Bar'am of 48 years ago. It will be a different Bar'am. Everything has changed. Even here in Jish, the young people have two sets of standards. For example, at home in Jish they will not walk down the street hand in hand; but when they go to Haifa they do. Things change. It won't be the same. I support you because fairness and justice must be done. But how many of your young people want Bar'am?"

"The young people are with us Natan." maintained George. "Most of the young people want to go back. The young people have taken the Kfar Bar'am situation into their psyche. They have received it from their parents. It is part of their identity. Like us they see it as an injustice which must be put right. We were loyal to Israel. We were on their side in 1948. It has to be put right."

The twelve of us listened to these interchanges, fascinated by the way history has hit these kind, long-suffering people. Yet there were no young people in the group chosen to meet us.

Before we left the church Bob outlined the earlier history of Jish. He told us that in 70AD one of the leaders of the Jewish revolt against Rome came from this area, and that Josephus mentions the town Giscala, which is equivalent to modern Jish. The Roman General Titus subdued the village in 67AD. However, the Jewish leader had already left the village at night, before the Sabbath, and went to Jerusalem to fight there against the Romans.

Bob added, "There is an ancient Christian tradition that Jish was the village of the family of St. Paul before they moved to Tarsus. This is why part of the letters of St. Paul are recited each time in the Mass. It celebrates local connection with the intellectual organizer of the Christian religion."

The Suleimans

As a group we had planned to have lunch in a cafe, but we were all invited into the house of the Suleiman family for coffee. Mr. and Mrs. Suleiman have both been teachers. He has retired from teaching Hebrew language and Hebrew literature at the Hebrew University, specialising in modern Jewish literature. Mrs. Suleiman taught in the senior school in Jish. Their daughter's wedding photographs were displayed proudly on the wall. She married a Jordanian and now lives in Kentucky, USA.

The Suleimans and Natan have been friends for years, working together in local politics, and Natan was a special guest at their daughter's wedding. It was lovely to see how some of the fissures between the different peoples of the land can be bridged by peaceful individuals. Traditionally, the northern villages of Israel have had strong links with villages in southern Lebanon. From time to time these contacts have been developed, and part of Natan's mission is to reunite families who are divided by the border. But everything is difficult. Everything causes tension. Nothing is simple. Good times and bad times follow in quick succession.

Mrs. Suleiman is an intelligent, serious person and I chatted with her about the church. I commented on the priest taking bread and wine, and the congregation receiving only the bread, explaining our practice in the Church of Scotland where we receive both bread and wine in the sacrament.

She asked me, "Do you adore Mary in your church?"

I gave an honest reply which I hoped would not offend. "Well," I said, choosing words carefully, "Of course Mary is important because she is the mother of our Lord, and we honor her and respect her because of that. But, no, she is not central in the way she perhaps is in your church."

This perplexed Mrs. Suleiman. "Oh, the Virgin Mary, she did so many miracles. She is so important."

On the opposite wall of the sitting room, beside family photographs, was a large framed line-drawing of an oriental gentleman. I asked Mrs. Suleiman who it was.

"He is a saint of more than one hundred years ago who came from Lebanon and who did many miracles, cured fevers, blindness, and raised people from their sicknesses."

I wondered what lay behind these accounts. Were they embroidered narratives? Or was the man used by God to do signs and wonders? Perhaps he was. God can do more with people who are humble and trusting, than with many in the West who have diluted that trust and expectancy with large doses of so-called rationalism and so-called realism. When God is in a life then the realism is of a different type.

Hospitality at the Suleimans was delightful. As we left their son wandered in. Apparently he cannot get a place at the University because of lack of money, and he badgered Natan about this. The young fellow is upset about the way he has been treated by the system, and felt that some of Natan's friends might be able to help.

Bar'am Village

On leaving the Suleimans, Clive, Marion, and I wandered out of the village for a stroll. We had brought our own bananas and bread and were able to leave the others queuing up at the falafel stall. I photographed a bright red old-fashioned lorry. Israel is full of old-fashioned lorries as well as ultra-modern Volvo monsters, and, due to the dry atmosphere, these veteran vehicles do not rust like they would in Britain. They stay serviceable and look good for longer.

We walked further out of Jish, with the sun beating down with its merciless heat. I really have to mention the heat yet again because only by doing so, and by repeating such descriptions, can I begin to convey the sheer intensity of light, brightness, and overpowering burning hotness.

On the other side of the road two women were picking figs, and one of them beckoned to us with great agitation. We went over. Both of them gave us figs, and were obviously trying to communicate something important. They kept giving us more figs as presents and clearly they wanted something. They did not want money. So what was it? Eventually we worked out that they wanted their pictures taken. The husband of one of the ladies arrived in (yet another) old, battered, white Mercedes, and the whole family posed beside the vehicle for Clive and me to snap them. I dug out a piece of paper from my camera-bag and they scribbled down their name and address in Arabic. When we rejoined the others Bob and Kareem deciphered it for us, so that we can send copies of the pictures to them when we go home.

ON THE RETURN JOURNEY to Kibbutz Malkiya we visited the ruins of Bar'am which is now under the Israeli Ministry of Tourism, and has become an official visitor attraction. But not a visitor site in connection with the evictions of 1948. Instead, the published information focuses on the ruined synagogue. Any reference to the events which have occupied our minds all day is restricted to the final paragraph: *"Until 1948 Bar'am was a Maronite Christian village. During the War of Independence, the villagers were evacuated and the site is now under the auspices of the National Parks Authority."* No mention of the people today. No indication of a continuing claim and a continuing problem. We asked Natan about the name Bar'am and he explained that it means, "Son of the People."

What will happen? Can the Israeli government ever decide to allow the people back? Would that be too dangerous a precedent? Would that be too great a weakness in the eyes of the right-wing whose support is essential in Israel's coalition governments?

We also stopped at the bus massacre site. The simple, sober sign reads: *"Here, on Friday the 22nd of May 1970, a murderous attack was made by assassins from across the border. Eight children, three teachers, and the bus-driver were killed on their way from Avivim to school at Dovev."* Natan worries that the memorial sometimes inflames wrong passions. For myself, living only a few miles from Dunblane, where sixteen children and their teacher were gunned down by a mad-man in the spring of this year, I could understand that.

The Army Base

Natan knows everyone. He is friends with the Camp Commander at a local army base, and so we were allowed to visit, even though the base is on active alert. But no photographs could be taken of electronic surveillance equipment, and so no cameras were allowed to point towards masts, aerials, or any high-tech apparatus. However, we were allowed to photograph the tanks which are used for mine detection. When I walked forward to get a close-up my feet sank nine or ten inches into the red-pink dust, the soil having been atomized into talcum by tanks grinding over it again and again. Crouching low-down for a wide-angle shot I heard a soft whirr, looked up, and found the tank gun barrel pointing straight at me with the business end only a foot away! The soldier in the tank turret grinned when he saw me flinch.

Another soldier explained the set up. "A Druze regiment is at the base just now, and you can see the Druze emblem of crossed scimitars on the barrack wall. Because it is a Druze regiment there are only men. Israeli women are in the forces, but not Druze women, only Druze men."

"So is everyone Druze here?"

"No, there are some Jewish soldiers, and of course some Bedouin soldiers. The army uses Bedouin as trackers and spotters for mines. Now, if you look behind you at the entrance to the camp, there is a demonstration area featuring common camouflage for land-mines and booby-traps."

He took us to the spot. As far as we were concerned there was nothing but rocks and stones, as elsewhere. Then he lifted up two of the rocks. One was real. The other was a hollow dummy made out of polystyrene. Unless we had seen it with our own eyes, we could not have imagined that a real rock and a polystyrene one could be confused. But the Bedouin can spot these straight away, and are even able to detect stones which have been recently disturbed: consequently, every morning they go into south Lebanon to see what Hezbollah have been up to overnight. And, almost every day, there is at least one death, either Israeli or Hezbollah. Occasionally flares are set off in the night sky if infra-red detectors indicate a human presence in the area. In their light any guerrillas can be spotted.

The Armoured Personnel Carriers at the base are stocked full of ammunition ready for action. The soldiers are friendly and relaxed. Yet, later today, or tomorrow, or next week, they might be in enemy territory and become vulnerable targets for Hezbollah. Again, no one jokes about security. Politics here is in the raw. It is far removed from the atmosphere of dinner-party conversations back home.

Clive asked, "Do you always shoot back when fired upon."

"Not always, because there might be a risk of hitting a little girl or civilians. The terrorists hide behind human shields, and that would create an International incident."

No doubt the soldiers were sincere. But, if what they said was Army policy, then why on earth did Israel bomb a UN Refugee camp in Southern Lebanon during the *Grapes-of-Wrath* offensive this year? Why did they go anywhere near it? Was Shimon Peres trying to look tough for the election? If so, it was in vain because he lost the election anyway.

INSTEAD OF GOING BACK to the kibbutz immediately, we motored beyond Malkiya because Natan wanted us to meet more friends. A short distance along the way is the tel which Johnny wants Bob to excavate, and beside the tel is the burial place of a Roman centurion. Part of the tel has been cut away by the road, revealing lines of ancient brickwork, carbon-dated to 4000BC, three thousand years even before the time of Deborah and Barak. Nearby is a mosque which is built on the legendary site of the burial place of Joshua. In Old Testament times this area was the fertile breadbasket of the tribe of Naphtali.

In the bus Natan told us a joke, "There was a Rabbi who had his prayer-shawl dry-cleaned. It was returned beautifully white, but the bill was £50. '£50!' said the Rabbi. '£50!' 'Yes Rabbi. £5 for cleaning, and £45 for unravelling all the little knots in it!'"

Soon we arrived at another settlement. It is a moshav, which is similar to a kibbutz, but allows individual wealth possession whilst its members still work in community. Basically, it is a co-operative. Natan phoned earlier to ask if we could come and so we were expected, but we had stopped so often to look at things that everyone was out when we arrived except a son of the house and his little sister. Natan was obviously a frequent and a welcome guest, so he took us on a tour of the house which was larger, more beautiful, and better appointed, than any house we had seen on a kibbutz. As we poked into the various rooms Natan sketched in the background.

"The mother of this family is a remarkable woman," he said. "She married at sixteen and a half, and she had five sons before having a daughter. The daughter is this little girl here who has come with us all round the house carrying her kitten." The little girl beamed up at Natan, who was obviously a favorite honorary uncle. Her older brother watched TV in the two-level lounge and he smiled at us as we passed.

"Sorry about tramping through your house!" we said.

"It's OK."

Perhaps Natan does this all the time with groups. Perhaps that's why the poor mother was absent!

AS WE TRAVELLED BACK to Kibbutz Malkiya, the late afternoon sun lit up Mount Hermon, and it occurred to me that Jesus was a tremendous traveller for his time. Perhaps part of Jesus' reason for dragging the disciples all over this country was to internationalize them before the great commission was given after the resurrection. They had to get used to travelling. They had to get used to meeting different people. They had to get used to dealing with cultural differences. Before Jesus challenged them to '*Follow me*' they only knew the communities around the Sea of Galilee. But, in following the Master, they went north, south, east, and west. They travelled to the Decapolis in Trans-Jordan. They visited Phoenicia in the north. They went through Samaria. They came to Jerusalem. This meant they were seasoned travellers after three years with Jesus, and could now deal with people, problems, and practicalities in a totally different way.

At Home with Natan

Back at the kibbutz, James and I examined the map, and discussed whether the Transfiguration took place on Mount Hermon or Mount Tabor. James favored Mount Hermon for four reasons. First: according to the New Testament, the Transfiguration took place immediately after events at Caesarea Philippi which is on its lower slopes. Second: atop Mount Tabor at that time was a Roman fortification and thus there would be little privacy for the event. Third: the biblical text says a *high* mountain, and Tabor is only 1,800 feet above sea level whereas Hermon is 9,200 feet. Fourth: it is characteristic for cloud to form on Mount Hermon whereas Tabor is usually clear.

Over against the Mount Hermon scenario, the Mount Tabor enthusiasts point out that, according to the biblical narrative, a full week elapsed between the happenings at Caesarea Philippi and the transfiguration itself, which week could have been spent in travel back to Nazareth which is adjacent to Tabor. As a counter argument, supporters of the Mount Hermon location say that the week was spent slowly travelling up the mountain, visiting and preaching in the small villages on its slopes before making the final ascent. However, was there actually a Roman fortification on Tabor? And Mount Tabor does have an old tradition connecting it with the Transfiguration.

Tonight has been our final night at Kibbutz Malkiya and, before our evening meal in the dining hall, the group was split up, with half going to the house of a Russian kibbutz member, and the other half, including myself, going to Natan's home. Natan's wife is in Tel Aviv 'grandbaby sit-ting' for their daughter and her husband who are in America on business.

We discussed politics, both British and Israeli, and Natan brought up the subject of various legal systems. He told us that Israel's justice sys-tem is complicated, because it has a mixture of Ottoman Law, British Law, and Jewish Law. Religious Law also has to be reckoned with even though Israel is officially a secular State.

But, for us, our host was himself a major point of interest. "Tell us more about yourself Natan."

"Well, I trained in law at a Catholic University in the States, and that is why I am so familiar with Christian worship as you saw this morning at Jish. I practiced as a lawyer in Chicago. And in 1967 I stood for, and was elected to, the Chicago city government."

Natan went over to the sideboard, brought out some old papers, and showed us an election leaflet for 1967, when he was elected as representa-tive for Ward 49. He was a Republican candidate, apparently one of only four Republicans out of a Council of fifty members. Although a Repub-lican, his candidature had been supported by independent Democrats. Natan said that these party labels were in fact used only loosely at that level of politics.

"Why did you come to Israel?"

"Well, for many years I practiced as a lawyer. But, you know, no one is interested in justice. They are only interested in winning their case. So I came over to Israel because I wanted to be part of a society, especially in the kibbutz movement, where there was real democracy and a sharing community. After coming to Israel I spent a number of years in South Africa as representative of the Kibbutz movement."

The titles on the book-shelves showed how well read Natan is, and, as he talked, our impression that he was a broadminded, fair man, increased.

"But what about yourselves?" he said. "How is Israel regarded in Britain?"

We hesitated.

I replied. "Well, Natan, years ago there was tremendous sympathy for Israel. At the time of the Six-Day War, the Yom-Kippur War, the Mu-nich Massacre, and the Entebbe Raid, Israel was seen as the small, vul-nerable nation fighting bravely for its life against powerful oil rich Arab countries and against the PLO. At that time, the word 'Palestinian' was synonymous with terrorism. But, Natan, now it has all changed. Today

Israel is seen as the powerful bully. The Palestinians are seen as the oppressed. I hope that does not offend you."

"We can be friends with the Palestinians," Natan said. "I have a simple creed. I take everyone as a friend unless proved otherwise."

He then thought for a moment.

"Remember what I said. When I was a lawyer in Chicago, no one ever came to me simply to see justice done. They came to win. Now, in the Middle East it is the same. Winning is everything. Only winners can make peace. You cannot initiate a peace overture if you are perceived as a loser. Therefore, after the Yom Kippur War in 1973 it was when Sadat of Egypt convinced his people that he had 'won' the war (which he had really lost), that he could afford to fly to Israel in that historic gesture and 'make peace.' No one can afford not to win."

"Lebanon was never a proper country. The League of Nations simply tried to make a Christian homeland for a Christian pocket in the Middle East. Lebanon is a tribal country. No one is 'Lebanese.' After Black September in 1970 when King Hussein expelled the PLO from Jordan they settled in Beirut, and the already weak political system there collapsed. Israel expelled the PLO from Beirut in 1982, but nowadays Lebanon is de-facto an arm of Syria although de-jure independent. The south Lebanese army which is 'Christian' gives Israel a buffer zone between Israel and the Syrians. But that is fragile. If there were real peace the water up on the Golan could be shared amongst everyone. Water is the key here. It always has been. It always will be."

"Some people think that Israel wants to destroy the Arab countries round about us. That is simply not true. What Israel really wants is for the standard of living in Syria, Jordan, Lebanon, Egypt, to increase, because equality of lifestyle will be a help to peace."

"Arafat is a problem. The EEC and Israel is prepared to pour millions of dollars into Gaza to renew the infrastructure: but Arafat only wants to complain about how Israel destroyed it. Arafat doesn't want to talk about the future. Your Prime Minister, John Major, took businessmen to Gaza, but Arafat wasn't interested in future development. He just wanted to talk and talk, on and on, again and again, about how Israel has destroyed the infrastructure in the past. If Arafat's men in the West Bank won't police their communities properly then the Israeli army will have to go in—with tanks if necessary—and disarm them."

That statement jolted us. "With tanks Natan! But that would result in more bloodshed! What kind of independence is that for the Palestinians?"

"Look, we did not give them independence. We gave them autonomy. But Israel must retain the right to impose order."

Is NATAN A HAWK or a dove? Is the Republican who was backed by Democrats a citizen of the world? Or is he simply an astute politician? He has given up material wealth in the States to pursue an idealist dream in Israel. He gets close to people and champions causes like that of Bar'am. But what makes Natan tick?

— Day 7 — Banias —

Monday 14th October

THIS MORNING NATAN WAVED us off from Kibbutz Malkiya. He and Johnny have been tremendous hosts, giving their time, sharing insights, and open to discussing differing views. Natan faces major heart surgery next year; whether in Israel or the USA remains to be seen. Kareem took the bus back down into the Hula valley, before turning north towards Dan and Banias which are on the extreme northern borders of Israel. *En route* Bob gave a masterly exposition of Genesis 1, dealing with it as a theological document specifically designed to counter pagan views of Creation. We scribbled down notes furiously because his exegesis was of the highest quality.

Bob also told us that, after World War One, when the British and French were drawing up maps of the Middle East, the British wanted the borders of Palestine to reflect the biblical phrase 'from Dan to Be'er Sheva.' Unfortunately, according to Bob, the clerk who drew the agreed line on the map used a blunt pencil when he came to the northern boundary, and the thickness of his blunt pencil line, when converted from the map to lines on the ground, was equivalent to 160 metres of disputed territory which, coincidentally, contains rich water resources. The breadth of a clerk's pencil line became one of the cocktail of factors which fan the flames of conflict in the region.

In Old Testament times, when the Israelites settled in the land following Joshua's conquest, the tribe of Dan were first given an area between what is now Jerusalem and Tel Aviv. However, the Philistines, who already occupied the coastal plain, made life impossible for them. Militarily the Danites were no match for the Philistines. Some Danites, like Samson, cavorted with the Philistines, but their position was always precarious. Eventually the tribe of Dan gave up the unequal struggle, left that territory, and decamped to the north where they expelled the Canaanites from the city of Laish and settled there. This is why, on maps at the back of many Bibles, the tribe of Dan is located in two places. Joshua 19:47 reads: "*When the territory of the Danites was lost to them, the Danites went up and fought against Leshem (Laish), and after capturing it and putting it to the sword they took possession of it and settled in it, called it Leshem Dan after the name of Dan their ancestor.*"

Tel Dan

Mid-morning, we arrived at Tel Dan. Bob explained that, before the Danites took over, Tel Dan (Laish) was a Canaanite high place, and has still to be properly excavated. He then showed us round the site, explaining its features and significance. Apparently, one day when the initial excavations were in progress, Gila Cook, the lady archaeologist who was recording artefacts by making drawings, noticed an inscription on a stone. She called over Abraham Biran, the project leader, and they examined the marks more closely. The inscription read: 'Bet David' which means 'House of David.' This was a major discovery, because previously there were thought to be no extra-biblical references to King David. Now there was.

We walked through a wooded area and alongside the River Dan, which is the largest and most important of the three sources of the River Jordan. Bob suggested an etymology for the river's name: "The rabbis of old asked why the Jordan (YRDN) is so named, and answered 'Because is descends (YRD) from Dan (DN).'"

I kept falling behind the rest as I tried to scribble down notes, not only about Tel Dan, but from Bob's bus lecture before I forgot the details. It's difficult writing up notes on a moving bus. So I wanted to get words on paper before they slipped my memory.

Dan is on the lower slopes of Mount Hermon, and when the snows melt high up on the mountain the water permeates down through the rock until it hits an impervious layer. It then bursts out of the mountainside as springs of water at places like Dan and Banias These springs made such sites favorite places for religions to erect temples to fertility gods and goddesses, and the strong roots of pagan culture meant that the northern tribes were always going to be susceptible to syncretistic religion.

The restored gateway of Tel Dan is impressive. In ancient times the city gate was the first line of defence in time of war. And in time of peace it was the meeting place for conversation, for gatherings of the city elders, for business, and for trade. It was also the Law Court, with a wooden canopy shielding the King when he sat judging cases. Yet, despite Dan's immensely strong defences, King Tiglath-Pileser III of Assyria over-ran it in 734/733BC.

AT THE CITY GATE is a Canaanite cultic shrine consisting of five standing stones, each only a foot or eighteen inches high, placed beside a flat stone. In Old Testament days standing stones were commonly used to mark sacred spots. However, whereas in Britain 'standing stones' are immense monoliths, in Israel the term is used of quite modestly sized rocks and boulders. Thus, for example, Jacob stood a stone up at the sacred place where he had an encounter with the Divine. Jacob needed no help to move the stone, whilst British standing stones needed the muscle power of scores of the able-bodied to manoeuvre them into position. Ancient standing stones in Israel also symbolized treaties or acted as boundary markers, so not every standing stone was religious. The location and context of a stone would show what its function was. Bob told us that standing stones can be identified as having religious significance when they have a stone ledge at the front, on which an offering could be laid.

Several hundred yards inside the Tel Dan gateway we came to the High Place where the framework of the ancient Israelite altar has been reconstructed in steel, and where, behind the altar, the Golden Calf of the Northern Kingdom would have been located. The Golden Calf was set up by King Jeroboam, who placed another in Bethel. This was one of a host of features of northern religious life which did not conform with biblical regulations. For example, the altar at Dan was of hewn stone, but hewn stone was condemned by the regulations because only unhewn, virgin stone was deemed to be appropriate. This made the Danite altar improper and its worship apostate; one reason among many why Dan was condemned by the prophets who wanted centralization of worship at Jerusalem.

"The altar had horns, just as the Ark of the Covenant had horns," said Bob. "But why was this? What were these horns for? Were they to tie the sacrificial goat to? Were they residual elements from bull worship? Or was the whole altar area meant to represent the head of a bull: with fire for the 'eyes', the horns for 'horns', the high place behind the altar for a 'brow', the smell of burnt offerings as the 'nose'? That might be what was intended."

According to Bob, the stonemasons of this area used a building technique in which a long stone is followed by a short one. The same concept was used in Solomon's Temple. There were so few trees in ancient Israel that they became expert stonemasons.

WE LEFT THE HIGH Place and walked back to the bus, passing derelict defence trenches guarding the Syrian border. Mount Hermon dominated the north. Looking over to no-man's land we saw deer and sheep grazing. On the other side of the hillock from the High Place, we passed a partially excavated site which has revealed a magnificent Canaanite entrance in dried brick, and yet only a flimsy covering guards this archaeological treasure from the elements. Bob gets so frustrated at Israeli archaeological policy which puts little money into preserving sites if they are not deemed to be spectacular.

"This is such an important site." said Bob. "Here we have an archway, constructed at least a thousand years before Roman arches, which previously were thought to be the first curved arches. This site is critical in the context of the ancient world. But what do they do? They give it a polythene covering!"

Banias

We moved on to Banias. This is Caesarea Philippi in the New Testament, and is where Simon Peter said to Jesus *'You are the Christ, the Son of the living God'*, to which Jesus replied, *'You are Peter, and on this rock I will build my church'* (Matthew 16:18). It was possibly the cultic site of the 'Ba'al of Hermon', and remained a religious center all the way through Canaanite, Greek, and Roman times. Its name was changed to Caesarea Philippi by Philip who was the Tetrarch of the area in the time of Jesus.

"In due course," explained Bob, "its name reverted to Panias after the Greek god Pan, but the Arabs pronounced it Banias because there is no 'p' sound in Arabic. In Arabic, for example, 'petros' becomes 'butros', 'Pepsi-Cola' becomes 'Bepsi-Cola' and so on."

Bob pointed out that in the first century AD the area governed by Phillip was predominantly pagan. This is why, out of the three sons of Herod the Great who gained 'kingdoms', Phillip was the only one to have his head on coinage. A strict Jew would never permit his image on a coin. Additionally, because Phillip's territory was less orthodox and more pagan, the Roman Emperor was openly revered as divine at Caesarea Philippi. Hence, it was a bombshell for Jesus to claim Messiahship in Phillip's tetrarchy where Caesar was revered as a god.

Bob suggested that we take time out for an hour and find a place to read and meditate on Matthew chapter 16 before meeting for group discussion. I took the opportunity to wander and examine the area further, as I wanted to see the niches carved in the rock-face near the great cave which used to have statuettes of the god Pan, having seen photographs of these niches in books on the Holy Land. Then I met up with Rosie, and we found a seat below a tree and looked together at the Scripture passage.

A lady climbed up the steps near us. "Shalom!" she said.

"Shalom!" Rosie replied.

"Is that a Glasgow accent?" said the lady.

"No," responded Rosie, "an Irish one!"

The lady introduced herself. "I'm Brenda, and I was born in England and brought up in Edinburgh."

"Where in Edinburgh?" I asked.

"Oxgangs."

"Have you been to Crieff?"

"Oh yes, we used to cycle to Crieff and stay in a Youth Hostel near there when I was a teenager."

"Where do you live now Brenda?" asked Rosie.

"Oh, I live at Kibbutz Sde Boker, away south in the Negev desert, which is the kibbutz where David Ben Gurion came from. I used to be Brenda Burns, and now I am Brenda Habshush because I married a Yemenite husband. We have lived fourteen years at Kibbutz Sde Boker, following on twenty years at a kibbutz near Akko. I joined the Kibbutz Youth Movement in Leeds and Edinburgh when I was young, and I have never lived in a town in Israel, always on a kibbutz."

"You know," said Rosie, "I think we go to Sde Boker in a couple of weeks' time."

"Come and see me when you're in the Negev!" and away went Brenda with a wave.

ROSIE AND I SAT under our fig-tree and talked about the Matthew 16 passage. Today, at Banias the water springs out of the rock to form a river. Apparently, in New Testament times it was even more spectacular.

At that time the river burst from the mouth of the cave like a roaring water-spout, and the temple to Pan was constructed at that spot, giving a spectacular setting for the pagan ceremonies which took place. Since then earthquakes have altered the water course and now the cave is dry, with the water emerging lower down, and very quietly. But in Jesus' day the water issuing from the cave was an extraordinary sight.

Alison appeared. "Hi Alison! Where are you going?" we asked.

"I spotted a small green-roofed mosque at the top of these cliffs. There must be a way up to it. Have you seen a path?"

"No, unless there's one further round the cliff. We haven't been that far."

"OK I'll have a look. See you later."

Alison strode off to the right to see if a way could be found there. All sorts of speculations came into our minds as we looked at the text. For example, when Jesus said to Simon Peter that *'flesh and blood has not revealed these things to you but my Father in heaven'* was he contrasting divine revelation with what happened in the temple to Pan where a priest 'revealed' wisdom similar to what happened at the Delphic Oracle? Or, was the water issuing out of the 'belly' of the mountain, like Jonah issuing from the 'belly' of the whale? Is that why Jesus refers in the same passage to the 'sign of Jonah'? And is that why, at Caesarea Philippi, Jesus called Peter by his full name Simon Bar JONAH which was not his normal practice?

When Jesus and the disciples visited Banias (Caesarea Philippi) the place would be crowded with people carrying out religious rituals. It would be busy, not only because it had always been a popular religious site, but because Phillip had made it the capital of his Tetrarchy. Was this busyness the reason Jesus took his disciples away from crowds, to a lonely place on the Mount of Transfiguration, in order to teach them what kind of Messiah he was to be? It was there he taught them that he would be a Suffering Servant, not a triumphalist Messiah as in popular perception. But he also wanted them to understand that, although there was to be suffering and lowliness, there was also to be triumph, and so Jesus revealed his glory in the transfiguration. In and through the suffering, servant King they would see the glory and majesty of the Lord in resurrection and victory.

Alison reappeared.

"Did you get to the top?"

"No. No route up the cliff-face. The path must take a more round-about way."

The three of us made our way back to the meeting-point to share our insights with the others. This was a place for profound reflection, and a multitude of thoughts were in our minds as the bus pulled out of Banias and climbed higher on the slopes of Mount Hermon.

The Golan

Part of Mount Hermon (including its summit) is in Syria, and soon the road swung over to the eastern side of the valley which separates the mountain from the Golan plain. With each mile we travelled further east, and behind us the great bulk of Hermon filled the western horizon. After passing through numerous Druze villages we were up on the Golan Heights and in the disputed area between Syria and Israel. The bus stopped near the border and we disembarked to look at the abandoned village of Kuneitra. A notice-board read:

You are standing on the eastern slopes of Mount Avital. In front of you lies the fertile Kuneitra valley, famous for its Israeli plantation of selected apples. Beyond you can see the ghost town of Kuneitra abandoned by the Syrians during the Six-Day War. Israel agreed to give Kuneitra to Syria after the Yom Kippur War. Now the border line between the two states goes through the town.

The board also gave information concerning the nearby extinct volcanoes, and concerning the ten windmills on the top of a hill called Mount Nei Rassan. The Golan has reliable wind, and the windmill system on Nei Rassan was the first site in Israel producing electricity by wind power. The board also makes the political point that the line of the extinct volcanoes gives a 'natural' boundary between Israel and Syria. The Syrians have built a new town of Kuneitra no more than a quarter of a mile away from the original. Both towns stood out in the sunlight as we looked across the Golan. One a ghost town. The other a living community.

THE PROBLEM OF THE Golan is a major difficulty, because the Golan has become a symbol of security: indeed, perhaps more of a *symbol* of security than a *necessity* for security. According to what Natan told us, this was why the assassinated Prime Minister, Yitzhak Rabin, told Israelis that the Golan could be handed back to Syria without the nation's defence being compromised. But many Israelis still remember that, in the years before the Six-Day War, the Syrian guns on the Golan Heights overlooking the Sea of Galilee used to fire shells down onto the lakeside Kibbutz Ein Gev. "They bombarded the kibbutz just for fun. Without provocation," Natan had said.

Bob added some of his thoughts. "Folks, tell me this. From a Syrian point of view, do you think that President Assad of Syria really wants the Golan back?"

We were of one mind. "Of course he does, surely?"

"Don't be so sure," Bob replied. "You see, the moment Israel and Syria sign a peace treaty resolving the Golan problem President Assad has no legitimate axe to grind with Israel. This is why some political commentators feel that the Israeli occupation of the Golan is a useful political lever for Assad. In the international arena it is useful to have something so obvious to complain about."

WE MOTORED OVER THE lava plain of the high Golan. The Golan Heights are mile after mile of brown, dry, dusty land. Pale fawn desert soil. Dusty dried grass. Dusty dead thistles. Black volcanic stones. Mile after mile of this brown, dry dust. Army bases. Tank depots. Dust. Dust. Dust. By mid-afternoon we reached the ruins of a fourth-century Talmudic village called Katzrin. Bob was particularly excited about this site because the Israeli Antiquities people have allowed some of the buildings to be reconstructed, and Bob feels more of that should be done in order to let these historical sites live. "Look at all the tourist buses and all the people coming here," he said. "This is what people like to see. And Israel has so many archaeological sites, so some could be rebuilt without losing anything."

In Talmudic times the village of Katzrin was one of twenty-seven Jewish sites in the central Golan, at each of which the Jewish inhabitants erected large and beautifully decorated synagogues. For centuries these lay undiscovered. Then, after the Six-Day War of 1967, Jewish archaeologists reached the Golan and started excavating. In 1976, the Katzrin synagogue was discovered. In Talmudic times the synagogue was the center of Jewish life, both in the cities and smaller villages. It was a place of worship and study as well as a general assembly hall and court of law. Then, further excavations of the Katzrin site during the 1980s, after the synagogue was cleared of its debris, opened up some of the rest of the village, though perhaps only 10 percent of the total. Two of the village houses have been restored, displaying typical house construction as of Jesus' day and for several centuries afterwards.

The village was abandoned during the mid-eighth century, probably as the result of a massive earthquake which struck in 749AD. Consequently, for half a millennium, the settlement was uninhabited. Eventually a mosque was erected in the ruins of the synagogue, and the village was resettled and stayed that way for several hundred years. In time it was abandoned again, and after a period of desolation, Bedouins settled on top of the ancient site. But the Six-Day War of 1967 changed everything.

After Katzrin we wound a twisting route down from the Golan and crossed the River Jordan where it flowed into the Sea of Galilee. In the first century AD the Jordan was the boundary between the region on the west governed by Herod Antipas, and the region on the east ruled by Philip. Any traveller going from east to west would have to pay border taxes at the first major town, which happened to be Capernaum. This was what Matthew the tax-collector was doing. He was '*sitting at the receipt of custom*' when Jesus said to him, '*Follow me.*'

Tabgha

Last year, on the Bike Ride, my wife Grace and a few others cycled round the northern end of the Sea of Galilee while the rest of us crossed by boat. I had always been struck by the color of the slides she took that day. They seemed to paint the reeds and grasses with a reddish tinge, and I had wondered if that was because the camera had a false exposure reading. However, today, when we traveled the same route (albeit in the reverse direction) I saw the afternoon sunlight coloring these reeds and grasses exactly as in Grace's pictures.

Bob meant to take us to the church and ruined synagogue at Capernaum, but we arrived at 4.15 pm, exactly the time it closed. So we went on to Tabgha, the site of the feeding of the five thousand with the loaves and fishes. A large tour bus labelled 'Knock Shrine Tour' followed our minibus into the Tabgha car-park, and the Knock pilgrims were ushered into Tabgha's delightfully peaceful church. But they were given no time for spiritual reflection. Their tour guide, a small, thin, wiry, sun-burned local man, was very agitated, urging them to move at the double:

"Please, come quickly. You must come now! Immediately! Come now for mass down at the beach! The priest is waiting! Come NOW! Immediately!"

So the pilgrims tumbled from their coach into the church. From the church into the souvenir shop. From the souvenir shop onto the beach. And, while they were down on the beach for a rushed mass, their guide joined his pals in the car park for back-gammon.

Tabgha is lovely, even though visitors are only allowed onto its beach if they are going to mass. In the Tabgha church there is a floor mosaic on the theme of Jesus feeding the multitude with the five loaves and two fish. On our first Bike Ride two years ago Grace photographed it, and, on doing slide shows for groups back in Scotland, I had wondered why the basket of loaves in the mosaic only shows four loaves not five. Are we to assume that the fifth loaf is hidden underneath? Seemingly not.

"Say folks," said Bob. "When we look at this mosaic we have to realize that in fact a theological statement is being made. Now, what stands directly next to the mosaic?"

"The communion table?"

"Exactly. And it was like that when the mosaic was laid down in the fifth century. The symbolism is quite explicit. The missing loaf from the basket is represented by the actual bread on the table for the Holy Eucharist. In this way the worshipping congregation of today is drawn into the mosaic and, symbolically, becomes part of the multitude fed by our Lord."

OFF-SHORE AT TABGHA, WARM water, caused by seismic activity deep underground, bubbles up into the Sea of Galilee, and the warmth of the lake at this point attracts shoals of fish. This is why the Tabgha site is regarded as having been a favorite fishing spot for Jesus' fishermen disciples.

"Folks," said Bob, "Behind us is the Mount of Beatitudes. Personally, I'm not sure if that's exactly where Jesus gave the Sermon on the Mount. However, I am fairly certain that when Jesus referred to a 'city set on a hill that cannot be hid', he was using the Decapolis City of Hippos on the far side of the Sea of Galilee as a visual aid because it stood out so obviously."

Bob pointed to the site of Hippos across the Lake. Even from our low vantage point, it was a clear landmark. I have been three times to Israel, but have still to go up to the Mount of Beatitudes. It has the reputation of being a beautiful place.

Tiberias

It was almost dark when our bus arrived in Tiberias and chugged up the steep streets which lead away from the lakeside, before pulling up outside the Daphna Hotel. A porter carried our bags to our rooms. He huffed and puffed to show how heavy the bags were, hoping to get a big tip for working so hard, so I gave him a few shekels. Before the evening meal James switched on the TV which was in our room.

"Bruce! Come and see this!"

This was our first experience of Jordanian television. It was amazing. The programme featured three extremely severe Jordanian army officers discussing safety in the home. Overloaded plugs, net-curtains hanging near a power-point, electrical flexes under carpets, and cushions piled close to fluorescent tubes, were shown for edification and warning. Each sequence started with a close up of the plug, net-curtain, flex, or cushion. Then the camera zoomed out for a wider shot. Then it led us round each danger point before zooming in again. Each hazardous scenario was introduced by more shots of deeply serious Jordanian Army officers either speaking direct to camera or interviewing a more senior officer who spoke with great solemnity on the subject. After dangers in the home, we were shown a man being pulled from the Dead Sea with two rescuers pumping his chest. Then there were pictures of fire-engines. Then scenes of scrub fires in the desert. And finally shots of sheep eating black plastic. Dire warnings for all!

At dinner James had our group in hysterics as he recounted the details. After the meal we crowded into Anne and David's room for coffee, with the Church of England clergy amongst us engaging in a discussion of the problems of a rural Deanery. All typically Trollopian. It was reassuring to escape to the atmosphere of the *Barchester Chronicles*, having watched Jordanian TV safety programmes.

LATER THIS EVENING, SOME of our group walked down to the lakeside, but I relaxed in the comfortable sitting area of the hotel foyer to write up more of my *Journal*, and to watch the various comings and goings. A German pilgrimage group was in the hotel, and they were meeting in its 'Carmel Lounge' for discussion and worship. It was lovely sitting there, listening to them singing and praying. Sharon, Clive, and Marion returned after their walk and we chatted over more coffee. The discussion led onto teetotalism. Clive led off.

"I was brought up as a strict Methodist teetotaller but I've changed on biblical grounds."

"On biblical grounds?"

"Yes, you can't get away from it. Scripture teaches us to enjoy wine as a celebration of God's gifts. The psalms are nonsense if you try and put a teetotal gloss over them."

"I suppose so," I said. "In essence, I suppose have the same view. I'm not teetotal in principle. But I just can't take much alcohol because I was never used to it."

"As with me," said Clive,

"You know," he continued, "an international perspective of Christian habits across cultures and denominations transforms some issues into non-issues. Take a simple example: when I was young our church was so strict about girls never wearing lipstick and all that. But it's a non-issue today! As for forms of worship, when you come out here and see the likes of the Maronite Church and all the different liturgies that take place in Jerusalem, it comes home to you what a wide and diverse family the Christian Church is. Somehow, our theology has to be able to embrace all this. If the good Lord accepts this wide family, then we have to as well! Not the sects and extremists of course. But there's a growing realization that the main-stream is really a wide river."

Rosie came and joined us. "Had a busy evening Rosie?"

"I've been telephoning home."

"Everything all right?"

"We've had a fire in the Rectory!"

"What!" we yelled.

Rosie nodded. "One of the boys was making chips when the chip pan went up in flames, and the whole kitchen is burnt out. It's in the newspapers. The Sun newspaper has a big headline about us, 'Holy Smoke' or something like that."

"Oh Rosie!" we gasped.

Rosie herself was remarkably cool and unflustered.

"Well, everyone's all right, and the kitchen can be repaired, so we'll count our blessings."

— Day 8 — Tiberias —

Tuesday 15th October

FREE TIME WAS SCHEDULED for the whole of today, but at breakfast a bus-driver came into the hotel dining-room and spoke to Bob, telling him a vehicle was available. Yesterday, Bob forgot that we were to have a free day, and when he took his leave of Kareem last night Bob said he was looking forward to having him with us. Kareem of course told Bob he was not scheduled to be with us, and that the bus company had no free buses today. In the light of this, a bus-driver arriving at breakfast telling Bob that his bus was outside was a big surprise. The driver left and Bob called us together.

"Well folks, this is a bonus. We have a bus today. So, if you are agreeable, I think that we could go by bus round the Sea of Galilee and call in at various archaeological and historical sites. We can perhaps get a boat back from Ein Gev to Ginnosar and the driver can go ahead and pick us up. Would that be OK folks?"

"Yes, sure."

We rushed to our rooms, threw a few things into rucksacks, and congregated outside the hotel at nine o'clock. However, even as we gathered we saw the bus drive off. We assumed the driver was away to fill it up with fuel, but after half an hour of waiting he had still not returned, so Bob did some phone calls.

"Folks! You just won't believe this. That bus-driver had nothing to do with us. He got the wrong message. And he came to the wrong hotel to pick up the wrong group! I'm sorry, we'll have to forget our plans."

In many ways it was a relief because we had visited so many archaeological and historical sites in the past week. Nonetheless, ever resourceful,

Bob chartered a 'Jesus' boat for us to sail on the Sea of Galilee. James did not feel well this morning and decided not to come on our boat trip. But, as we walked down the steep streets to the waterfront he caught up with us. He was feeling much better.

The Sea of Galilee

The boat was for our group alone, and we appreciated being by ourselves out on the water. As we boarded, the boat was flying an Israeli flag and a German flag. Obviously a German tourist group had been the last set of passengers.

The captain welcomed us. "You English? I put up your flag."

"Hold on!" I said, as he was about to change the German flag for the Union Jack.

I rummaged in my rucksack and produced the Lion Rampant.

"Ah! What is this?" said the captain.

"It's the Scottish flag."

"You all from Scotland?"

"Some of us."

The captain tied the flag to the hoisting cord, then ran it up to the mast head: and the red lion on its yellow background flew proudly above us for the voyage. It was a special time on the boat, with worship and prayer. Bob explained more background to the gospel writings in the context of Jesus' Galilean ministry. The whole experience breathed the presence of God.

AFTER RETURNING, ROSIE, TONY, and I walked with Bob to the Tiberias Hot Springs which are a mile out of town going south. We passed the old walls of Tiberias, which are built out of the black volcanic stone so common in Galilee. These black walls of old Tiberias are in stark contrast to the white, limestone walls of Akko and Jerusalem.

The heat of the sun was intense, and the pavement and roadway reflected the heat back up at us as we walked. On the way we met a large black dog with two lively pups. She had a rope-cord trailing from her collar, perhaps having broken away from a lamp-post or a tree to which she had been tethered. Perhaps her pups had wandered out of her reach, making her wrench the rope free in her determination to stay with them. Further out of town we met a tiny pup walking along the pavement on its own. To whom did it belong? This little pup trotted along the pavement, hopping either side of the railings which bordered the waterfront.

On our walk to the hot springs we passed various tourist beaches, all of which were totally deserted. The riots which preceded our arrival in Israel had discouraged visitors from coming. The hot springs of the lakeside are one of the reasons why Herod Antipas moved his Galilean capital from Sepphoris to Tiberias, since at Tiberias even the winters are mild. So, Herod Antipas had a town built on Roman lines, with Roman lifestyle, and Roman baths fed by the naturally warm water.

"Put your hand in the water here." Bob said.

We did so. Ouch! It was piping hot! Not just warm. Really hot!

Bob smiled, "This water has a temperature of fifty degrees centigrade when it comes out of the ground."

I was taken aback by the heat of the water. It looked like a normal stream, apart from its sulphurous smell. We then walked back to the center of Tiberias feeling tired because of the burning heat. Back in town I bought bread and bananas at the supermarket. Two loaves of bread and three bananas came to only 2.95 shekels. Supermarket shopping is much cheaper than buying food at the street stalls. On the other side of the main road we spotted a lady sitting on a three-legged stool, preparing food with her back to the street. Unremarkable, apart from the lady being one floor up, and her three-legged stool six inches from the edge of an unguarded open ledge. One false move backwards and she would plunge to the street below.

LEAVING THE OTHERS, I wandered into the entrance of the Church of Scotland's Sea of Galilee Centre, and sat down on a bench to eat my lunch. A lady came out of the office, not to ask who I was, or what I was doing there, but purely to be friendly.

"Are you all right?"

"Yes thank you. I'm enjoying the shade. It's so hot!"

"Would you like a drink of water?"

Only then I saw she had a glass of water in her hand.

"How kind of you. Thank you very much."

It was a lovely, thoughtful gesture. Rosie appeared and sat beside me.

"You know Rosie, the lady in the office has been so kind. She came out with a glass of water simply because she saw me sitting here. Isn't that great?"

"It's better than my experience!"

"Oh?"

"Yes, I was wandering about the town center when some youths began to pester me. So I've come up to the Kirk for 'refuge'!"

We finished our simple lunch, and Rosie set off up the hill to the hotel, while I tried to hail a taxi to take me to the Mount of Beatitudes. The accepted technique of taxi-hailing is to stand in the middle of the road and wave at every white car that passes, hoping one of them is a taxi. My attempt was unsuccessful. This was partly because I waved at the wrong cars, and partly because my waving was half-hearted since I was beginning to feel increasingly uneasy about being on my own, with a camera, and going off in a car. So I abandoned the plan and walked back to the Daphna Hotel. Then I changed and joined the others at the hotel swimming pool.

The Lakeside

Before the evening meal James and I tuned in again to Jordanian television. Tonight it had their equivalent of *Blue Peter*. Youngsters in the studio clapped and shouted at the antics of the programme presenters. Then suddenly, on screen came the picture of a mosque and the call to prayer sounded out with words from the Koran in Arabic across the screen. Five minutes later, an equally abrupt change brought us back to 'Blue Peter.'

After dinner we walked down to the lakeside, and I wore the kilt to celebrate our last night in Tiberias. On the way I chatted to Anne who is deeply involved in pastoral and preaching work at the churches where her husband David is the vicar.

"You know Bruce, in pastoral counselling situations, it is so important simply to be able to talk, but to give folk openings to speak if they want to."

"That's right Anne," I agreed wholeheartedly. "And yet, not everyone has a natural ability to chat. I know that I struggle. And often I'm aware that there are times when, as well as needing someone to listen, people also need someone who can talk and who can put in words what they are finding so difficult to express. Sometimes people find it so hard to put their feelings into words and they need someone else to express what they are thinking."

"I think that being a woman helps in a lot of cases," said Anne. "Recently I visited a young mum who had miscarried. I'm the right shape, you see, Bruce. I'm small and dumpy. And I'm like a granny to a young mum in a situation like that. It helps a lot."

ON THE WAY TO a lakeside cafe we visited the Church of Scotland bookshop. There we met Phil Hair, Church of Scotland minister at Ullapool in north-west Scotland. Phil is leading a Holy Land pilgrimage tour, and his group are having seven days in Jerusalem, three days in Nazareth, and four days in Tiberias. So far they have had a tremendous time, both as holiday and pilgrimage.

Another bookshop on the waterfront caught our attention. It was a Christian 'Zionist' bookshop where nearly every book focused on the End Times and was anti-Palestinian. James was appalled.

"Look Bruce! Look at this! How can they call this a Christian bookshop! There is no sensitivity at all in this place to the Palestinian people!"

I had to agree, "Yes. It's a bit extreme."

"You know," continued James, "too many Christians seem to think that support for Israel equates to support for God. But God wants justice for the oppressed, not just a blind tribalistic support for one side. What about the Arab Christians? They must be offended by all this stuff! Now, look over here!"

James pointed to piles of book celebrating Israeli military victories.

"How on earth can it be appropriate for a Christian bookshop to sell books glorifying the victories of the Israeli Air Force?"

I decided to be devil's advocate. "Well, James, I suppose they would justify stocking them by saying that these victories were God's work, and therefore part of the divine plan."

"But Bruce, even if it were valid to argue that God defended Israel during the Six-Day War and that the Israeli Air Force was used by God, not all Christians agree on this. It is such a sensitive issue. Even if it were so, does this up-front Zionistic, militaristic eschatology encourage reconciliation and harmony? Would it be right for a Christian bookshop in Germany to sell secular books glorifying Allied Bombing raids in World War II even though we believe God gave the Allies victory over the Nazis?"

We did not buy anything in that bookshop.

David and Alison found us a cafe with a wonderfully helpful waitress. She directed us to seats overlooking the lake, and we pushed the tables together. In the balmy, warm, soft evening air of Tiberias, we drank coffee and chatted happily as the lights of Ein Gev twinkled on the far side of the lake.

WHEN WE ARRIVED BACK at the hotel Sharon and Rosie were drinking coffee down in the foyer. Sharon was excited and grinning from ear to ear.

Rosie explained. "Romance is in the air! It's a long story!"

Sharon interrupted, "Bruce, do you remember that on last year's Bike Ride there was a lawyer from Edinburgh called Paul? Well, since then, Paul and I have been friendly. But before I came out on the Study Group a week ago things went wrong between us. That's why I've been a bit subdued."

Sharon had indeed been quieter than last year on the Bike Ride.

"So, what's happened?"

"Well, tonight Paul telephoned me."

"Here? Tiberias?"

"Yes! And he's coming to Jerusalem at the end of the week! Just to make up between us! I'm so excited!"

Apparently, since the Study Tour started, Sharon has been sharing her troubles with Rosie with whom she is rooming for the month. And some other things now fell into place. For example, I had telephoned Grace from Kibbutz Malkiya, and tonight's turn of events explained something Grace had said. "You know, Sharon," I said. "Grace said to me on the phone that Arlene from the EMMS in Edinburgh was asking where our group were staying. I thought she was just asking out of interest. But obviously Paul contacted Arlene to see if she could find out where we were!"

Sharon was over the moon. We could see that Rosie would get little sleep tonight with so much for them to talk about and with planning to be done, all of which would go on into the early hours. Sharon thought for a moment. "When Paul comes, should I play hard to get?" Thankfully she was grinning as she said it.

— *Day 9 — Bet She'an* —

Wednesday 16th October

THIS MORNING'S JORDANIAN BREAKFAST TV had a choice. Popeye cartoons on one channel, or heavy political interviews on the other. We watched the interviews for a while. The interviewees were allowed to talk on, and on, and on, with the interviewers totally passive. Not so much a political cross-examination as a government information service. "Israeli TV doesn't seem to have breakfast TV," I said. "Good for them," James responded, "I wish ours didn't."

This morning we left Tiberias and made our way south. Jerusalem was our destination for tonight. On the bus I noticed, not for the first time, how Tony has a tremendous ability to ask relevant questions immediately. While the rest of us are digesting Bob's information, Tony has already weighed it up, spotted implications, and formulated his question. Bob deals with these supplementaries skilfully, but Tony's ability to produce them is impressive. In contrast, Dee is quiet. Each day she busies herself recording events on her camcorder. Yet she has a quiet authority. She has an ability to persuade shopkeepers, traders, or unhelpful officials, to assist without having to argue in any confrontational way. She simply takes her time and exudes infinite patience.

WHERE THE RIVER JORDAN leaves the Sea of Galilee at its southern point, a baptismal site has been created with access to the river. As Bob reminded us, Jesus was possibly baptized much further south, near where the river passes Jericho, but now that bit of the Jordan is part of the international frontier between Israel and the land of Jordan and is out of bounds.

At the river, bright sunshine filtered through overhanging trees. It sparkled on the water's surface. Several pilgrim groups were at the baptismal site. One was a South American party who were having a service led by their priest. As they sang they held candles and stood in a circle by the edge of the water. The priest baptized them one by one by pouring water over their heads. It was extremely moving. At another spot a group were in the water and 'baptizing themselves' by plunging three times into the river in trinitarian symbolism, making the sign of the cross before each immersion. Bob explained that they were probably engaged in a renewal of baptismal vows rather than baptizing themselves for the first time.

Bet She'an

We then motored down the highway to Bet She'an. For me this is a familiar road, having cycled it in 1994 and 1995 on the Bike Rides. It seems such a short distance by bus. We soon reached Bet She'an which has roots far back in Israel's history due to its strategic position guarding the eastern entrance to the Jezreel Valley which stretches across Israel, connecting the Jordan Valley with the Mediterranean coastal plain.

"Bet She'an means 'House of She'an.'" explained Bob. "Who or what 'She'an' was no one knows. The name is ancient, probably referring to a Canaanite god of the era before the Israelite invasion. For some time Bet She'an was called Scythopolis. This is because in Roman times Dionysius was the patron god of the city, and, according to legend, he buried his nurse there, with Scythian archers guarding her grave. Hence the name Scythopolis."

Outside the main archaeological area Bob took us to the impressive Roman Amphitheatre.

"Folks, this place hosted the full range of Roman pleasures. And we know for certain that Christians were thrown to the lions in this very amphitheatre. Now, these people were not always killed. The Romans often 'rescued' them after a limb had been mauled from their bodies, and, if they survived, they were set free to be outcasts living in misery in the desert in the south of the country."

"Why were the Romans merciful?"

Bob shook his head. "The Romans were not being merciful. The opposite in fact. The continued existence of these victims was designed to be a deterrent. The Romans knew that, whereas a glorious martyrdom might attract followers, the sight of a maimed, broken, destroyed human being is less likely to. If you dehumanise a person and make them repugnant, then the causes they stand for become unattractive. Hitler knew that. So did the Romans."

BOB WAS INVOLVED PROFESSIONALLY in excavating Bet She'an for eight years, and he had so much to tell us about the site. Bet She'an is impressive. The Roman and Byzantine remains on the lower level are breathtaking. Bob's speciality is the excavation on top of the high tel which forms a backdrop to the Roman/Byzantine city. And one of the things which impressed us about Bob at Bet She'an was his ability to summarise and communicate his vast knowledge of the site in a compact punchy presentation. Having worked there for eight years Bob must have been overflowing with data. It would be so easy for someone with his depth of knowledge to overwhelm his listeners with information. But his talk was concise and relevant. It held our attention from start to finish. Bob is a first class teacher.

The first major building inside the Roman city is the magnificent theatre. It was built on three levels, the lower of which alone remains. That itself is a marvellous sight. Nowadays it hosts concerts, and this morning lorries and tractors were moving staging and lights ready for the next event. We sat down on one of the rows while Bob told us more.

"Folks, where we are sitting is only one of the sections of the theatre. The Crusaders took stones from the upper sections to construct building elsewhere. Now, these Roman theatres were almost always built on an artificial slope like a modern football stadium, whereas Greek theatres were almost always built into a natural hillside. As you know, during the time of Jesus strict Jews would not go to these theatres. But do you know why?"

"The nudity?"

"Partly. But the real reason was the theology of the gods as portrayed in the plays. Greek and Roman theatre focussed on the capriciousness of the gods, who deal with human beings as if they were playthings. This attitude was in direct opposition to biblical theology in which JeHoVaH is understood as a God who is constant and faithful. The alien pagan theology was offensive to Jews as much as, if not more than, the nudity involved in the theatre."

"But some Jews went to the theatre?"

"Sure. Hellenistic Jews living in Bet She'an would go to the theatre. Do you know what these Jews were called?"

"No."

"They were called 'Jews living as Romans.' Now, Paul, even though he was brought up in a Hellenistic environment, always remained an orthodox Jew as far as these things were concerned."

"But here's another point," Bob continued. "Orthodox provincial Jews would not even go into the cities of the Decapolis, and so, when Jesus took his fishermen disciples into the region of the cities of the Decapolis, he was breaking some big taboos in order to engage in mission. Jesus was not approving of the Hellenization of the area. Nor was he approving of the lifestyle of these cities. But he was teaching the disciples that, in order to reach people, you had to go to where the people are whether you like these places or not."

IT WAS SEARINGLY HOT at Bet She'an as Bob opened up the philosophical and political ramifications of the clash of cultures in the biblical centuries. By now, Bob was deep into his teaching mode.

"Folks, who started the Hellenization of Israel?"

"Alexander the Great?"

"Yeah, sure. Now, can you tell me what was different between Alexander's conquest of Israel and the other conquests Israel suffered at the hands of the Babylonians and the Egyptians and so on? Any ideas?"

We thought hard. "Was his conquest more thorough?"

"In a way. But the real difference was that no other conqueror of Israel tried to change the people. The Babylonians didn't try and make them Babylonian. The Hittites didn't try and make them Hittite. Neither did the Egyptians, the Persians, the Syrians, or the Assyrians try to make the people into images of themselves. But Alexander the Great was different. He was a man with a world view. He wanted to 'civilize' the world, not just conquer it. And in Alexander's mind 'civilizing' equated to 'Hellenization.' Alexander's conquered peoples were intended to become 'Greek' in the fullness of time."

This was an angle I had not heard before, but it made sense.

Bob continued. "Alexander knew that Israel was not as malleable as other peoples he had conquered. They would not abandon their God or assimilate him into a Greek pantheon. Neither would they compromise their way of life. Israel was unique in that even the hellenized population did not abandon their religious beliefs, unlike the other nations he conquered who did. So, what Alexander did was to set up cities of Hellenistic culture to act as magnets of 'improvement' and as model towns for the surrounding peoples to learn from. Alexander believed that over a period of time the 'higher culture' of these centers would pervade the whole land. Alexander wanted hearts and minds, not just gold and glory."

WE MOVED AWAY FROM the theatre and Bob pointed out the bath-houses of the Byzantine period when the city had a population of over forty thousand. Slave and free alike came to the bath-houses, with separate days for men and women. One series of booths had been a brothel for both heterosexuals and homosexuals. Wall inscriptions referring to days and nights of pleasure with wine, women, and boys were quite explicit. Inside the bathhouses and dwelling houses most of the floors had mosaics. Some mosaics named individuals who donated money for the city. These references are useful for modern archaeologists, helping them to date buildings accurately.

The main street, or Cardo, of Bet She'an is in two parts which, unusually, are offset. The offset is because the large tel was in the way when the Cardo was built. The tel is much higher than the surrounding Roman city, and in Old Testament times it was up on the tel that Saul's body was nailed to the city walls by the Philistines after the disastrous battle near Gilboa in which Saul and his sons, including Jonathan, perished. Saul's body was tied to the highest point as a visible deterrent to anyone else who thought of challenging Philistine authority. The pillars which used to colonnade the Cardo, its side-streets. and its reflecting pools, have fallen down due to earthquake activity, though several have been reset upright by the Israeli Antiquities Authority. In the height of its glory Roman Bet She'an was an outstanding example of opulence and luxury.

In the burning, overpowering mid-day heat, we climbed the Tel. The sun blazed in a cloudless sky. This was October and the heat and dryness was intense. What must it be like in July or August? Etched on the skyline of the tel was a dead tree, which is called the 'hanging-tree' because when the film 'Jesus Christ Superstar' was made it was used in the scene where Judas hangs himself. Bob was in his element.

"The earliest occupation of the tel was 5,000BC. Three terraces have been excavated. The Lower Terrace dates from 2,900BC. The Middle Terrace was from 1,450BC—when the Egyptians maintained a garrison—until about 1150BC. And the Higher Terrace is from the end of the Egyptian period to the rise of Israel, the time of Saul."

Compared to the spectacular Roman remains far below us, the small clay walls of the settlements atop the tel seem insignificant. But this is where the real history of Israel took place. The excavations up there have much more to do with the history of ancient Israel than the Cardo and bath houses have.

Bob had more to say. "The bulk of the pottery discovered in this higher terrace is Canaanite," he emphasized. "And so, even in Saul's day it was still a Canaanite city though under Philistine authority. Now, over there, see the pale pink bricks at the top of the Tel? These are from Solomon's time, and it was during his administration that Bet She'an was conquered by Israel and came under direct Israeli rule."

Remarkably, the Israeli Antiquities Authority is hardly interested in the Tel, concentrating on reconstructing the Roman city because that brings more tourists and more revenue. Yet that cuts across Jewish national philosophy in which roots, and history, and possession of the land, are so important. Surely many Jews must be interested in the Tel.

BOB ELABORATED. "ARCHAEOLOGISTS GET really excited when they discover the remains of burnt barley or burnt wheat, since these are ideal for Carbon-14 dating. Burnt grains are better than charred trees, because charred trees need to have the outer rings available for accurate dating to take place, and outer rings are not always there. On the other hand, wood dates back further than grain, so there's a trade-off between accuracy and antiquity. But I settle for accuracy."

"But is the dating really accurate?"

"Yeah, sure. Modern accelerators can give dating measurements to within twenty-five years of a date four thousand years ago!"

We were impressed.

"2,900BC is early Bronze Age for the Middle East," Said Bob. "This was when there was a change from agricultural villages to urbanization of a sort. But the village communities were an egalitarian society, whereas the small cities usually had a chief's house showing that a hierarchical system had emerged. Chief's houses were followed by walled cities. And the emergence of walled cities was followed by wars between these cities for more land. At Tel Bet She'an the first settlement was Canaanite, and then the Egyptians took over. In turn, the Egyptians pulled out when the Philistines occupied the coastal plain. There is no evidence that the Philistines ever settled at Bet She'an, but they controlled it."

Bob then pointed to the foundations of a small temple from that period. This temple had three 'rooms': an antechamber, a sanctuary, and a holy of holies. It is not known which god was worshipped here but the bronze leg of a Ba'al figurine has been found nearby. This temple is in poor shape because it was severely damaged in an earthquake which made it sink in the middle and twisted the walls. Bob explained that although this whole temple is no more than the size of a large room, its three main sections correspond to the sections of Herod's Temple albeit Herod's Temple was on a massive scale.

"You know," he went on, "We have spent years excavating the Bet She'an Tel, and it is an immensely important site for the early history of Israel and occupation of the land. Yet the Israeli authorities are allocating no money to preserve the excavations."

Bob pointed to the diggings with an air of resignation, "In due course these mud walls will crumble away. All the money at Bet She'an is being poured into the Roman and Byzantine ruins which are more spectacular. But you can see for yourselves, a lot of tourists have made their way up here onto the Tel despite the heat and despite the lack of information. If the Israeli Antiquities people value their own heritage these ancient walls would prove an asset in every way. At Tel Bet She'an they have a unique feature to preserve. We've tried to tell them this. But, so far, no effect."

Sachne Springs

We lunched at Sachne Springs which I have visited twice before on the Bike Rides. The place is a tropical paradise of palm trees, warm water, bathing pools and waterfalls. There was a large crowd today. A disc-jockey was playing 50s' and 60s' hits at full volume. It all added to the atmosphere. In Israel you move between centuries, eras, cultures, and civilizations, at a dizzy speed.

On the way from Bet She'an the bus had been stalling and juddering, so we were not surprised to find it completely broken down when we were ready to leave for Jericho. A replacement bus was radioed from Nazareth, and, while we waited, Bob gave us a lecture on the Psalms of Ascent as we sheltered from the sun under a sycamore tree. The Psalms of Ascent are the psalms which were sung by Old and New Testament pilgrims as they approached Jerusalem. Jerusalem was our destination today, and it was fitting to have that lecture before we set off for Zion.

West Bank to Jericho

Our backup bus took us down the West Bank, following more of the 1994 and 1995 Bike Ride route, with Sharon and I exchanging information on familiar landmarks. On the way Bob pointed out Wadi Jabbok over on the Jordanian side of the Jordan. It was at the Jabbok that Jacob wrestled with God, and Bob shared with us his way of interpreting the significance of that event.

"Folks, Jacob's wrestling with God can be seen not as rebellion, but as a legitimate struggle with the Almighty, in which a human being encounters the Divine and grows through active interaction. Perhaps the wrestling is saying that God gives us a humanity which is intended to engage with him. He doesn't want us to be totally passive."

"Now, a New Testament parallel to this concept of 'wrestling with God' would be the incident where the four friends are so determined to bring their paralysed companion to Jesus that they cut a hole in the roof to get access to the Lord. They didn't give up without a struggle. And their struggle was rewarded. Three things happened to Jacob after his wrestling with God. He came away more mature. He came away wounded. And he came away changed."

As we approached Jericho the sun sank low on the horizon. From the bus we saw Bedouin leading their herds of sheep and goats back to the enclosures for the night.

"See these flocks of sheep and goats?" commented Bob. "Now, the sheep stay together in a bunch, following one another; but goats wander all over the place. This was why Jesus used sheep to typify obedience; and goats to symbolize waywardness."

The low light of the setting sun silhouetted the shepherds and their flocks in dust clouds thrown up by the animals as they trotted along. We had a brief visit to the ruins of Tel Jericho, and then motored up the old Roman Road of Wadi Kelt. There were precipitous ravines on either side, and the bus lurched round the corners with its front end repeatedly overhanging. I had the dubious privilege of being in the front seat, experiencing the full drama of the ride.

Halfway up Wadi Kelt we stopped opposite St. George's Monastery where twelve Orthodox Monks live. The sky ahead was filling with stars, and a red glow on the horizon marked where the sun had set. The lights of Jerusalem could be seen. A large cross, erected near where we stopped, towered over us in the fading light. Three Arabs who had been pushing their broken-down car uphill rushed over and clamoured to sell us beads and head-dresses.

It was a brilliantly warm desert evening, and the wilderness of Judaea stretched all around. This was where Jesus stayed for forty days and forty nights after his baptism. This was where he hungered, and thirsted, and was tempted and tested. This was where, by the pale moonlight, the stones of the desert could look like bread, enticing him to turn them into something edible to break his fast. With these thoughts we continued our journey up to Jerusalem and sang praise songs as we approached the city.

Christ Church by the Jaffa Gate

For the next eight days we are staying at Christ Church, inside the Jaffa gate of the Old City. When we arrived today, a Messianic congregation was worshipping in the sanctuary, with a time of prayer taking place. We found our rooms. Then there was a delicious evening meal. David Pileggi, whom we had last seen at Stella Carmel, welcomed us and said that at 8.10 am tomorrow he was leading a tour to the tunnel, the same tunnel which was the cause of riots last month.

"Shoresh, we are going to join up with another Shoresh group and do this together."

"But should we be going there at all?" asked Alison. "I mean, if there was such strong Arab opposition to the Israelis opening a second entrance to it, should we ignore the Arab feelings? In the past week we have seen the hurt felt by many Palestinians and Arabs."

James also was uneasy about going to the tunnel. And for the same reasons. As a group we discussed the problem. I decided to go on the tour because I felt that the people who caused the trouble before we came out were extremists. Seemingly the tunnel has been there for years, and all that the Israelis have done recently is to open another entrance to avoid congestion. Am I right or am I wrong? It's difficult to know out here.

AFTER SUPPER JAMES, CLIVE, Marion, and I walked round the outside of the walls to the Damascus Gate. When we returned, a disturbed man was sitting on the ground outside the gate of Christ Church. A man and a woman were trying to help him, but he was cursing and swearing in English, obviously very disturbed. It was a jolt to hear profanities, because for over a week we had been listening to people speaking Arabic and

Hebrew which we do not understand and we had been deaf to anything which might be irreverent speech. We did not know what was wrong with this poor soul. A beggar at the rich man's gate? A sinner outside the 'courts of the righteous'? A sick man needing to be healed in his soul? Here we were in Israel, in God's Holy City, only a hundred yards from Calvary, and what did we do? We wandered back into Christ Church and hoped that the two other people would help him. I felt a huge contradiction between all that we were learning, and our poverty of action when faced with this needy person.

Sharon and I started having a contest under strict rules to see how many people we meet have been to Scotland. Expatriates do not count. Tonight, when we came back from the walk to the Damascus Gate I found a note pushed under the door: 'McAuslane 4, Ritchie 2.' Along with the score Sharon communicated some good news. When I arrived at Tel Aviv off the flight from the UK my sleeping-bag was missing: but, when Paul comes tomorrow to see Sharon, he is bringing his sleeping bag over for me. I need one on the Bike Ride.

Jerusalem

— Day 10 — The Tunnel —

Thursday 17th October

THIS MORNING WE WENT through the tunnel. In the end all of us did it except James who remained profoundly uneasy about the high-handed way the Israelis went about opening the new entrance to the tunnel in the Muslim quarter. "Look Bruce, I've been re-reading Elias Chacour's book *Blood Brothers*, and in the book he makes it clear that the evacuation from Bar'am in 1948 was not as voluntary as Natan led us to believe, never mind the appalling way the Bar'amites have been treated ever since!"

"So you're not coming through the tunnel?"

"No. I don't see how I can."

Bar'am was Elias Chacour's village. Over the years he has learned to forgive. But the arrogant use of power by the Israelis, which he describes in his book, has made James really unwilling to come to the tunnel.

"Bruce, I know that the tunnel doesn't go anywhere that a fair-minded Muslim needs to be sensitive about; but it's simply that the actions of the Israeli government before we came out here were just another example in a long line of incidents in which the feelings of the Arab community have been arrogantly swept aside."

"Maybe you're right James. I suppose I just want to see all I can."

SO JAMES STAYED BEHIND as we joined up with the other Shoresh group and made our way towards the Western Wall where the tunnel starts. The other group was American and the leader looked familiar. Mindful of my competition with Sharon I spoke to him.

"Hello, I'm Bruce."

"Gee, good to meet you Bruce! I'm David."

"Have you been to Scotland David?"

"Sure Bruce. I studied there at Edinburgh in the seventies."

"David, by any chance did you study at New College?" New College is the Divinity Faculty of Edinburgh University.

"Sure did Bruce. Sat under the Torrance brothers. They were great theologians."

"David, I was at New College from 1973 to 1976. I thought you looked familiar. You know, I think I played table-tennis against you between lectures!"

As we walked David and I chatted about life in New College, when we were training for the ministry.

The Tunnel

At the tunnel entrance a small, skinny man handed each of us a glossy colored information leaflet. The leaflet is produced using ultra-high quality photographic paper. Generous resources are obviously being made available for anything to do with the tunnel. It seems that the Israelis are making a statement about their right to do what they want in 'their' city. The little thin man went with us all the way.

Although James wasn't with us, Alison was.

"I wonder if I should be here," she said. "But I'm determined not to come out the new exit at the far end, because that's what upset the Arabs."

In the event Alison *had* to go out the new exit because it was too difficult to turn back.

"I shouldn't have come. I've asked the Lord to forgive me for doing this."

Alison was really upset about the way she had had to compromise her good intentions.

THE ISRAELIS CLAIM THAT the only reason why they have made the new exit is in order to create a one-way system through the tunnel. Before they opened the new exit there was major congestion as groups tried to pass each other coming from, and returning to, the single entrance beside the Western Wall. That may be true, but the Arab community sees sinister motives.

The tunnel starts at the left-hand side of the Western Wall and comes out opposite the Church of the Flagellation in the Via Dolorosa. This morning there were plenty of police and soldiers about, but no sign of trouble anywhere. In the tunnel we got down to actual first-century street level and touched the very bedrock of the hill on top of which the massive Temple was built. Deep into the tunnel David Pileggi got Tony to stand at one spot and David from America to stand at another spot fifteen yards further on.

"OK Shoresh," said David. "Look at Tony and David. Where they stand marks the edges of one of Herod's stones, called the Master Stone."

"One stone! Just one stone?"

"Yep. This particular stone is all of one piece. It is forty-five feet long, eleven feet high, and weighs three hundred tons."

Halfway through the tunnel a small Jewish crypt marks the nearest known point to the ancient site of the Holy of Holies. Some Muslims are worried that extremist Jews will use the tunnel as a place to mine underneath the Dome on the Rock Mosque and blow it up, clearing the Temple Mount for the building of a Third Temple.

As a guide David Pileggi has a unique style. Bob Mullen's style is to give us a clear, logical, tidy presentation of the facts allied with devotional insights. David's method is to narrate the 'adventure story of history.'

"Hey Shoresh, listen, this is what happened."

Then David thumps the wall, or model, or door, or table, with his massive bear-like paw of a hand, wipes the sweat off his brow with his forearm, peers at us through half-closed eyes, and engages us in the story, the philosophy, the politics, the scheming, and the plotting of first-century Jerusalem. He is scholar, poet, and story-teller all in one, and I regret that my summaries of his talks are only a pale shadow of his original presentation.

"Look Shoresh," David expounded, "Solomon's Temple, the First Temple, was wrecked when the nation was exiled to Babylon. Now, when the people returned the Second Temple was built along the same lines. But Herod wanted to rebuild the Second Temple into something much grander. And he had two reasons for wanting that. What were the reasons Shoresh?"

We shook our heads.

"Well Shoresh, two reasons. First, Herod knew that the Jewish people did not accept him as a real Jew. His family were recent converts to Judaism. But Herod reckoned that if he built a superb Temple for the people then that would help him to be accepted as a legitimate king. So the first issue was legitimization of his rule. The second issue was history.

Herod wanted to be remembered in history. But what could he do to make his mark? Look Shoresh, what was the normal way for a king to become memorable?"

"Military conquest?"

"Exactly. But Herod's country was under Roman rule so he couldn't go out and conquer other nations, which was the standard means for rulers to make an impact. But what he could do was build. So Herod paid for the rebuilding of the Temple. Herod also sponsored buildings throughout the Mediterranean lands. All over Mediterranean countries you can find plaques on buildings which read 'This Temple/Theatre/etc. has been built by the generosity of Herod, King of the Jews.' For example, Herod paved two and a half miles of Antioch's streets with marble. Nowadays Coca-Cola sponsors the Olympics. Back then, Herod sponsored architecture."

"OK Shoresh. So Herod wants to build a Temple for the people. The biggest, best, Temple ever. Now, what's the obvious problem?"

"Money?"

"Nope. Try again."

"There already was a Temple standing?"

"Exactly! The problem was that there was already a Temple on the site. Now, sure, Herod wants to make it bigger, and Herod wants to make it better. But the religious leaders don't trust Herod. They don't believe that he will carry through his grandiose scheme. After all, he wasn't a religious guy. So, understandably, they are extremely reluctant to allow him to pull down the existing Temple preparatory to building a new one. Now, this created a real problem. Herod couldn't build his new Temple on any other site because the Temple had to be built at exactly the same place on the land bought by King David for this purpose centuries before. So how does Herod win their trust?"

We shook our heads. None of us knew.

"Well, Shoresh, what Herod does is to spend eight years cutting and preparing vast stones. And when the religious authorities see all the preparations he is making, and therefore that he is really serious about the scheme, they let him proceed. Now, during all the years of dismantling and rebuilding, the daily sacrifices continue without interruption, and so although Herod's building was technically the third building built as a Temple on the site, it is classified as part of the Second Temple period because there was continuity of worship all through the time of reconstruction."

"Now Shoresh, look at these stones laid on top of each other."

In the dim light of the tunnel we looked up at the ancient stones laid down by master masons twenty centuries ago.

David went on, "Shoresh, when each huge block of stone was put in place, iron pins were fixed into the top of it, sticking upwards. And so, when the next stone was placed on top, the higher stone was temporarily perched one or two inches above the lower stone. Then the sheer weight of the top stone slowly crushed the iron pins; and, in the time it took for that to happen, the engineers could fine-tune the exact placement of the top stone before it settled. Each course of massive stones was offset half an inch inside the line of the lower course, and this both added stability and enhanced the aesthetic appearance. We can't see the effect of the half-inch offset in this limited space. But, down at the south-eastern corner of the Temple Mount it becomes obvious."

IN THE TUNNEL WE could also see part of the water aqueduct which carried water into the Temple. Water was needed for ritual purification and also for washing away the blood of the sacrifices. Originally the water came from near Bethlehem and the aqueduct had to follow a wandering route with a vertical fall over that distance of only a few metres.

"OK Shoresh, the standard of civil engineering involved was remarkable. The Romans knew about syphoning and so it is highly probable that parts of the channel were air-tight, helping to move the water over the various contours from Bethlehem. The total distance covered was seventy kilometers rather than the twenty kilometers as the crow flies."

Information. Understanding. Analysis. These poured out of David. He pointed out that when Jesus cleansed the Temple, and turned over the tables of the money-changers, that took place either on the exterior southern steps or outside the Treasury area; certainly not in the Temple proper, because no money was allowed within the Temple precincts. This reminded David of other issues.

"Now Shoresh, you know that in the Temple there was the Court of the Women and the Court of the Men?" We nodded. "Now," David added, "these male and female areas were not totally segregated." This surprized us.

"But David," Alison asked, "did the women not have to stop in the Court of the Women and go no further? That's what we've always understood?"

"No Shoresh, it wasn't as strict as that. To begin with, it's obvious that the rule was not an absolute rule because a woman had to go through the men's court when she presented a sacrifice, for example after childbirth. And there is other evidence to suggest that women were regularly found in the court of the men."

"So Gentiles could go into these inner courts as well?"

David shook his head,

"Oh no! That really was strict. Really strict! Gentile exclusion was absolute! That's why Paul got into such trouble when people thought he had taken Trophimus from Ephesus, an uncircumcized Gentile, into the Temple."

WE EMERGED FROM THE tunnel into a quiet Via Dolorosa. Two policemen relaxed on chairs by the exit. Looking up, we saw a heavily armed policeman on the roof overlooking the tunnel exit. Janet Francovic was with us and she told us about a Palestinian pottery shop which she wanted to visit, so we went with her. Inside the Damascus Gate were milling crowds, fruit sellers, street-traders, and money changers. The sun was high. The scene was colorful and noisy. The interior street of the Damascus Gate is one of the most exciting places in the whole of Jerusalem. Passing through dense crowds we left the Old City and walked north up the Nablus Road, but I began to feel unwell. So I left the others and started back to Christ Church. On the way I had to pass a group of twenty or so youths who were arguing violently with one another. Several of them were fighting, punching, and kicking each other. Even though I crossed to the other side of the street it was unnerving having to walk close to them on my own. Eventually I got back to my room, and after a lie down felt much better. It was probably a case of foreign food and the heat finally getting to me. Especially the heat.

Old City Rambles

After my rest James and I visited the Church of the Holy Sepulchre. The Church of the Holy Sepulchre was founded on the traditional site of Calvary by Helena, mother of Constantine the first Christian Roman Emperor. I had a rough idea of the route to follow through the maze of streets, and when we saw a group of visitors gathered round the Eighth Station of the Cross we fell in with them because they would be heading for the church as the climax of their walk up the Via Dolorosa. Following the pilgrims, we moved through the streets, passing numerous stalls and their pushy stall-holders, but after some time we had still not arrived at the church, so I spoke to one of the pilgrim group. He spoke no English, and my French was limited.

"Allez-vous a l'eglise Holy Sepulchre?"

"Mais non! a l'hotel!"

James and I hurriedly doubled back and found the church ourselves.

LAST YEAR I TOOK a photograph of an Orthodox priest in the courtyard of the church, and this year I brought back some prints for him. The corner of the courtyard where my man had been sitting last year was being repaired, with workmen busy tearing up the flagstones. In the huge crowd I could not see him anywhere.

"There he is!" said James.

Sure enough, there he was, in full robes, standing speaking to another elegantly robed senior ecclesiastic.

I pushed through. "Excuse me, I have a photograph for you."

"Pardon?"

"I have a photograph for you. I took your photograph last year. Here it is. Do you like it?"

He was delighted. I had not seen him standing up before, and he was much shorter than I imagined.

"Thank you very much indeed," he said, bowing as he spoke.

"Not at all. Thank you," I replied. "May I ask your name?"

"Daniel. I am Bishop Daniel."

"Thank you Bishop Daniel for allowing me to take your photograph. May the Lord bless you."

He bowed again, and smiled.

WE BOUGHT BREAD AND bananas for lunch. This afternoon was free from lectures, giving an opportunity to explore the nearby Armenian Quarter of the Old City. Grace and I had never gone there on our previous visits to Jerusalem, but, because the Quarter is adjacent to Christ Church it was easy to get to. Dozens of political posters are pasted to the walls of the Armenian streets, and these posters are of two types. The first is a map of former Armenia and Turkey with the words: *'Remember April 24, the Day the Armenians mourn the deaths of the first Genocide of the Twentieth Century.'* The second poster reads:

'Justice! Now! One and a half million Armenian men, women and children were killed in the first genocide of the Twentieth Century, planned and executed by the Turkish Government in 1915 as a brutal 'final solution.'

*Another million were driven from their ancestral land where they have lived
for thousands of years before the Turks arrived. Today, a determined Armenian people has risen from the ashes of the 1915 Holocaust to remind the regime in Turkey that we will not forget until justice is done, and Turkish held
Armenia must be returned to the Armenian people. The world community
must recognize that the use of genocide as an instrument of national policy,
by any nation at any time, must be universally condemned and the guilty
state must be denied the territorial, material or political fruits of genocide.'*

Grace's parents were friends for many years with a lady called Arsine Alexander, whose family had to flee Armenia during the persecu-
tions referred to in the posters. She was a small girl at the time, and,
after some time in Greece, the family moved to Scotland where Arsine
trained in social work. There she met Grace's mother who worked in the
same department. In T.E. Lawrence's book *Seven Pillars of Wisdom*, he
describes meeting Armenian refugees in the Syrian desert, who were
fleeing the Turks. They were destitute, homeless, and without a land to
call their own. And, from time to time, they were willing volunteers for
Lawrence in raids on Turkish outposts.

There are very few side alleys off the main road which goes through
the Armenian quarter. Instead, on each side of the roadway are large com-
pounds containing the Armenian Monastery, the Armenian Cathedral,
and the buildings of the Armenian Patriarchate. The afternoon sun was
unbearably hot and I bought a cool pineapple drink from a cheerful shopkeeper. I chatted to him, keeping the competition with Sharon in mind,

"Have you ever been to Scotland?"

He grinned, and pointed to the whisky bottles on his stall. "No, but
Johnny Walker is my best friend!!"

He was so pleased with this joke that he repeated it several times.
He was friendly, and I told him about Arsine in Edinburgh. He nodded
and emphasized the injustices done to the Armenian people. So many
peoples within the walls of Jerusalem. So many cruelly treated by history.
Jews, Arabs, Palestinians, Armenians.

THE STREET THROUGH THE Armenian quarter loops past the Zion Gate
into the Jewish Quarter. From there I was soon back in the Souk and
decided to revisit the Church of the Holy Sepulchre because I love to
watch the cosmopolitan crowds. I found the steps which lead from the
Souk up onto the roof of the church: this is where the Ethiopian monks
have their community. Many years ago they had a place inside the church

itself, but taxes and ecclesiastical pressures forced them out of the building and onto the roof. I sat on a chair on their rooftop courtyard watching comings and goings for over half an hour. I kept the camera ready and snapped photographs as the monks grew less aware of my presence. In the center of the courtyard is the Copula around which the Ethiopians process with lighted candles on the night of Good Friday.

The door to their chapel was closed when I first arrived, because the chapel is shut during lunchtime each day. One of the black-robed monks was leaning against the wall, reading from a small, ancient prayer book which had pale brown leather covers. He was happy to be photographed. Then three dark-skinned youths, dressed in casual western clothes, came into the courtyard. They bowed respectfully to the monk, and he bowed back to them. Then they clasped hands in a fellowship greeting, and sat on the ground and conversed with him.

Another monk, dressed in a grey gown, came out from his cell, hobbled over to a vacant chair, and sat in the shade of a sycamore tree. Bearing in mind that the 'ground' is the roof of the church below, the tree has flourished remarkably well. The monk in the grey robe limped badly, and used a stick to help his walking.

A group of American tourists arrived up the steps and tried to get into the chapel, but it was still closed. One of the tourists approached the grey-robed monk, and asked, "Can I take your photograph?" The monk shook his head. The tourists left but I stayed, relishing the warmth of the sun, and enjoying the feeling of peace of this quiet rooftop refuge. The three youths had by now finished their conversations with the first monk, so they bowed to him and left. With no one to talk to he was restless. He read his book for a few minutes. Then he paced about the rooftop. Then he disappeared and reappeared whirling a prayer necklace. Then he disappeared again, this time to reopen the chapel. I followed him through the chapel, down the inner stairs to the lower chapel, and from there out into the sunlight of the familiar main courtyard of the Church of the Holy Sepulchre.

A white bird and a black bird perched together on a ledge over the main doorway of the church. Rich sermon illustration! Going inside, I saw two armed policemen sitting on a wooden bench next to the doorway. Catholic pilgrims gathered around the rock slab which, according to tradition, was where Jesus' body was laid after he was taken down from the cross. The pilgrims placed necklaces and olive-wood crosses on the rock slab, and anointed it with holy oil.

AFTER THE EVENING MEAL at Christ Church we met in the lounge for a lecture from Joseph Francovic on the Rabbinic background to the parable of the Prodigal Son. On the wall of the lounge a plaque read:

> *Glorious Lord Jesus,*
> *Thy death we show forth,*
> *Thy resurrection we proclaim,*
> *Thy coming we await.*

Joseph's exposition was brilliant, combining high scholarship with devotional insights. We used English texts, but Joseph translated directly from the Hebrew and Greek as he went along, employing not only the biblical texts, but a variety of Rabbinic writings. After Joseph finished David Veness opened up about some personal issues. "What you said tonight, Joseph, helped a lot." Tony and our other David prayed for David and Alison and their family, then David went off to tell Alison what Joseph had been saying. Alison, Rosie, and Sharon had been attending a celebration service in the church led by the Romanian Christian community.

— *Day 11 — The Citadel —*

Friday 18th October

PAUL ARRIVED LATE YESTERDAY afternoon, and Sharon went to meet him at Tel Aviv. Since then they have been having long walks, long talks, and long hours together. As a group we get on well together, but Clive looked tired today. Last week he was energetically cheerful, but a stomach bug has left its mark. All of the group who come from England are involved in the renewal movement of the Anglican Church, and several are from churches which have started a two service pattern on Sunday mornings in order to deal with the 'new wine in old wineskins' dilemma of contemporary church life. It's a great crowd to be part of. The folk are realistic and genuine. No one has a narrow theology of either a liberal or fundamentalist type. And there is an eagerness to learn, to assess, to grow, and to look for ways we can use the material for our congregations.

At breakfast one of the Christ Church staff read the day's Scripture portion from *Daily Light* before leading us in prayer. Like the St. Ninian's Christian Centre in Crieff, where Grace and I live, Christ Church has volunteer staff from different parts of the world. The dining-room also doubles as the Christ Church museum, though the exhibits on show are quite modest, consisting mainly of framed photographs and documents hanging on the wall. Christ Church is not focused on the past. It is much more concerned with what God will be doing in the future!

Wandering and Wayfaring

After breakfast I strolled into the Souk. It is adventurous living in the heart of the Old City, because, whenever we want, we can wander its streets, filling in a spare half hour here and there, and able to see much more than if we had to make special excursions from a hotel or hostel on Jerusalem's outskirts. It was 8.45 am. and stall-holders were starting to open up.

As I ambled down the narrow alleys the familiar invitation was extended, "Come inside. Please sir, no need to buy." But I had heard that before, many times. Two years previously Grace and I accepted such an open invitation and went into a souk bazaar which sold Arabian clothes, and was full of exotic and beautiful costumes. The stall holder took us to the rear of his shop, assuring us repeatedly that there was no obligation to buy. Then he showed us pictures of his wife and family and confided that custom was poor, tourist numbers were down, that it was hard to feed his children, and that people from Scotland were lovely, generous people. When we excused ourselves and made to leave his shop, he raged at us for being so mean.

Yesterday James bought a kippur head-covering, and the shopkeeper who sold it to him looked up as I passed.

"Good morning sir." I said.

"Good morning. Come inside. Please sir, no need to buy."

"No thank you." I walked past resolutely.

All down the tapering street shop-keepers displayed their wares. Beautiful chess-sets carved from olive-wood. Colorful Armenian pottery. Richly embroidered Bedouin clothes. Traditional long dresses. Modern waistcoat-style tops. And, of course, printed T-shirts emblazoned with slogans: 'Don't worry America, Israel is behind you!', 'Jerusalem Hard-Rock Cafe', 'My mother went to Jerusalem and all I got was this lousy T-shirt!'

Within this mixture of ancient and modern, ethnic culture and absorbed culture, live and move the people of Old Jerusalem. When H.V. Morton visited Palestine in the 1920s and 1930s, Jerusalem had barely changed for a thousand years. But, since the Second World War, the city has been heavily influenced by universal modern culture; and yet its roots and its history manifest themselves around every corner.

What am I searching for? I am well aware of what I would like to find. I want to see glimpses of the images my imagination associates with traditional middle-eastern life, with its color, noise, and atmosphere. And I do see these because they still exist. But the Old City of Jerusalem is not a museum. It is a real place. It is a home and a place of work for people today. The elegance of Arabic clothing is so beautiful, and delights the eye, that it is a pleasure to simply walk the crowded alleys amongst these people.

Deeper into the Souk the butchers in Meat Street were unloading animal carcasses. Flagstones, red with blood, were washed down with power hoses. In one dimly-lit thoroughfare a copper-smith was starting the day's work. His shop was stacked from floor to ceiling with metal articles, with himself crammed in a corner working on his lathe, and his only illumination a single naked light-bulb.

AT THIS TIME IN the morning the courtyard of the Church of the Holy Sepulchre is deserted, and when I went into the sanctuary it was quiet, peaceful, and beautiful. This is the best time to go to the church. Contrary to the experience of many pilgrims who visit Jerusalem in a hurry— perhaps on a rushed day tour from a cruise—the Church of the Holy Sepulchre does have a devotional atmosphere. But you have to be there early. You have to be there when it is quiet. Just like this morning. And yet, even though the hour was early, already there was a small queue of pilgrims waiting to see the traditional tomb of Jesus. They waited quietly and reverently for their turn to enter the sepulchre. A black-robed monk emerged from a gloomy corner of the church into the half-light, then turned and went back to his station. Inside the main doorway an Ethiopian monk in bright yellow robes was sitting on a bench, so I sat next to him.

"Good morning." I said, "Do you speak English?"

The monk did not, but hailed a man who was passing, and who was fluent in both English and Amharic.

"Good morning, what can I do for you?" he asked.

"I would like to speak to my friend here, but he speaks no English. Can you help?"

"I will be privileged to help the holy Father. I am also from Ethiopia and I am studying in Tel Aviv. I am at your service."

The monk spoke to him, and he translated.

"The Father, he says that he is called Abu Gebreselassie, and this is his first time in the Holy City. But he is very sad."

"Oh! Why?"

"The Father, he bought a golden incense burner from a trader in the bazaar because he wishes to take something back to his monastery from the Holy City of Jerusalem. But the trader charged him four hundred shekels. And after he bought it he discovered elsewhere that the true cost is much, much, less. He is very sad because it cost a lot of money. But he is even more sad because in the Holy City he thought people would be good and kind, for it is the City of our Lord."

I tried to make the monk feel better by admiring his purchase. "May I see your incense burner?"

It was in a black plastic bag, but he took it out and showed it to me. I examined the burner, pointed out its striking features, and said how lovely it was. I think this made him feel more cheerful. Then we exchanged addresses because he was planning to come to Scotland in the New Year. "May I take your photograph?" I asked.

He was delighted. Hiding the black plastic bag, he produced a small cross which he held over his chest as he looked intently into the camera. Ethiopian monks are serious people. Where a Scottish or English cleric would normally smile when meeting new people, these small, sun-burned, poor monks from Africa have a grave and solemn demeanour which never leaves them.

AFTER I LEFT ABU Gebreselassie I made my way back to Christ Church via a leather worker's shop. Yesterday I bought a belt from him, but when I got back to my room at Christ Church I realized the belt was far too long and wanted to change it for a shorter one. The leather worker was quite amenable, but never smiled. The man selling kippurs again acknowledged me as if we were old friends as I rushed by, trying to be in time to join the rest of the group for our guided tour of the Tower of David museum. As I pushed through the crowds I heard his voice again, "Come inside. Please sir. No need to buy."

The Tower of David

Christ Church is directly opposite the Citadel, or Tower of David, and, after everyone had arrived, David Pileggi guided us through the fortress and its fantastic museum. In truth, the tower has nothing to do with King David of the Old Testament. It is part of the remains of Herod the Great's Jerusalem palace. Herod built three high towers at his palace, each of which he named. One after his brother Phasael. Another after his beloved wife Mariamne the Hasmonean. The third after his friend Hippicus. The present so-called Tower of David is the only remaining one of the three, and is probably the Hippicus tower. When Titus destroyed Jerusalem in 70AD he razed the city to the ground apart from the Citadel, and Titus had two reasons for leaving it intact. First, he wanted a place to garrison his troops. Second, he wanted the Herodian towers to stand out as examples of how heavily fortified Jerusalem had been. The implication being, that if such a strong city fell to Roman power then it was futile for others to resist the legions. Titus was also anxious that posterity would not belittle his campaign. So the Herodian towers were to be a witness to the strength of the city he had overcome, and a testimony to his military prowess.

David's running lecture encompassed the whole history of Jerusalem, and was delivered in his remarkable, idiosyncratic style. One of David's sentences stood out. It came when we were in part of the museum which featured ancient Jewish tombs in Jerusalem. Rosie asked him about the authenticity of the Garden Tomb site as the place of Christ's burial. David paused, sighed, and rubbed his eyes before replying.

"Look Shoresh! Listen! OK, the Garden Tomb site is really beautiful, but it's the wrong period to be Jesus' tomb. It is First Temple period not Second Temple period. When Catherine Kenyon, *that pistol packin', gun tootin', rum drinking, rebellious daughter of a Bishop,* examined it, that's what she discovered." Few phrases cap David's description of the eminent and legendary lady archaeologist.

"I can tell you about something which is truly genuine though," said David. "At the base of the Scottish Church in Jerusalem there is an ancient graveyard. And in that graveyard archaeologists discovered an amulet from the seventh century BC which, when the metal was unrolled, displayed the words of the Aaronic blessing from the book of Numbers written in Hebrew script. Now Shoresh, that artefact is the oldest portion of Scripture in the world, predating Qumran by several hundred years."

After David's historical, sociological, and theological guided lecture we broke up and roamed the museum on our own. I was struck by a notice on the ramparts which read: *This corridor leads to the Machicolations: parapets from which hot oil, molten lead or stones, were dropped on the enemy.* Barbarism is fascinating when it is historical. But if it is contemporary like the barbarism in Rwanda, or Bosnia, or the Warsaw Ghetto, it is sickening.

LUNCH WAS BREAD AND bananas inside the Jaffa Gate. We sat on a low wall outside David's Tower and watched the breadseller. Grace and I noticed him last year. He cannot speak, being dumb though not deaf, and communicates with his customers by hand-gestures. The street-traders know each other well, having worked alongside one another at the same stances for years. Together they operate an informal 'neighborhood-watch' system, though it is the tourists and not the locals who really need to be protected from the petty thieves and pick-pockets operating in the Old City.

Two camels with highly-decorated saddles sat inside the gate. These were for tourists. The camels are a new feature at the Jaffa Gate, for we did not see them last year, or the year before. Adding to the bustle were the wheelbarrow men who trundle their slim barrows into the Souk delivering goods to the traders. If the streets are quiet the men allow their barrows to freewheel down the Souk. In order to freewheel, they lean on the load, feet off the ground, and then activate a 'brake' by jumping onto a small rubber tyre which drags along the ground behind them. Goodness knows what happens if they miss the drag tyre when an emergency stop is required.

At lunchtime Paul and Sharon went into a falafel shop and, on hearing their accents, the shopkeeper asked, "Are you Scottish? Do you come from Pitlochry? I was once engaged to a girl from Pitlochry, but it fell through two months before the wedding. It was not to be! This is the will of Allah!"

JAMES GOT INVOLVED WITH a Jeweller whose shop was up a side-street near the Jaffa Gate. James was passing when the shopkeeper came out to him. "Can you speak English please?" asked the shopkeeper.

"Yes, what do you want?"

"You help me. This my new shop. I need to write English signs. You help me."

James helped the man and the jeweller was delighted.

"Now," he said, "I reward you. You are a good man."

James beamed. The jeweller gave James one lapus lazuli bead.

Then he said, "Aha! you need to hang it on something. You buy a chain from me."

So James bought a reasonably priced chain.

"Now," continued the jeweller, "Something for your wife. Here is a lovely necklace. Only £30."

"No," said James, "I can't afford that!"

"Oh sir," replied the jeweller, "You offend me! You are rich man!"

"I am not a rich man!" James retorted "I am a Church of England priest!"

"No, no, my friend. I mean that you are a rich man in your heart!"

This was an unexpected line of reply. So James tried to reason with the jeweller,

"Look, I have brought money to buy books to study from, not to buy necklaces."

The jeweller thought for a moment, and in a quiet, concerned, confidential tone said, "Tell me, how much *can* you afford?"

"Well, twenty pounds I suppose," said James.

Before he realized what he was doing, James had taken out his wallet and the jeweller had sold him a necklace, and, when asked for change, gave him two earrings instead of cash, insisting what a bargain James had. The whole incident took half an hour. Fortunately, the articles were truly of high quality. But the business ethics were zero.

TODAY I PURCHASED TWO books in the Christ Church bookshop. These were recommended for our course, and were written by Brad Young: *Jesus, the Jewish Theologian*, and, *The Lord's Prayer from a Jewish Perspective*. James bought these titles yesterday, and I had glanced at his copies last night. In reaching for one of the books, which was on a shelf over the sales counter, I accidentally spilt the assistant's coffee cup.

"I'm terribly sorry."

"No, no, it's all right," replied the assistant as he wiped up the mess.

"Look, I'll buy the books the coffee spilt on."

"No, no, not at all."

The people in this bookshop are really nice, even if they too sell videos of the Israeli Air Force.

Synagogue and Shabbat

Today is Friday, and in the evening we visited a synagogue for the service which marks the start of Shabbat (Sabbath/Saturday) which begins at sunset, or, strictly, one hour before sunset in order to avoid the danger of inadvertently trespassing into the holy day. One of David Pileggi's Jewish friends, Rabbi Henry, came to Christ Church in the afternoon to talk to us about the significance of Shabbat for Jews.

"This evening you are going to Shai Agnon synagogue. It is an Orthodox synagogue named after the first Israeli writer to get the Nobel prize for literature. The synagogue is in a nice neighborhood. There will be lots of singing. People will be dressed nicely. No one carries money into the synagogue. Everyone is equal there. All are kings or queens in the Lord's house. It is a foretaste of the world to come. It will be a happy time."

"Shabbat is interpreted by some Jewish theologians as Israel's Bride," explained Rabbi Henry further. "But why is this? How can a day of the week be a Bride? Well, it is because all the other days of creation have a partner, whereas Shabbat has no partner except Israel, the people of God. For example, the first day has the second day, the third day has the fourth day, and the fifth day has the sixth day. But the seventh day has no other day to pair with. Instead, Israel is her partner."

"Is Shabbat still important in Judaism?"

Before Rabbi Henry answered, David broke in, "In my view the Jews have a unified body of religious practice, not a unified body of belief. What Jews have in common is circumcision, Shabbat, and prayer. Would you agree with that Henry?"

"To a certain extent David. But we have Torah as well. And we have the fundamental faith of the Shema, '*Hear O Israel, the Lord your God is one God.*'"

"Yeah. Sure. Torah is central," said David. "But Torah is a huge discussion area! Nobody agrees on interpretation. Argument is everything. In my experience a Jew has the philosophy that argument is for the sake of heaven; and, as iron sharpens iron, you get to the truth through argument. This is part of Jewish culture. Now, if you say 'I don't want to argue about it' that is interpreted as meaning 'It can't be true, for its not worth arguing over.'"

Rabbi Henry came back on David's comments. "Look, we Jews love to argue. We love to discuss. We love to raise points. And if one Rabbi disagrees with another Rabbi over the interpretation of Torah, so much the better. That gives us even more to talk about!"

THE SHAI AGNON SYNAGOGUE is out in the suburbs, and on the way we passed St. Andrew's Scots Kirk which overlooks the Hinnom Valley. It was a long walk to the synagogue and we arrived after the service had started, but that did not seem to matter. Before going into the synagogue itself, David divested us of cameras, and then went to his own house looking like an exaggerated cartoon of the archetypal American tourist, camera-heavy and laden with baggage. When the service was over David came with the minibus and fifteen of us squeezed into it for the journey back to Christ Church.

At the synagogue the women were separated from the men and looked on from the side through wrought iron railings, while the men occupied the central area with their sons and daughters. Girls are allowed into the central section until they become twelve years old plus one day. At that point they also have to go to the female section. However, not all synagogues have this rule: and in all non-Orthodox synagogues the men and women sit together.

A Rabbi read prayers at the start and in the middle of the service, but was quite inaudible. During the readings and prayers there was a huge amount of coming and going, with conversations between groups of men continuing even as prayers were read. The singing rose and fell throughout the service. Sometimes it was wholehearted. At other times it was weak. Occasionally it lifted in crescendo with everyone taking part. Then it would fade away. Rabbi Henry came and sat beside us. At one point we had to stand up and turn round to face the back of the synagogue.

"Why are we doing this?" we whispered to him,

"This is the part where the congregation turns to the sunset," he whispered back. "We are acknowledging that Shabbat has truly begun. This synagogue is on the western side of Jerusalem. Therefore, it faces east towards the Temple Mount. Therefore, the sunset is behind us. Therefore, we have to turn round."

During prayer the people rocked back and forwards.

"Why do people rock like that during prayer?"

"The rocking back and forward is in time to the heart-beat, as part of the rhythm of life, and it helps you to introspect and engage with God more deeply. It is such an automatic thing for me to do that I am now unaware of it when I am praying."

At the close everyone shook hands and greeted one another saying 'Shabbat Shalom.' Children went up to the front to have a look around, rocking back and forward as they stood. The Torah Scroll is kept at the front of the Synagogue. On the wall on either side, the Ten Commandments are inscribed in Hebrew. In the synagogue there is democracy of dress. All the men wear white, open-necked shirts like the Israeli politicians we see on TV. No one is meant to carry money into the synagogue. That was why David divested us of our waist-bags as well as our cameras. And yet the ladies in our group saw men signing cheques in the synagogue as the service was taking place. There was much hand-shaking and meeting people all through the service. The ladies in the female sections behaved in the same way. They moved around, chatted to friends, and joined in the singing as they chose.

At one point a man stood up to give a homily. He also spoke inaudibly and, when asked to speak louder, shrugged his shoulders and said that people should sit nearer the front. But that was impossible, because the place was packed. It is so difficult to evaluate Synagogue worship. There must have been religious piety underlying the service and the experience of worship; but I found it hard to understand why so many people were not focused on praying and listening to the homily. I suppose I still have a lot to learn.

AFTER WE RETURNED TO Christ Church we had a Kiddush Shabbat meal, which is the meal celebrated by Jewish families on Friday evenings to mark the start of Shabbat, and I sat beside an elderly man called Oscar who came from Switzerland.

"Are you with a group Oscar, or are you on your own?"

"I am on my own Bruce. I am retired now. So I have much freedom. I am staying in Israel for a few weeks with no special plans."

"What was your profession before you retired?"

"I worked with language schools, setting up conferences and student exchanges all over Europe. You are from Scotland I believe. I have set up many conferences in Edinburgh. It is a lovely city."

The Kiddush Shabbat meal was led by a man named Anthony who spoke with a strong South African accent. Two candles were lit. Anthony explained that one candle represents man, and the other candle represents woman. This is because men and women were God's supreme creation on the sixth day of creation, and also because it is important on Shabbat for families to be together. Anthony led us in the Jewish prayers appropriate for Kiddush, and, after some singing, the meal started.

"At Kiddush there is a special blessing over the salted bread as well as the normal blessings over the wine," Anthony told us. "According to tradition, the reason we bless the bread as well as the wine is in order that the bread will not feel 'left out' or 'jealous'!"

He then broke the bread and shared it with all at the table. We ate the meal, and there was more prayer at the end. After the meal Anthony stood up and read out a fax-message.

"I am afraid I have serious news for us all. In my hand I have a fax which has come from a well-informed source. It says: 'Syria is amassing troops near southern Lebanon and is preparing for a blitzkrieg war on Israel with the objective of occupying southern Lebanon in a forty-eight-hour campaign. These things will happen before the 5th November which is the date for the US Presidential elections.'"

He read the fax with gloomy seriousness, creating a profound sense of foreboding. Then he took off his glasses and folded them into his pocket before speaking again.

"The Lord has not confirmed this message to me personally. I believe that there will indeed be a war, but the action will take place *after* the 5th November. I repeat, the Lord has not confirmed the original message to me, and so the invasion may not be imminent."

Even so, the news was disturbing.

Anthony continued. "We are fortunate in having a leader such as Benjamin Netanyahu. Remember the meaning of his name. The name Benjamin means 'Son of the Right Hand,' and Netanyahu means 'God gave.' The Lord has raised up a Leader from among his people for this hour. Blessed be the name of the Lord. But, I repeat, the Lord has not confirmed this fax personally to me. But its message is true because Assad of Syria wants a limited war to improve bargaining power vis-a-vis the Golan."

I am afraid I cannot take Anthony seriously. There may be a war. There may not. There may be conflict. There may not. But I do not believe that Anthony has special knowledge. Unfortunately, many Zionist Christians see Benjamin Netanyahu as another Churchill. They see him as a misunderstood realist whom God has raised up in place of the appeaser Yitzak Rabin. In my view that is misguided.

— Day 12 — Bethlehem —

Saturday 19th October

THIS MORNING WE WENT to Ein Karem. During the journey, for our now regular minibus seminar, David Pileggi told us that the stones for the Second Temple altar were cut from the rock of the Ein Karem valley because, according to tradition, that was where Abraham met Melchizedek, and in Jewish tradition Melchizedek is regarded as the archetypal perfect priest before God. Until 1948 Ein Karem was a Christian village; but Christians saw the signs of the times and fled the area to avoid the fighting which broke out between the Jews and Arabs in the War of Independence.

Ein Karem

After we reached the village, and the bus was parked, we walked down a narrow lane to a disused mosque and found a corner in the courtyard. David sat on the ground with his back against a blue steel door, and, in the morning warmth, we had another of his extended open lectures.

"Hey Shoresh," he drawled. "According to tradition Ein Karem is the home village of John the Baptist's parents, Elizabeth and Zechariah. But who decided that? It was the Crusaders who got that idea. That tradition did not really exist before then. Look at the Bible. What does it say? It simply says that John's parents lived '*in the hill country of Judaea.*' In fact, the early Church Fathers thought that his birthplace might be near Hebron. So, is Ein Karem the birthplace of John the Baptist? Well, it might be or it might not be. Either way, we can talk about the significance of

John the Baptist. John was a mover. He was an itinerant preacher. And he baptized all up and down the Jordan valley, not just in one place."

David was in full flow as we scribbled our notes. A Muslim family wandered past, and the children looked at us curiously then walked on.

David continued. "Look Shoresh. If Elizabeth and Zechariah stayed in Ein Karem, then, given that Ein Karem is close to Bethlehem, Mary and Joseph could have gone on to Elizabeth's home when they found nowhere to stay in Bethlehem."

I was unsure about David's argument because Bethlehem and Ein Karem are not that close, and with Mary so near to her confinement any extra travelling would be avoided. Moreover, did Mary and Joseph really have a problem finding a place to stay in Bethlehem? David himself made this point later on.

"Look Shoresh. Regarding the Mary and Joseph incident. The Bible simply says there was *'no room in the Inn'* or rather *'no room in the guest-room.'*

David paused before continuing. "In fact, Shoresh, accommodation was provided rapidly for Mary. I reckon that the family of the house at which Mary and Joseph called took one look at the pregnant girl and brought her into their own living quarters rather than put her in with a crowd in the guest-room. That was the significance of saying that the 'guest-room was full.' The biblical text means to imply that there was no privacy for an expectant girl about to have a child, and so the family invited Mary into their own large living-area for the birth. So we have to paint a different picture in our minds. It was on the lower level of this large living-area, with the warmth of the house-sharing animals around her, that Mary gave birth. Local culture would *never ever* have turned away a pregnant woman in Mary's condition. It would be unthinkable. Mary and Joseph were welcomed at Bethlehem, not rejected."

"So, David," one of us asked, "the question of going on to stay with a relative perhaps never arose? Especially if Joseph had to be in Bethlehem for the census?"

"Sure. And another thing, Shoresh," added David, "various churches commemorate John the Baptist's birth in Ein Karem, but they are closed on Saturdays. Can you guess why?"

"Out of reverence for Shabbat?"

"No. Because too many Jewish tourists were coming to see them, and they couldn't cope with the numbers!"

"So they closed their doors!"

"Yep, because too many people want to see them. Real missionary outlook! What a lost opportunity to show hospitality and build bridges. Instead, they close down!"

Abu Ghosh

From Ein Karem the minibus took us a winding route to the village of Abu Ghosh. David wanted us to see the monastery there because, when we return from our week in the desert, Christ Church will be full up, and we are to stay out at the Abu Ghosh monastery. David is keen to reassure us that we will enjoy it, and this quick visit was fitted in to set our minds at rest. In the Old Testament the Ark of the Covenant rested at Abu Ghosh, which at that time was called Kireath Jearim. From there, King David took the Ark to Jerusalem. The Roman Catholic monastery, where we are to stay, has a high tower, and, on the tower is a statue of Mary holding the Christ child, with Mary herself standing on top of the Ark of the Covenant. The theological symbolism of the statue expresses the belief that, in the same way as the Ark carried the old covenant (the tablets of the Ten Commandments), so Mary was the ark which carried the new covenant (Jesus). And similarly, as the New supersedes the Old, so Mary stands supreme.

Abu Ghosh is a few miles west of Jerusalem on the way to Tel Aviv, and in Turkish times villagers collected unofficial tolls from travellers going between the two cities.

"Under the Turkish occupation this used to be a real wild town," said David, "The name means 'Father of the Fist Fight', because so many travellers were attacked on their way past here."

Today Abu Ghosh is mainly a Muslim village with several Jewish kibbutzim around it, including a settlement of Jews from Kurdistan. According to David, during the 1948 War the Muslims of Abu Ghosh allowed the Israelis to use the village as a military base, not because they were sympathetic to Zionism, but because they knew which side was going to win. Moreover, they felt no real solidarity with the other villages in the area.

David gave his opinion. "To my mind, the people here, both Muslim and Jew, are dedicated to making money. Their peaceful co-existence is due to this mutually shared objective. There is no real integration of the various communities of the town."

If David's aim in taking us to Abu Ghosh was to reassure us about the standard of accommodation, then his good intentions backfired. No one was able to meet us at the monastery. No one could let us into the main building to see the rooms. And, because of rebuilding work, the only available toilets were outside, dilapidated, and ghastly. What lies in store when we come to stay for real?

IN THE EYES OF its inhabitants, Abu Ghosh has another claim to fame as a biblical site. On the first Easter Sunday Jesus met with two disciples as they walked from Jerusalem to Emmaus, and Abu Ghosh is thought by some to be the site of Emmaus. In later centuries a Crusader church was built in the village to mark this. However, as we motored through a valley nearer to Jerusalem, we passed the site of another village, named Motza, which Josephus identified with Emmaus. Motza is also David Pileggi's preferred location.

"Look Shoresh," he drawled. "The Motza site is nearer Jerusalem. It has an ancient spring. It is on a Roman Road, a main highway. So it was a natural place to walk to. I think Motza was Emmaus. Now, whether identification with Emmaus is valid or not, Motza was still a significant place in first-century Jewish religious life because reeds cut at Motza were used in the Temple worship. On the Feast of Tabernacles water was taken from the pool of Siloam and poured on the altar of the Temple, and around the altar were placed these reeds. Interestingly, the Pharisees and Sadducees disagreed about the liturgy of this event. The Pharisees poured water directly onto the altar, whereas the Sadducees would only pour water around the altar."

THE NEXT PLACE TO visit today was to be Bethlehem, and on the way there we passed through Gilo, the southernmost suburb of Jerusalem, and which features in the life of King David. Two of David's commandos came from Gilo, as did the man who gave bad advice to David's son, Absalom, encouraging Absalom to revolt against his father. As we went towards Bethlehem from Jerusalem we appreciated the dramatic nature of the surrounding countryside, especially the Judaean Wilderness on our left.

When the tall cone of the Herodian came into view, David took up the bus microphone. "The Herodian was one of Herod's wilderness fortresses, Machaerus and Masada being others. There were seven in all. And the Herodian is where Herod the Great was buried."

We passed Rachel's Tomb, now heavily fortified against suicide bombers. Old books on the Holy Land show photographs of Rachel's Tomb standing in splendid isolation between Jerusalem and Bethlehem. Today it is surrounded by barbed wire, sand-bags, machine-gun stations, and soldiers' huts. David talked to us about the tomb.

"Look Shoresh, it's quite true that Rachel was buried on the outskirts of Bethlehem, but she wasn't buried at this place. This building, which passes for Rachel's Tomb, is actually the tomb of a Muslim Sheik, but it was bought by some Jews several hundred years ago, and the tradition grew up. So we have this scenario where Jews come and pray at a Muslim shrine!"

Bethlehem

Bethlehem is a town of forty-five thousand inhabitants, and, like all West Bank cities except Hebron, is now under the control of Yasser Arafat's Palestinian Authority. Foreign tourism is vitally important to Bethlehem for two main reasons. First, there is the financial boost that visitors give to the beleaguered Palestinian economy. Second, there is the public relations dimension: every tourist who leaves Bethlehem with a good impression of the way the Palestinian Authority runs its towns is a potential ambassador for the Palestinian cause.

The traffic into Bethlehem was extremely heavy, so our group abandoned the bus when it halted in a traffic-jam. Sharon and Paul were absent, but we had been joined for the day by Oscar whom we met at the Shabbat meal, and by a young woman from Australia called Jenny. Leaving the bus, we went up a side street to a shop described by David as the 'Best Falafel Restaurant in the World', otherwise known as *Afteem's Falafel Shop*. The owner pushed tables together to give us one big table, and David took the bulk orders. After chat and refreshments, we strolled deeper into town.

THE CHURCH OF THE Nativity in Bethlehem's Manger Square is one of the oldest churches in the whole of Christendom, and has survived earthquake, fire, and conquest. The first major building on the site was early fourth century, and built by Helena, the mother of Constantine. However, long before Helena, the site had been revered in primitive Christian tradition as the Cave of the Nativity by the indigenous Christian community. The pagan Emperor Hadrian then unwittingly ensured that the site would not be lost when he maliciously erected a temple to Adonis and planted a sacred grove of trees with the intention of desecrating the site. Ironically, his hostile action ensured that the spot remained clearly marked. Hadrian's planting of the trees was not just an anti-Christian action, but an anti-Jewish one as well. He saw Christianity as just another Jewish sect, and this was why he built pagan shrines on the Temple Mount and on the sites of Jesus' birth and death.

We went into the church through the low doorway, which was built low to stop men on horseback riding into the church, and is now taken as a parable of humility when approaching the manger. A small number of tourists were wandering amongst the ancient pillars of the dimly lit interior. David pulled us into a quiet corner.

"Look Shoresh, you've seen all sorts of places in Israel which claim to be where this happened or where that happened. And most of them have a 'tradition' attached to them. But how do we know if these traditions are true? Well, there is a rule of thumb which is pretty accurate. If a tradition was established *before* the fourth century legalization of Christianity, then it is a reliable tradition. But, if a tradition emerged *after* the fourth century, then it may well be a suspect tradition. You see, before Constantine adopted Christianity, persecution was always just round the corner, so you did not publicize yourselves unnecessarily. But, after Constantine's Edict of Toleration, when his mother was travelling all over the place building churches on sacred sites, it became a real temptation to invent a tradition for your town, or at least elaborate on wishful thinking that 'here Jesus did this, or there he did that.' So, traditions that emerge after the fourth century have to be taken with a pinch of salt, whereas traditions which existed before that date can be regarded as pretty authentic."

That all sounded reasonable to us. David continued.

"Shoresh, nowadays, as late twentieth-century people, we don't trust the reliability of tradition because we are not an oral society. But it was different in Jesus' day. At that time oral tradition was efficient. Another point is this: Bethlehem was really small in Jesus' day. Really small. And, unlike some biblical sites, there is no *double* tradition for the place of the nativity. It is, and always has been, the only site ever claimed for the event."

More tourists came in, and a priest at the far end of the church started a service for some of the pilgrims. For our group, David was in full flow.

"OK Shoresh, when was Jesus born? I mean, what time of year was it? I reckon it was probably the month of May. You see, the Romans were really practical in their system of governance. First, a census would not be timed for winter, because travelling would be too difficult. Second, you cannot ask people to move around during the busy part of the agricultural year, or when harvesting fruit crops. Third, the Bible tells us that the shepherds were in the fields; now the only fields were grain fields, and so we have a scenario where the sheep have been let into farmers' fields just after the harvest to eat up what remains. Thus it had to be after Pentecost, but before the summer heat."

Tony wasn't too sure, "David, but what about the time of the Feast of Tabernacles in October? Does the Bible not make a word-play on the phrase *'he tabernacled amongst us'*?"

"Nope," replied David, "I don't think it would be so late in the year. Now, concerning the church here. In the fifth century the Emperor Justinian tore down the fourth-century church in order to build a bigger and grander church. That again is ironic since the essence of the birth narrative in the Gospels is quietness and humility."

Rays of sunlight angled down from high windows. Shafts of light cut their way through incense clouds, creating blocks of brightness on the ancient stone floor. Perhaps where we were standing had once been a street. Perhaps it had been the street Mary and Joseph walked up when they arrived in Bethlehem so long ago. Majesty and mystery. How could Mary's womb contain the maker of the world, and yet the same Lord be still ruler of heaven and earth? This is what Reformed theologians term the *extra Calvinisticum,* expressed in a hymn by the line, *'See within a manger lies, he who made the starry skies.'*

David continued. "Look Shoresh, in 613AD the Persians invaded Palestine and destroyed every church they found, save one. This one. Why did they leave this one alone? Well, when they rode up to the Church of the Nativity they saw a mosaic depicting three people dressed in Persian dress, the Magi. What did they say to each other when they saw the mosaic? They said 'Hey, these are our guys. This must be one of our places. Better not touch it.'"

The columns in the church are Crusader columns. The lead for the roof came from England. The wood was sent from Venice. It was here that the Crusaders crowned their Kings. They were not crowned in Jerusalem, because in Jerusalem our Lord was crowned with thorns. Instead, Crusader Kings came to Bethlehem for their coronations.

We went to a lower level to see the cave where the manger is supposed to have been. A silver star is set in the floor at the exact spot where, according to tradition, Jesus was born. On coming up we found ourselves in the Armenian chapel where a huge crowd of tourists were watching the Armenian monks. Four monks were having a service. One of them, robed in black and with a black hood over his head, read aloud. Then the monks started to chant and wail. As they chanted a diminutive old man in an old, worn, drab, dark, untidy gown came over to the side to light a pedestal candle from another candle which he held in his hand. It took him a long time to do this, and the chanting and wailing continued with passion and volume. The old man then walked past us waving an incense burner, going round and round the perimeter of the Armenian chapel, waving the incense, and ushering us out of the area.

"Quick please! Quick please! Out! Out!"

The crowd retreated to the very edges of the chapel. The wailing became louder and stronger with all the main participants now involved. Eventually they were reassured that their own area was clear, and that the tourists were standing in the Orthodox sector, rather than in the Armenian one. The little man circled the area one more time. He was 'cleansing' it with more incense, so that the service could proceed without defilement. The wailing stopped and the monks now chanted in softer voices. But this worship was for them. It was not for us. We were on the outside. We were not wanted. We were a nuisance. So we moved on.

WE EMERGED FROM THE dim interior of the Church of the Nativity, into the brightness of Manger Square. I spotted a traffic policeman in smart Palestinian uniform and crossed the street to chat to him. With a broad, beaming, welcoming smile, he took me over to the police-station where two armed Palestinian policemen on either side of the doorway allowed me to take their photographs. Another young unarmed policeman greeted me. He had little English but was eager to strike up a conversation.

"My name is George. I am your friend. I would like to show you my church."

Yet another George! If in doubt the name may be George! George and I marched across Manger Square, and walked up an alley for several hundred yards. We soon arrived at George's church, or rather outside its gates, since it was closed and the gates were locked.

George turned to me. "Twenty dollars please. I have been your guide!"

"I don't have that kind of money on me!"

"Well, ten dollars please."

"George, you said you were my friend. This is not what a friend does. I have another friend who works in Gaza helping the Palestinian people. We are friends. You are a member of the Palestinian Police. You look after visitors. Yes?"

I trusted that I sounded more confident than I felt. But what I said was quite true. Alyson King, one of the young people in our church in Crieff was working in Gaza during her student's vacation helping to teach young Palestinian children, and I was hopeful that this name-dropping might give George second-thoughts. He seemed to be a new recruit to the Police, and it was likely that all during his childhood he had earned money from tourists. My approach worked, with George becoming embarrassed at what he had demanded.

"I am very sorry. You are my friend."

He then dipped into his pocket and brought out a Palestinian Police badge and gave it to me. "My friend, you have this. From your friend."

We walked back towards the square. On the way I was talking to George about home when a woman came out from a doorway. "Excuse me, excuse me," she called out. "I hear you speaking. I have been to Honduras, Scotland, and Holland. I have family in Britain." We chatted with the lady for a while, and then moved on. I told George about Alyson, the young person from our church working in Gaza. That impressed him.

The Cooperative

We left Bethlehem and went to a co-operative on the outskirts of the town, where seventy-two Palestinian families are involved in producing olive-wood carvings for shops and bazaars. David Pileggi introduced us to one of the men who showed us round the main workroom where the olive-wood figures are carved and varnished.

"Where does the olive wood come from?" Marion asked.

"At the moment the main supply is from new Jewish settlements. When these new settlements are built they cut down the olive trees and the co-operative buys them."

"Can you use the wood straight away?"

"No. The olive wood is stored for four to five years before we use it. Now, look over here. A machine carves five figures at a time to give them the basic shape. Then the figures can either be machine-finished or hand-finished before the varnishing. If the figures are hand-finished, we use an implement like a dentist's drill."

He demonstrated the technique, and, after showing us the workshop, we were taken upstairs into his home where we could buy articles at cost price. We met his family who were really welcoming. On the wall of their main room was a picture of Jesus. Next to it, the Palestinian flag. Symbols of the two things most precious to them. Their faith. Their nationhood.

I then spoke to a lady called Rema, and we chatted generally about Britain and Israel, contrasting rain with sunshine, green grass with desert sand. Rema has been to Turkey and Arizona in the USA visiting relatives. I said that Arizona, Turkey, Israel, were all hot and dry, whereas Britain can be so wet. The conversation was relaxed, but then Rema became serious,

"Yes. But you have peace. We have no peace. You have hope. We have no hope. We have no place to go. The USA is all for the Israelis. Perhaps Europe is on the side of the Palestinians, but we have little hope for the future."

On another wall of the room was the framed photograph of a young man.

"Is he your son?" I asked Rema.

"No, he is our neighbor's son. He died at the hands of the Israelis."

By this time everyone was listening intently as Rema unburdened herself. "The Intifada started in 1987, and in 1989 the Israelis provoked tax problems with our Co-operative. Then they came and took one of our people and put him in prison for four months. They took the car. They took goods from the shop. Our whole community lived in fear."

"We have despair like the despair in the book of Job. Israelis are up. Palestinians are down. For example, we used to have plenty of water. Where has the water gone? It has been piped away from us to the new settlements. Then people come from the West and they see Israeli towns with green grass; and they see Arab towns with nothing but dust, and they say 'See how lazy these Arabs are.' When my husband was in prison Israeli soldiers came to our house. Myself and the children, we hid. We were afraid that we too would be taken to prison. My sister is in Arizona, but we cannot all go to America. We have nowhere to go. This is our home. This is where my father and grandfather and our family have always lived. It is our home."

Rema and others posed for a photograph before we drove off. They are all lovely people, and there is a gentleness and grace about them which lends integrity to what they say. Today the olive harvest started. According to reports, it is to be a good harvest this year. From the bus we saw dozens of colorfully dressed workers, busy in the fields gathering the crop.

Downtown Jerusalem

After the evening meal at Christ Church James and I walked to the King David Hotel. We marched in boldly as if we were residents and no one stopped us. The walls of the Servitor's office are decorated with photographs of dignitaries who have stayed at the hotel: President Clinton, the British Royal Family, Israeli politicians, former US Presidents, and a host of other world leaders. Everything is plush and luxurious. Even the toilets of the King David Hotel are five star. Outside, we looked at the window displays of the many gold and silver shops which are nearby, and then walked to Ben Yehuda street to see what was happening. On the way we passed a Taxi office so I went in.

"How much would a taxi from Jerusalem to Tiberias be?"

"360 shekels," the man in the office said.

When I leave the Study Group and join the Bike Ride I have to get to Tiberias, so I need to explore travel options in case I run into transport problems. However, 360 shekels is more than £70, and so I will definitely go by bus.

In Ben Yehuda Street there were huge crowds, and loads of street entertainers. Saturday night is a good time to be in Ben Yehuda Street because Shabbat ends at sunset and people come to celebrate as night falls. One crowd was gathered round a duo playing accordion and violin. Other groups watched various street-performers. Some trainee jugglers practiced their act. Another man sold balloon sculptures. A big crowd listened to four students playing brass instruments and going through a classical repertoire. But the largest audience was listening to a man and woman singing 'Sonny and Cher' style with guitar and keyboard. The atmosphere was good-humoured, well-behaved, and totally non-threatening, even though the place was thronged with thousands. Here were the privileged of Jerusalem: rich, talented, well-educated. Music sounded from every retail outlet, and James and I went into an English Language bookshop to browse. A police van and an Armoured Personnel Carrier with soldiers carrying machine guns were strategically placed at the main junction. We looked at a pavement jewellery stall full of beads and necklaces, before returning to Christ Church.

Tonight I packed seven films for Paul to take back to the UK when he leaves tomorrow. All he has to do is to post them to Fujifilm, and the transparencies should be in Crieff by the end of next week. Sharon is going with Paul to Tel Aviv to see him off at the airport. We hope things went well for them both. They certainly seem happy.

THIS YEAR THE OLD City is strangely quiet. Much quieter than during the last two Novembers when Grace and I stayed on in Jerusalem after the 1994 and 1995 Bike Rides. This is concerning since October should be a peak month for tourists. The shops in the Old City are open from 9 am till late afternoon as usual, but the streets of the Souk are much emptier. Many tourists have been put off by the uneasy political situation, by the fragmentation of the peace process, by the furore over the tunnel, and by the riots and deaths in Hebron three weeks ago.

Illogically, despite few tourists, the street traders are reluctant to reduce prices, and even less happy to be bartered down. Not for them the normal economic theory of supply, demand, and market forces! In their mind fewer customers means that prices have to be higher, even though it should be a buyer's market. But normal prices can be had at a pleasant little supermarket we have found in the Armenian Quarter, which sells water, coke, chocolate, and biscuits at reasonable rates, and with no hassle. Its owner is, of course, called George.

— *Day 13 — Christ Church* —

Sunday 20th October

THE ANGLICAN CHURCH IN Jerusalem has two centers of operation. One is St. George's Cathedral and Hostel on the Nablus Road, which is traditional Church of England, with a pro-Palestinian tendency. And the grounds of St. George's are a miniature copy of gardens to be found anywhere in England, with a rose-garden, quadrangle, and cloisters. Concerts of organ music are held regularly in the church and the Cathedral is a natural gathering place for expatriates and British visitors to Israel. Grace and I stayed there for a week in 1994.

Christ Church, in the Old City, is different. Its roots are in the nineteenth-century Anglican mission, and so Christ Church is orientated towards the Jewish community whilst conscious of the injustices being suffered by Palestinians. When I came on the Shoresh Study tour—aware that it was Christ Church based—I wondered if it might ignore Palestinian problems. But our many visits to Arab communities have shown that Shoresh has an awareness of issues affecting both communities. Christ Church also has connections with the Renewal Movement, and manifestations of the charismatic gifts of the Spirit are regular occurrences at its events.

Worship at Christ Church

Sunday service at Christ Church started at 9.30 am, and the church was packed. The preacher was Murray Dixon from New Zealand. At breakfast Murray approached Tony and me, asking us to read the lessons during the service. The praise was led by a music group comprising two violins, guitar, piano, trumpet, and singer. As people came into church the music group prayed together at the side before leading the worship. During the service members of the congregation gave words of prophecy in tongues, and interpretation was given, also from the congregation. I read from Isaiah 60. Tony read from Luke 15, the parable of the Prodigal Son.

After the sermon we shared in communion, and the clergyman who presided for the Eucharist invited all of us to say together words in the liturgy which are normally reserved for the priest to say alone. This was to emphasise the New Testament principle that all of God's people form a royal priesthood.

We went forward to the altar rail to receive the sacrament. I like this Anglican way of celebrating the Lord's Supper. My own Presbyterian liturgy emphasizes that, by remaining in our pews and waiting for the bread and wine to be brought to us, we are reaffirming that God takes the sovereign initiative in coming to us in Christ. In contrast, the Anglican practice of going forward emphasizes our active response to God's free grace. I find the action of going forward, kneeling, taking the bread and wine, and receiving a word of blessing from the priest, a strongly meaningful experience. The whole service was exceptionally moving, and we concluded the Eucharist by singing 'There is a Redeemer' which we have often sung in Crieff at our early service.

MURRAY DIXON PREACHED ON the Parable of the Prodigal Son, under the title of 'The Waiting Father.' His headings were: Repentance, Reconciliation, and Restoration. Murray is sharply aware that some Christians are so obsessed by the place of the Jews in God's plan for Israel that they forget about the Palestinians. So he started by telling us some family history.

"My wife and I had to let our own son go into the far country. There comes a time when you have to do that. But it is terribly, terribly painful. Our son went into the New Zealand Territorial Army and, as we had feared, he succumbed to drink and to the whole lifestyle which goes with that culture. We simply had to wait and pray. But, praise God, he came back. In the end he saw that that kind of life made no sense and was going nowhere. But all we could do was to wait."

"The pain and vulnerability which we went through made us aware of the pain and vulnerability felt by others in many different situations."

"Jewish Christians in the third and fourth century were vulnerable. They were criticized and rejected by other Christians. And, instead of being embraced by their brothers and sisters in Christ, they were rejected by Gentile Christendom. They were rejected by their own people—us. There is so much hurt in Christian history. Jewish Christians have suffered in the past and still suffer in the present. Similarly, today we must be aware that the Palestinians are vulnerable and in pain. Let me tell you of an incident which took place here."

"An Arab who works here at Christ Church was grabbed by the local police and taken up to the police station just outside our gates. He was beaten up in full view of everyone. I heard the commotion and ran to where this was taking place, but could only watch. Nonetheless, I made sure that the police saw that I was watching. The Arab was beaten up. Then he was let go by the Israeli police when he had signed a statement saying that he had not been maltreated. I brought him back into Christ Church, sat him down, and we looked after him and gave him coffee to drink. He was shaking and sobbing. He didn't say anything and then, after a long time, still sobbing, he said, 'I forgive, I forgive, I forgive.'"

"Another Palestinian Christian, this time from Bethlehem and who had attended Bethlehem Bible College, was arrested for no reason by the Israeli Police, and spent over fifty days in solitary confinement. Eventually, after seventeen days, his lawyer was allowed to see him and came with new clothes and his Bible, but these were taken away after the lawyer left. Then he heard someone speaking to him from outside his prison window. It was a Jewish soldier who whispered, 'I am a believer, here is some bread for you.' The prisoner was suspicious, so the Jewish soldier ate part of the bread, and drank some of the water, and then the prisoner ate and drank the remainder. Yet the prisoner was still suspicious that the whole thing might be a set up by the police, so he prayed for a sign: 'Lord, if this is from you, let the soldier bring chocolate.' A few days later the Jewish soldier re-appeared—with chocolate! Eventually the Palestinian prisoner was set free, and after his release spoke about his experience to the Principal of the Bethlehem Bible College. Sometime later, the Principal told these things to a gathering of Messianic believers. The Jewish soldier was there and introduced himself to the Principal after the meeting."

Murray reflected on the implications of these incidents.

"The Jews are Abraham's descendants through Isaac. And the Arabs are Abraham's descendants through Ishmael. There must be blessing on both Isaac and Ishmael in Jesus. This is the teaching of Isaiah 60. What a revelation it was to me when I discovered the message in Isaiah that the descendants of both Isaac and Ishmael are to be blessed. Jew and Arab are both part of God's positive plan. Both lines—not just one—of the Abrahamic promise will come to Zion for blessings which are yet to be fulfilled. Repentance. Reconciliation. Restoration."

This was powerful stuff and food for thought. And any theological interpretation of current events has to take account of Murray's emphasis on the implications of Isaiah's prophecy.

Sunday Saunter

Following the church service there was orange juice and biscuits outside in the sunshine, after which James and I walked through the Armenian Quarter past the Zion Gate to a restaurant for lunch. We then made for the Temple Mount, and on the way passed an old man and a small boy gathering olives from a tree between the roadway and the city walls.

"Excuse me, may I take a photograph?" I said. They were pleased to be asked, but posed too stiffly in front of the olive tree. "Please, just continue with your work." That made a much better picture and both James and I snapped them.

Coming into the Old City through the Dung Gate gives access to the Western Wall, and for many years a man dressed as King David, playing a harp, and warbling self-composed 'psalms', has made the pavement between the Dung Gate and the Western Wall his stamping ground. We wanted to photograph him rather than listen, and he was delighted to pose after some shekels were thrown into his open suitcase. His 'Thank you' was in a broad Australian accent.

A ramp adjacent to the Western Wall area slopes up to the vast Temple Mount area, now dominated by the magnificent Dome of the Rock shrine. The Temple Mount is where Herod's Temple once stood. Conditions were ideal for photography, and I sat on a low wall watching the crowds. The area is so vast that it is easy to spot individuals isolated against an attractive background. These make excellent compositions. In the busy, crowded streets of the Souk the sheer volume of people pressed close together makes it difficult to get full length people shots. Up on the Temple Mount photography is much easier.

We walked over to the eastern side of this vast space. From there we had a magnificent view of the Mount of Olives. Between us and the Eastern Wall of the Old City was an olive orchard, and to the left of the orchard was the Golden Gate. Many times I had looked over from the

Mount of Olives at the outside of the Golden Gate, but now we could see the interior of that blocked up entrance. According to some folklore the Messiah will enter Jerusalem through the Golden Gate, and one of the stories which tour-guides recount is that Muslims have created two barriers to try to stop this happening: first, they have closed up the gateway; second, they have created a Muslim cemetery all along the foot of the eastern wall outside of the city, thinking that a Jewish Messiah will never walk through a Muslim graveyard. David Pileggi pooh-poohs stuff like this, which is peddled to tourists, pointing out that neither Jews nor Muslims actually hold these theories!

James went to one of the gate-keepers to enquire about tickets for the Dome on the Rock. "Excuse me sir, how much is it to get in?"

"Twenty-two shekels. I take you. Come in. come in."

We reckoned that twenty-two shekels was too much.

"No, not today, thank you." James said politely.

"Stupid man!" the gate-keeper muttered as we walked away.

I HAVE BEEN TO the Temple Mount area before, but this afternoon saw it in a different light. The Muslim community treat it as a public park as well as a holy place, and a number of boys were playing football on the open expanse. Two other children were flying kites not far from the mosque itself. The whole place is seen by Muslims as a safe area where they can worship, meet, play, pick olives, walk, and be their own masters. Israeli police do have a presence on the Temple Mount, but concern themselves strictly with security matters, allowing the Muslims a high level of autonomy. And it is quite clear that they use it as a Muslim city within the Old City, within the city of Jerusalem.

James was wearing shorts. So when we came onto the Temple Mount the gatekeepers gave him a petrol-blue skirt to cover his knees. When we left the Mount he handed in his skirt. Unfortunately, on turning a corner we came to a dead-end and were faced with a solid wall punctuated only by doors to male and female toilets. The route was not an exit after all, only a lane that led to the public WCs. We turned back, but, in order to access any other exit, we had to return to the Temple Mount and of course James was not allowed onto it without a skirt covering his shorts. But he had his skirt no more! It had been handed over to someone who by now had disappeared. In this Catch-22, we visualized James trapped there for ever in limbo between the Temple Mount and a cul-de-sac.

One of the Arab gatekeepers shouted, "Stop! Stop! You cannot go up there with shorts!"

"But I handed my skirt in and it's gone now!"

"You cannot go up these steps onto the Holy Place."

"But I don't have a skirt! Do you have one I could borrow!"

"No, we have no skirts here. You get them at the entrances."

"Yes, but I can't get to the entrances without going up the steps. I made a mistake and handed it in!"

"You cannot go up there like that!"

The gatekeeper was adamant, and the impasse took a full ten minutes to sort out, but eventually another skirt was produced. Leaving the Temple Mount we came across a woman begging in an alley near the Church of the Holy Sepulchre. She had a child with her, and sat at the same spot each day. That was her life.

No sooner had we returned to Christ Church than we heard the sound of bagpipes. We rushed out and ran the short distance to the Jaffa Gate where a huge crowd was gathered. The pipes were being played, and drums were being beat, by a troop of Palestinian boy scouts. I squeezed through the crowd, past soldiers and police, to see what it was all about. In the center of this enormous, cheering multitude was the new Maronite Bishop on his processional way to his official enthronement at the Maronite Patriarchate in the Old City, and he was flanked by a dozen robed clerics representing different church groups: the Roman Catholic Church, the Orthodox Church, the Egyptian Church, and of course Maronite priests and nuns. We tried without success to spot Father Elias from Jish.

At the rear of the throng, white doves were released as signs of peace. And, on either side of the Bishop, dwarfed by soldiers, police, clerics, and crowds, there were young girls, dressed in white, who carried baskets full of rose petals which they threw over the new Bishop and the crowd. Other attendants tossed handfuls of rice into the air. The women in the procession chanted in a high-pitched Arabic wail like the one we heard in the Maronite church a week ago. During all of this the drums beat, the pipes played, the crowds cheered, and the Bishop smiled and waved beneficently.

The Bishop's official ceremonial guard comprised eight burly men with dark coats and red Fez hats. His unofficial protectors were Israeli police. The new Bishop wore a brilliant red cloak and a magnificent red mitred hat. I pushed past the TV crew for a close up photo and then held the camera over the heads of the crowd to get more shots. Then the procession moved up the lane next to Christ Church, squeezing along its narrow confines on its final leg to the Maronite Patriarchate. The noise died down. The crowds thinned out. The Israeli police stood around for a while before dispersing and returning to normal duties. The police in the Old City are nearly always either Druze, Bedouins, Christians or Muslims from the north of the country. Quite a few are army veterans.

St Andrew's Hospice

Tonight there was a service of healing at Christ Church, but I decided to walk over to the Church of Scotland Hospice at St. Andrew's Kirk, where Grace and I stayed for four days in 1995. Whenever we come to Israel two of our church members in Crieff, Stuart and Pat King, give us a jar of coffee to take to Bill Gardiner Scott, the retired Church of Scotland minister in Jerusalem who married them and baptized their eldest daughter Alyson—the one who worked in Gaza earlier this year. Two years ago Stuart and Pat also gave us tinned ham and pork for Bill, as these are difficult to purchase in Israel. It was only after we handed them over that it dawned on us that we had carried these items through the Arab Quarter, onto the Temple Mount, and past the Wailing Wall en route!

St. Andrew's was quiet. All the guests and staff were out, except for Alexis, the Warden. She gave a warm welcome, invited me in, and we chatted over a glass of wine. The Hospice was full despite several long-term USA bookings being cancelled following the Hebron riots, their places having been filled by people coming at short notice on cheaper flights. St. Andrew's, like the Anglican St. George's, is supportive of the Palestinian cause and the concomitant theology of non-violent liberation.

Alexis and I chatted about politics.

"As you know Bruce, we are quite pro-Palestinian, but we are aware that it's not all one sided. In the Palestinian Authority regions some of the Palestinian Police are being really brutal with their own people. Cigarette burns are common on people released from their jails."

"Mind you, Alexis," I replied, "I suppose they're copying what they have learned from Israeli police methods! Maybe that is the only role-model of policing they know about? Though I've heard that some of the Palestinian Police commanders came with Arafat from Tunis."

I told her that Shoresh is trying to be balanced, if such a thing is possible in Israel. I told her about Murray Dixon's sermon this morning and how he had deliberately talked about Palestinian Christians suffering Israeli brutality in order to counter the Christian-Zionist-Triumphalist attitude of many fundamentalists who come to Jerusalem. Alexis was pleased to hear about Murray's approach.

"Bruce, one of the big problems is with people who come for a week and 'know everything' at the end of it," she said. "Here a week, know everything. Here a month, not so sure. Here six months, totally confused! It's really important to be in the middle and not exclusively identified with either community. If the Church of Scotland has any role out here it is to be an agent of reconciliation, and we can only do that if we relate to both communities."

Alexis went on. "Benjamin Netanyahu is a disaster. He is not even his own man, and many young people who voted for him are now totally disenchanted. I believe that his private life is in ruins. According to rumour he doesn't pay bills. But he performs well on TV. That's why he got elected. But he's caved in to the ultra-orthodox."

The hospice bell rang, and Alexis answered it. She returned with a couple looking for a place to stay. I took my leave and wandered back to Christ Church. St. Andrew's is a wonderful place. I love its lounge. Its soft lighting. The large portrait of General Allenby looking down from the wall. The wicker chairs grouped round the fireplace. The homely hot-water urn in the corner, on permanent stand-by for cups of coffee.

Back at Christ Church we sat outside enjoying the balmy air of the evening. Marion leaned across the table. "Bruce," she said, "that man over there is from Nazareth and works at the hospital." So I went up to him and spoke slowly in simple words,

"Hello—are—you—from—Nazareth?"

"I—did—the—Bike—Ride—last—year—and—the—year—before."

"Great to meet you," he responded, "I'm from Yorkshire, and my wife from Hereford."

I had spoken pidgin-English to someone, who, in the pale lamplight, looked dark and middle-eastern, only to find he came from the UK! He works in the emergency baby care unit which is the specific department of the Hospital we are raising money for this year. His wife knows Jayne Neilson from Crieff who worked at the hospital for two months earlier this year.

— Day 14— Ophel —

Monday 21st October

TODAY, THE WHOLE MORNING was filled with lectures from Joseph. His material is first class, but it can be hard work concentrating in the heat. Each day in Jerusalem we have had several lectures, not all of which are recorded or referred to in this *Journal*. These are in addition to on-site talks given during field-trips. The lectures are excellent, of an impressive academic standard, and with highly usable material. For the classes we gather outside in a small courtyard at the rear of Christ Church which is surrounded by hanging vines; or we convene indoors at an open area on the upstairs landing. Joseph is a remarkable scholar. His tools are the Hebrew Bible, the Hebrew Midrash, the Hebrew Mishnah, Hebrew Rabbinic writings, a comparative Synopsis of the Gospels in Greek, and a few marginal notes of his own written in ink and pencil. Armed with these, he lectures, discusses, and debates the issues with clarity, coherence, direction, and spiritual insight.

Archaeological Extravaganza

This afternoon David Pileggi took us on an archaeological expedition. Our first stop was at the Temple Mount excavations, where the southern and western retaining walls of the Temple Mount meet. This is at an area called Ophel. The heat was almost unbearable as we gathered in the lee of Herod's massive structure. We sat on blocks of stone beside a first-century pavement which had been excavated only a few years ago. This is far below the twentieth-century ground level, and is a street which Jesus might have walked many times, right at the base of the walls of the

Temple Mount. In Jesus' time one side of the street was dominated by the towering height of the Western Wall, and the other side lined by a series of booths. The booths were separated by stone blocks, whose lintels are still in place as if the booths have been newly made and awaiting occupiers to sell spices, clothing, food, or trinkets.

"David, surely these stones must have been reworked. Their lines are so sharp. They look new and fresh."

"Not really, Shoresh." said David. "You see, this street here was repaved after the time of Jesus' crucifixion but before Jerusalem was destroyed in 70AD. After the Romans took Jerusalem they destroyed the buildings on the Temple Mount, and the stones of the Temple buildings were flung into the streets below, covering them up. So the newly paved streets were only used as public thoroughfares for a very short period. That is why the pavement is relatively unworn. Over the centuries rubble and dust piled on top, and, until recent excavations, the street was unknown."

"The retaining walls here were built by Herod. Now, at this point we have to go over some ground we've covered already. As you know Herod was unpopular and, by biblical tradition and precedent, had no business being King of the Jews, so he had to legitimise his rule somehow. Herod's big problem was legitimization. His family was not even loosely connected to the royal Jewish house, so his reign had to be put on a better basis. Now, Herod was a Hellenist through and through. He was not like King David. He did not 'pine for the Temple Courts.' He was not really religious. So how could he legitimise his regime?"

"Well, Herod tried several ploys. First, he married Mariamne who was one of the last of the Hasmonean princesses—by the way, Herod married nine others after her. Second, he got involved in rebuilding the Temple. This was Herod's master stroke. And he was helped by a precedent, because Ezra's temple had already been modified by the Hasmoneans in 24 to 22BC so alterations had taken place before."

"But rebuilding was a massive task. Even after he persuaded the religious authorities that he was serious about the enterprise, he had a huge programme to carry out. To begin with, Herod had to dismantle the existing Temple structure before rebuilding. Then, through the whole period of rebuilding, sacrifices had to take place daily continuously without a break. On top of that, Herod had to train several thousand priests to do the building work so that no profane hands would be employed in the project. Most of all, Herod's great vision of artificially extending the

Temple Mount platform had to swing into action, and that involved building arches upon arches to support the extended platform area above."

David broke off and indicated the walls behind him, "So, Shoresh, behind these walls is essentially empty space, or rather arched spaces, with the arches existing for the sole purpose of supporting the extended platform of the Temple Mount above."

"Shoresh, there are four levels of arches inside the walls. Filling the void with rubble would have produced too unstable a base, so proper arches had to be constructed by Herod's engineers. These are called 'Solomon's Stables' but they have nothing to do with Solomon. The Crusaders used them as stables, and during the Crusader period a military order of fighting monks inhabited the Temple Mount."

David continued. "Folks, although Herod extended the Temple Mount area, he was not allowed to make a bigger Temple building because its dimensions are fixed in the Bible. But Herod could, and he did, go to town on the surrounding areas. The builders' work rate meant that in only one and a half years the new Temple building was erected, but it took many more years to decorate. And it took twenty-nine and a half years to build up the Temple Platform. All this needed money, and Herod funded all of this without taxing the people." David then paused and asked us a question.

"Shoresh, how did Herod get the money?"

"Personal wealth?"

"No, not as such."

"Taxing the upper classes?"

"He wouldn't dare!"

"Temple taxes?"

"He wouldn't dare touch these either! Any other suggestions?"

No one could come up with an answer. David grinned. He had stumped us.

"Shoresh, it was taxing the trade-routes. That's what Herod did. The lucrative trade-routes were from southern Arabia and Yemen to the Mediterranean coast. Most of the way the route was in Nabatean territory, but the final leg went through Herod's lands to the port of Caesarea, and that was where he made the money."

David then turned our attention back to the site. "Folks, the site we see today is complicated. It has Second Temple period ruins. It has Byzantine ruins. It has early Arab ruins. However, we can usually identify the Herodian stones because these have a frame-border like this one here."

David pointed to one of the stones which showed this feature clearly. By now he was sweating heavily. Down in the archaeological diggings the heat of the sun was overpowering, and there was no escape from it. The heat hit us directly. And it bounced back from the stones. It was like being in an oven. I was beginning to wilt.

David went on. "One more thing Shoresh. See this frame-border. Herod saw this style in Rome and brought it back here. But he only used it for religious buildings. Herod had impeccable aesthetic taste even if he was not a wise choice to marry! He was a monster and a murderer. But, then again, history is full of examples of monsters with impeccable aesthetic tastes. Now Shoresh, here's an important point: Byzantine Christians largely ignored the Temple Mount because they reckoned that God had finished with Israel. So they used it as a rubbish dump. It was the Muslims who restored it."

WE MOVED FURTHER DOWN the first-century street, with David pointing out other features. "Shoresh, this was Valley Street. Jesus walked here, though not on these actual paving stones because, as we said, the pavement was re-laid about 60 to 65AD, and, as we said, had very little wear and tear before 70AD. Now, why was the street re-laid?"

"Earthquake damage?"

"No! Think! Think about people! When the Temple Mount was finished there was huge unemployment with twenty thousand redundant labourers. What do you do if you are in government? Do you ignore twenty thousand people with no work and no income? You can't. The potential for civil unrest has to be avoided. So, loads of job creation schemes were needed for these people, and this project of relaying the pavement, and ones like it, were part of the answer. Unemployment and social conditions resulting from unemployment were significant factors behind the revolt of 70AD. The Jewish revolt did not originate from religious or nationalist factors alone. You mustn't think that. There were socio-economic conditions feeding into the unrest as well."

David pointed upwards, "Now, see that stump of an archway coming out of the wall."

We all looked up.

"That's Robinson's Arch. If you look carefully you can also see an indentation in the wall, just below the arch, going the full length of this side of the wall. That is the line of a piped Arabic water channel."

Someone pointed to a hole in the stonework about twenty feet above us, where the Western Wall and the Southern Wall met. The hole made a tube through the stonework, six inches in diameter, with one end on the western face a foot from the corner, and the other likewise on the southern face. David explained it was a tethering-point since, during the Byzantine period, ground level was up there. During that period the spot where we were now standing was under metres of rubble and dirt. So people in the Byzantine times tethered their horses and camels to the corner of the wall using that hole.

David brought us back to political and theological questions.

"Now Shoresh, if the Jewish people viewed the Temple as a physical proclamation of the glory of the Lord, how did Jewish theology cope with the Temple's destruction? The First Temple, Solomon's Temple, was rebuilt, but this one was not. So how did Jewish theology cope with that? Well, the Babylonian Talmud gave several answers to this problem. It said that the First Temple was destroyed because of bloodshed, murder, and idolatry—in the population and priesthood alike. And the Second Temple, according to the same source, was destroyed because of 'hatred without a cause', i.e. internal divisions! There were also claims of sexual immorality in the Temple's priestly order. So, in effect, the Babylonian Talmud tried to say that because the Temple had not really been a manifestation of God's glory then its loss did not detract from God's majesty."

"Another point. In the first century you never walked from the Temple Treasury directly onto the Temple Mount itself. Instead, you came out of the Treasury, and entered the Temple by going up steps at the Southern Wall. At the Southern Wall there were two sets of doorways. One set was for entering the Temple, and the other set of doorways was for leaving. However, if you were in a state of mourning you entered by the way-out and you left by the way-in. That meant people realized you were mourning and could give you a blessing or alms as you passed by."

"When you entered the Temple you took no money, went barefoot, and wore white clothes. You entered the Temple without bag, money, staff, or shoes. So, when Jesus sent the disciples out on mission without bag, money, staff or extra tunic, he was not just advocating a simple lifestyle or teaching the disciples to rely on dependency on God, though that was how St. Francis, and others, interpreted Jesus' words. It was more than that. Jesus was proclaiming that the whole world is God's Temple. The disciples were to approach the world in the same manner as they would approach the Temple. This is because God is served in the world, not just in the Temple. And the people of God are found in the world, not just in the Temple. But Jesus was not against the Temple, he was simply against the Temple regime."

"Shoresh, think for a minute about the destruction of the Temple in the year 70. Liberal theologians reject the authenticity of Jesus' prophecies about the destruction of the Temple, and say that the gospel writers wrote these words after the event and put them into the mouth of Jesus. But prophecies of destruction were not uncommon. Long before 70AD other sages were warning about the possible destruction of the Temple. Josephus wrote about these warnings. There was one man who walked around Jerusalem for fifteen years crying out 'Woe unto Jerusalem!' foretelling the ruin of the Temple long before it happened."

WE NOW REACHED THE ancient steps which had once led up to the Temple entrances in the Southern Wall. The entrances have been blocked up for many centuries, but the steps by which pilgrims ascended and descended are still in place. Across the Kidron Valley, and to the east, is the Mount of Olives. Due south is the 'Hill of Evil Counsel' where, according to tradition, the authorities plotted the arrest of Jesus.

David signalled to us. "Shoresh, see the Hill of Evil Counsel over the valley. Nowadays the United Nations have their headquarters there, and, at one time, the more cynical modern Israeli news agencies used to preface a news report with the words, "Today, the United Nations, from the Hill of Evil Counsel, said such and such.'"

The meeting of the eastern and southern walls of the Temple Mount make a high corner which the Bible describes as the Pinnacle of the Temple. Tradition holds that James, the leader of the fledgling Christian community in Jerusalem, was thrown to his death off the Pinnacle of the Temple. He was not killed outright but writhed on the ground in agony until a Fuller came and put him out of his torment by clubbing him to death. Josephus records that James was well respected by all Jews in Jerusalem, both 'messianic' and 'non-messianic.' David emphasized that James was killed by the official High Priest out of jealousy, taking advantage of a delay between Roman Procurators of Judaea. But when the new Procurator arrived the people demanded that the High Priest be removed.

All along the southern area, below the steps, we saw the ruins of ritual immersion baths (Mikvah). Today, there are the remains of fifty ritual baths in that area. But there may have been as many as one thousand in the time of Jesus, and if, as many think, they were also used for Christian baptism then the number baptized on the day of Pentecost could easily have been accommodated by them. David made this point. "Years ago, before these ritual baths were excavated, some scholars made an issue of the fact that no one had found any location in Jerusalem where several thousand people could be baptized by immersion in one day. But now we know that was eminently likely."

In Jesus' day Mikvah baths were not in the open. People had to take all their clothes off for the act of purification, after which they donned a white robe to enter the Temple. For Mikvah purifications people immersed themselves by themselves, hence it has also been suggested that some early Christians baptized themselves. It was important for the ceremonial bath to be done by the person himself or herself in order for ritual cleanliness to be achieved, and it is possible, though not certain, that John the Baptist got pilgrims to baptize themselves, rather than assist them in the fashion we are aware of today.

Tony asked, "Was there nothing distinctive about Christian baptism?"

"Look," replied David, "The definitive feature of early Christian baptism was not its ritual but its theology. It was done 'In the name of Jesus.' That was what was revolutionary. Eusebius of Caesarea, who had access to the great library of Caesarea, said that the main point of Jesus' Great Commission to the disciples was that teaching and baptizing was to be done in *his* name, for his sake. This distinguished it from standard ritual immersion. To be baptized in *his* name is a huge theological statement. It affects everything."

"And, Shoresh, another thing. While immersion in a Mikvah was done frequently, Christian baptism was a rite of initiation and done only once."

The Jewish Quarter

We left the Ophel excavations and made our way into the Jewish Quarter and the Herodian Houses. These have foundations of first-century villas which were only discovered after the occupation of the Old City in 1967, when Israelis began to excavate in preparation for the building of the new Jewish Quarter. Modern houses and streets have been built since, but the extensive first-century remains are preserved under the new structures, with access for the public. Some of the Christ Church volunteer staff had joined us for this afternoon's explorations, one of whom is a girl called

Unk who comes from Holland. Unk and I were so busy taking photographs on the way to the Herodian Houses that we became detached from the group.

One of the shops in the Jewish Quarter has an intriguing notice in its window. The shop sells models of Second Temple artefacts, and the sign states, 'Buy now! Prices go up when Third Temple is built!' The words were amusing for us, but are threatening for Muslims. They fear that extremist Jews will burrow under the Temple Platform, blow up the Dome of the Rock, and force a situation where they will be expelled from the Temple Mount and a Third Jewish Temple built in its place. Another thing we wanted to photograph was a billboard featuring a picture of an old Jew, who lived in New York, has died, but is believed by some to be the Messiah and that he will reappear. All of this resulted in us losing the others, but, after rushing through the streets and asking policemen and soldiers for directions to the Herodian houses, we found them again.

David led us underneath the present Jewish Quarter to the first-century foundations of Roman-era villas. At that time this had been a neighborhood of the rich and influential, with the foundations revealing houses with multiple rooms, mosaic floors, and Mikvah baths in each house. David leant over a handrail, and gave his analysis.

"Shoresh, these houses here are luxurious. They are only a short distance from the Temple itself. And they have two Mikvah baths in each house. So what does that tell us? First, it tells us that the owners had wealth. Second, it tells us that they had scrupulous religious practices. So, these are houses belonging to Sadducees. The Sadducees were obsessed with ritual cleansing, and so their houses had numerous ritual baths, whereas normally there would only be one Mikvah for the whole of a village."

"The Pharisees and the Sadducees both wanted to stem the tide of Hellenism, but had different ways of trying to keep the general populace faithful to the Torah. The Sadducees focused on urging people to be ceremonially pure. In contrast, the Pharisees picked up the theme of 'a holy nation and a royal priesthood', and the Pharisees took this message to the whole country, encouraging the people to make themselves a 'holy priests to God' keeping separate from outside influences."

"The Sadducees were brutally pragmatic," David emphasized. "They saw it as their duty to keep the Temple functioning by whatever means necessary, even if this meant collaboration with Herod, the Romans, or whoever. For them, the end justified the means. In actual fact, the Sadducee group comprized only a small number of families. But they were rich and had immense power. Financial bargaining with Herod secured the High Priestly position, and it was the Sadducees who were responsible for financial crookedness in the Temple Treasury where people were exploited when they came to worship."

One of the group commented, "David, I think that sometimes we confuse the parts played by the Sadducees and the Pharisees in Jesus' story."

"Yep," replied David. "We sure do! The Pharisees believed that religion should be free, whereas the Sadducees charged for it. The Sadducees also rejected the oral law, and they may well have rejected the prophetic writings as well, all of which the Pharisees accepted."

"Moreover, the Sadducees rejected the ideas of Afterlife, Final Judgment, and Angels. So they lived for today. Their theology was akin to the modern idea of 'name it' and 'claim it' that you find among some Christians. For them, the fact they were rich proved that God had blessed them, and they interpreted material prosperity and lavish houses as signs of Divine favor and blessing. Health, wealth, and happiness! On the other hand, the Pharisees emphasized holiness, purity, and morality, with rewards and punishments to be given in the life to come, not in the here and now."

"Shoresh, look at the story of the Good Samaritan! All Pharisees would be required by the oral law to help the wounded man, even if he had died and his corpse caused them to become ritually unclean. That's what they did. And people knew that. Jesus therefore was not attacking the Pharisees in that parable. Rather, Jesus was gunning for the Sadducees, because, for a priest, a dead man was so ritually unclean that to touch him would impose a seven-day period of 'quarantine' before you could be 'cleansed.' And for a Sadducee it would not be worth such inconvenience for a nobody who was going to die anyway. For a Sadducee, the ministry of the Temple was more important than a single man dying by the side of the road."

This analysis was making so many things click into place. And David was not finished. There was more.

"Shoresh, the Sadducees didn't worry about Jesus until he attacked their Temple empire. But once Jesus attacked the money-changers and spoke of the Temple being destroyed, then, in their eyes, he went from being unpopular to being dangerous. There were many Messianic rumours in the air on that fateful Passover. Jerusalem was buzzing with excitement. And the Sadducees did not want the Romans alarmed by possible unrest or by talk of revolt. This was why Caiaphas and Annas decided that it was '*Better for one man to die, than the people to perish.*' Of course, by the 'people' they meant themselves. In truth, they were frightened that their privileges would be taken away."

"Similarly, a Pharisee would *never* turn a Jew over to the Gentiles. They would *never* do that, just as in the twentieth century extradition of a Jew to another country is virtually unknown. But the Sadducees were different. Survival of their power-base was paramount."

"Take the question of who were in the crowds during the Passion Week. We know that the Thursday/Friday crowds were different from the Palm Sunday crowd. When Jesus was arraigned on the Thursday Night/ Friday Morning there might only have been fifty people in the crowd, probably Temple employees who were dependent on the Sadducees for their wage and daily bread. Certainly, there would not be any of the pious religious pilgrims for the Passover because the pilgrims would still be sleeping after the Passover feast. Also, the official Roman day started long before the pilgrims would be up and about. The people who had been in the Palm Sunday crowds would still be in bed. Moreover, what kind of Jew would ever say '*We have no king but Caesar.*' Every single day Jews recited the Shema, '*Blessed art Thou, O Lord, King of the Universe.*' With that daily affirmation of faith, and daily declaration of the uniqueness of the Lord forming their core religious values, good Jews would never shout '*We have no king but Caesar.*'"

"Read the reactions to the crucifixion carefully. By the time Jesus is crucified it is later in the day, and by then the pilgrims are outdoors again, and they are shocked. Those in power scoffed. But the pilgrims were aghast."

AFTER WE LOOKED AROUND David called us together again. He had more to say. "Shoresh, here's something to ponder if you have a sense of history attaching itself to a place. The High Priests Annas and Caiaphas were Sadducees. Their villas were in this area, cheek by jowl with Herod's Palace. This was where Jesus was brought to be questioned by the High Priests. Right on this spot perhaps."

The caretakers wanted to close up the Herodian Houses for the day, and so we moved back up into the streets of the new Jewish Quarter. David had opened our minds to so much today. Was it really here, at this place, that Jesus was brought from Gethsemane? If not here, then close by. Awesome thoughts. Awesome realities.

After we dispersed Clive and Marion went for a walk in the strictly Orthodox area of the new City, but some of the streets were sealed off by security forces. They did not know why. Perhaps a common occurrence.

The Concert

Tonight, Dee arranged for us to go to the YMCA, for a concert of Israeli dancing. The YMCA in Jerusalem rivals the King David Hotel for luxury, and its concert hall is an extraordinary auditorium which tonight was packed with over five-hundred people. The lady MC asked where people were from. Most were from Europe. Several from the USA and South Africa. And a large number had come from South America. In the concert itself the dancing was fantastic. It was fast, rhythmic, expressive, colorful, and excitingly varied, and the programme notes took pains to emphasise the unity of the peoples of the land.

Israel is the meeting point between two cultures: the East and the West. The folk dances of Israel express the vitality, the pluralism and the hopes of its people. They express the beauty of the Holy Land which has gathered to its bosom Jews who were exiled from its shores and dispersed throughout the world for generations. Israeli folk dances have been influenced by the pioneers who came from Eastern Europe, by Hassidic Jews, by Jews from Arab countries, and by the folk dances of the Arabs and Druze living in Israel.

The YMCA is directly opposite the King David Hotel where President Chirac of France is currently staying during his State Visit to Israel, which started today. When we left the concert there were security forces all over the area. Traffic was at a standstill, police cars had blue lights flashing, and queues of stationary vehicles stretched far into the distance. We made our way on foot through the Hinnom valley back to the Old City.

— Day 15 — Yad-Vashem —

Tuesday 22nd October

WE HAD MORE LECTURES from Joseph this morning on the Rabbinic background to the New Testament. In the course of his exposition I learned that in Judaism the Historical Books in the Old Testament are viewed as part of the Prophetic Writings, because they were intended to be theological commentaries on the nation rather than simply factual chronicles.

This afternoon we had free time. Some of the group visited the Knesset, but Tony, James, and I decided to go to the Holocaust Museum at Yad Vashem. We took a number 20 bus from outside the Jaffa Gate and held on tight as it roared through the streets. This suggested to James the *Three Laws of Jerusalem Bus Driving*. Law One: the narrower the gap, the faster the bus must travel. Law Two: please do not speak to the driver *unless* the bus is moving. Law Three: it would be appreciated if passengers would hold the steering-wheel while the driver gives change. The flat rate charge anywhere in Jerusalem is 3.70 shekels. A year ago, when Grace and I were in Jerusalem, it was only 3 shekels. Is the increase due to inflation caused by pressure on the economy? Or simply a catch-up after several years?

The Holocaust Museum

Yad Vashem is on the outskirts of Jerusalem on the slopes of Mount Herzl, and the museum presentation is relatively low key, allowing the appalling facts to speak for themselves, and by the time a visitor has read all the information boards, looked at the photographs, seen the objects on display, and absorbed the data, a profound impact is made on the emotions.

I took photographs of various large scale pictures which are on the wall because I am compiling a set of slides for use in an audio-visual presentation of *Anne Frank's Diary*. The light levels were low, and I was reluctant to use flash because that would create 'hot spots' on the images; so I held the camera tightly and braced myself against the wall before firing the shutter. I also planned to photograph some of the abstract sculptures in the Yad Vashem gardens, but most were out of bounds, as also was the Hall of Remembrance. This was because President Chirac was coming later in the afternoon to pay his respects.

However, the Children's Memorial Hall was open. The interior of the building is in total darkness apart from six candles whose flames are reflected by a series of mirrors in such a way that, as a person walks through the darkness, they are surrounded by flickering points of light, above, below, to the right, to the left, stretching far into the distance in every direction. In the darkness, voices read out the names, ages, and countries of individual children who perished in the Holocaust:

"Aaron Cohen, 12 years old, Poland."

"Anna Weinberg, 5 years old, Holland."

"Esther Goldberg, 13 years old, France."

And so on.

Name after name is spoken. Over one and a half million children perished in the Nazi abomination of The Final Solution. When a people has such a recent history, and with suffering on the scale of the Holocaust, it is no wonder they trust no one.

President Chirac's visit curtailed our plans, so we wandered back up the long Yad Vashem driveway to the main road. The military cemetery where Yitzak Rabin is buried is adjacent to Yad Vashem and we decided to go there. Sharon and Paul had been to it, and reported that candles and flowers still surrounded the memorial. Last year, when we entered Jerusalem on the last day of the Bike Ride, we went to Rabin's grave. His funeral had taken place only four days earlier, and the place was thronged with silent crowds of sobbing, weeping people, young and old, lighting candles, saying prayers, laying flowers, reading tributes. It would have been good to see it again. However, Chirac was due to visit Rabin's grave as well, so that was out of bounds also.

Evening Gossip

At Christ Church, everyone gathered in the lounge before the evening meal. Sharon and Rosie had been in the Orthodox Quarter.

"It's so shabby, and poor, and rundown!"

David Pileggi agreed. "Yeah, there are some Israelis who accuse the Orthodox of being 'benefit scroungers.' The ultra-Orthodox are an odd group. Did you know that some of their women shave their heads on marriage and wear wigs and headscarves?"

"Why do they do that!"

"For reasons of modesty."

"So, is that why the women all seem to have thick, well coiffured hair styles? Are they all wearing wigs? And if their natural hair is shaved off to avoid the risk of pride, why then buy deluxe wigs?"

"Search me. I suppose the theory is that the wigs make women equal in beauty."

"There are notices up saying 'No Cameras.'" said Rosie,

"Sure. And don't go there on Shabbat. Some Orthodox throw stones at cars on Shabbat."

"There is to be a rally tonight in Ben Yehuda street," said Sharon. "What about going to see what happens? I think it has something to do with a soldier killed in Nablus a few weeks ago. But the people who mentioned the rally said something about Holy Books."

David knew all about this. "What happened," he explained, "was that Israeli soldiers were guarding Joseph's Tomb in Nablus when they were cornered and shot at. But, as well as a soldier being killed, some Jewish Holy Books were burnt, and as a result of this two things have happened. First, a 'shrine' or 'money collecting spot' has been set up near Ben Yehuda Street for the soldier's family. Second, the Holy Books have to have a proper 'funeral.'"

"A funeral for books!"

"Yep Shoresh. Any Writings with the name of 'God' in it have to be disposed of properly and reverently. There are some Orthodox Jews whose entire mission in life is to ensure that all Jews and all Holy Writings have a proper burial. So, for example, after a bus bomb attack these people will search for every scrap of human flesh they can find to give it a proper burial. And they do the same with holy books that are no longer useable."

David turned to Sharon. "Are you sure the rally hasn't taken place already?"

"I'm not sure. I don't know."

David nodded. "I think it took place last night."

David and Alison had gone to Bethany to see a child whom they sponsor through the Bible Lands Society. Dee went with them to capture it all on video, and they had had a wonderful time. "The little girl was really shy at first," said Alison, "But our relationship with her became really good as the day went on. The children were lovely."

Dee added, "The nuns told us that they normally keep their crosses inside their habits. On one occasion, when a little girl saw the nun's cross she cried out 'Kill! Christians kill!' Muslim children have been brought up to remember the Crusaders. For them, the cross means death to Muslims."

"It was also quite sad," said David. "The parents want their children to have US citizenship so that they can get out of Bethany, because they see a future with no hope in it. In the West Bank recently people have been murdered for food, and this was never known before. Life is desperate because the closure of the West Bank has gone on for so long. People just can't get to work, so they have no income, and no means to earn a livelihood. The Headmistress at the Bethany School said that if a Palestinian goes into Jerusalem avoiding the check-points and is discovered, they have to pay a huge fine on the spot or be thrown into prison. People watch TV, and they see places where people live in freedom, and they want to get out."

A discussion started with David Pileggi on the whole Middle East situation, and David shared some of his thoughts with us.

"Look, war with Syria is likely. What Anthony said the other night at the Kiddush meal was pretty accurate although I don't go with him all the way. All of us who live here are pretty gloomy about the future. War won't happen until after November 5th, the US Presidential elections. But after that date the bargaining positions are weaker, and each side will have less reason to negotiate. At the moment the American Presidential candidates can be pressurized to make promises to various sides in order to gain the votes of different parts of the US electorate. But after they are elected that lever goes."

"The atmosphere in Jerusalem is really nasty just now. Nastier than I've known for over ten years. Remember the Arab whom Murray Dixon referred to in his sermon on Sunday? Well, that Arab was in fact an Israeli citizen, yet he was still beaten up by the Israeli police. You see, there had been a knifing of a Coptic priest, and when the police were making enquiries this man was uncooperative when he was questioned. So the police decided to teach him a lesson. But he had nothing to do with the murder. And there was no excuse for the beating the police gave him."

"The paramilitary police are unpredictable, though not the regular police who are quite professional. This is because they are low-grade recruits. The best recruits go into the equivalent of the SAS or paratroops. Relationships between army and police are pretty well non-existent. Leadership is atrocious. Yasser Arafat is useless! Benjamin Netanyahu is a bird-brain!"

"Tony, you and James and Bruce were out at Yad Vashem this afternoon. Well, out there they make a big thing of the fact that the British stopped Jewish immigration into Palestine from 1939 onwards. But why did the Brits do this? It was because the Brits wanted the Arabs to come on their side. The Arabs were willing to ally with anyone who opposed their colonial masters. The old adage here was in operation—the enemy of my enemy is my friend. And so the Arabs were ready even to support Hitler. In fact, in 1942 the Grand Mufti of Jerusalem said that all Jews should be killed and anyone doing this does Allah's will. Ten years later the Arabs were happy to support Stalin. Even nowadays, a huge number of Arabs admire Saddam Hussein."

"Why?"

"Well, they see Saddam Hussein as a man who took a stand against the West. And he was against the Shi'ite regime of Iran."

"Look folks, Islam is a religion of *Power*. Power is fundamental. And Islam is a religion that highly values political power which comes when a nation is ruled by Sharia Law—there is no split between religion and politics in Islam. This is fundamental. So, nothing other than Sharia can be allowed to rule in the house of Islam, even if the governments are headed by secular Muslims. And, of course, even worse are non-Muslim ruled states such as Israel and Lebanon. The only principle which is consistent behind all the wheeling and dealing is the axiom: No other authority must rule in Islam's sphere of influence."

David looked at us.

"This is why Lebanon's 'Christian' society is being wiped off the map. Israel is next. The 'Jewish' society has to be dealt with, so that Islam can have total authority here. If Algeria falls to fundamentalists, then Tunisia and Egypt follow. Mubarak of Egypt is ruthless with fundamentalists.

But the West doesn't make a great issue of human rights in Egypt except nominally. Have you heard much news reporting about the abuse of civil rights in Egypt? Of course not, because the West wants Mubarak to deal with extremists."

David posed a question. "During the Gulf War why didn't Israel retaliate to the Scud missiles Iraq threw at them? "

"Because of US pressure?"

"Yeah, sure, it was because of US pressure. But also because they had no option. If Israel did an air strike on Iraq what air-space could they use? If they flew through Jordanian air-space King Hussein of Jordan would have to send his fighters up to intercept the Israelis, otherwise he himself would be toppled from the throne, because Jordanians feel close to the Iraqis. And if King Hussein goes, that is disaster for Israel. Israel needs King Hussein even though Israel and Jordan hate each other. Then again, if Israel sent her planes through Syrian air-space, Syria would have withdrawn from the Gulf War alliance. Again, if Israel flew down the Gulf of Aqaba and through Saudi Arabia to attack Iraq, then Saudi would have withdrawn. Israel had no options."

"Quite simply, the Arabs want the Jews out. It took a hundred years to eject the Crusaders from Palestine, so, in the Arab mind, there is plenty of time to deal with the Jews."

— *Day 16* — *Brothers* —

Wednesday 23rd October

BEFORE OUR FIRST LECTURE today, I took another saunter through the Old City. The shopkeepers were opening up their stalls, and a teenage youth carried cups of black tea on a brass tray to various traders, giving them an early morning refreshment. A woman with her baby was already at her begging point, and several rolls of film, pulled out of their canisters, lay beside her. I assumed this was a warning, 'No Photographs!' In contrast, some stalls had trays with masses of film for sale, and the prices in the Souk were half the price being charged at Yad Vashem and the film was not old, out-of-date stock. As well as some people, quite understandably, not wanting to be photographed, there is also a fear of the 'Evil-Eye' which feeds the notion that you lose something if an image is taken of you.

At the Jaffa Gate, porters, with their narrow barrows, were waiting for delivery vans to come with supplies for shops deeper into the Souk, and in the Jaffa Gate square two men with drum-sets were setting up. A few soldiers walked past. Outside the Gate workmen were busy making a new underpass. Some of them were riddling soil into wheel-barrows, like archaeologists sifting through the debris of an excavation, but their methods were too rough and ready to be that. I puzzled why they were doing this, so I called out to them, but they did not understand my question.

Then I strolled up the lanes of the Greek Patriarchate district, all of which were eerily quiet. The Greek sector has a large proportion of flower stalls, men's smoking rooms, and barber shops. As noted previously, political posters are on every wall. Orthodox monks, dressed in their long black robes and wearing their tall flat-topped hats, made their way with busy, purposeful strides. After exploring the alleys, it was time to return to Christ Church for lectures.

Claire Pfann

Our first lecture was given by Claire Pfann who did her Master's thesis on the use of the word 'Brother' in the Acts of the Apostles. Claire's argument is that originally the term 'Brother' was only used by Jewish Christians to describe other Jewish Christians. As regards Gentile Christians, they were not accorded that title at the beginning, and, until the watershed Council of Jerusalem of Acts 15, Gentile Christians were made to feel outsiders. One of Claire's points was that today the roles are reversed, and it is now Jewish believers who feel they are outsiders and put under pressure to deny their Jewishness before gaining full acceptance in the Christian community.

"You see, in the Early Church, Gentiles were wrongly asked to become 'Jewish' before they were fully accepted. But in the twentieth-century Church, it is Jews who are wrongly asked to deny their Jewishness to be the same. Identical error. But in mirror image."

Claire delivered her lecture like a machine gun. Her speech speed was supersonic. Fortunately, the lecture was clearly structured, and easily followed.

We chatted afterwards. "Have you been long in Israel Claire?"

"Fourteen years I guess. I became a Christian in the USA in the early 70s through Arthur Blessett's work. Anyone remember him? Remember the Jesus People?"

I recalled Arthur Blessett coming to Edinburgh during his world tour. It was while I was doing my science degree. His appearance in UK cities, carrying his huge wooden cross made a big stir. Thousands and thousands of bright, red, circular stickers with the logo 'Smile—God Loves You' appeared everywhere.

Ofer Amitai

The second lecture was quite different. David Pileggi introduced us to Ofer Amitai, who is a Jewish Christian with a unique background. His father's family left Poland in 1935 when they realized that the future of Jews in Poland was grim; his mother's line had lived in Israel for two hundred and fifty years. His grandfather had been a prominent Israeli at the time of the founding of the State of Israel, and his father had been military governor of Jerusalem at the time of the Six-Day War in 1967. Ofer shared with us what it means to be a Jewish Christian in Israel. He was born in Israel in 1951, and grew up in a secular Jewish family. By 1977 he was a Christian, living in the United States, with a calling to ministry. He told us that God led him to Bible School, and he stayed fourteen and a half years in the USA as a Pastor.

"But God has now called me back to Israel," said Ofer. "I was not keen to come, but God's love prevails. In the United States I worked and ministered with Gentiles, and I believe this has helped me to have a balanced outlook."

This quiet, small, slight, softly spoken, gentle human being is a real man of God, and the grace of Jesus shone from him.

"My friends, what do we need to make a bridge between Gentiles and Jewish believers? What is needed are three things: Patience, Love, and Lowliness in the Holy Spirit. These are the things. Otherwise it is impossible to relate to a Jewish Christian, and you become either sentimental or pro-political. To be pro-political means that you become a person who takes the side of either the Jew or the Palestinian. I cannot be political. I came back to Israel two and a half years ago, and the Lord instructed me to be quiet and to learn."

Ofer then analyzed what he saw as the place of the Jews in God's continuing plan under three headings: Scattering, Gathering, and One-ing. He did his biblical exegesis with quiet spiritual insight and sharp intelligence. A special person.

"God's sovereign way of uniting people is not by coming to a compromise, but by having a new emerging into something else," Ofer explained. "What do I mean? I mean an emerging from ourselves into the mind of Christ. Nothing born of self brings unity; but a yielding to the head who is Christ can bring unity. Outwardly this looks impossible. But God is never discouraged. The scriptures teach that God says, 'I *will* . . . do this, and this, and this.' The fountain which cleanses in Jerusalem between Arab and Jew, between Gentile and Jew, will be belief in Jesus. But the method will be by Patience, Love, and Lowliness. Arab and Jew, Gentile and Jew, will always be separate until they are united in Jesus."

Ofer then elaborated on his view of recent times. He explained that, from the 1970s onwards, a tiny new body began to emerge in Israel. These were Jewish believers in Jesus. This was the first time in many centuries that Jewish believers in Jesus lived in Jerusalem. This was largely the result of Gentile missionaries who came and prayed for years and years and years. Sometimes these people never made one convert. But they prayed and prayed and prayed. On that foundation God birthed these 'children' and now forty to fifty congregations, amounting to about four thousand souls, are in the land. Ofer again emphasized, "We need patience, love, and humility to do all this."

He went on, "You know what picture comes to my mind when I think of the body of Christ in Israel? It is like a Wild West town. People from elsewhere in the world swagger into Israel with six-shooters, shouting about prophecies and apocalyptic scenarios. This means that it is so difficult for people here, who are being birthed into Christ, to grow up in safety. In the Gentile-Jewish scene there exists a feeling of being swamped by ministries which come with their own agendas. Westerners find it difficult to come with a humble attitude. They are more likely to say 'let me tell you how to do things.' People who come from abroad, who believe they have been 'called' here, find it hard to maintain a servant attitude. This Western 'know-it-all' mentality confuses the body of Christ in Israel, because the body of Christ which has been birthed in Israel is a very fragile body."

We sat spellbound as Ofer spoke to us. Ofer emphasized another point, that the body of Christ in Israel is a mixture. There is no ecclesiastical structure. "You are what you are, what the Lord has made you. Nothing works except the real thing. You see, society in Israel is very, very tight. In the USA people are allowed to be what they want to be, and individual rights are all important. But in Israel the group or nation is everything. If you do not conform you are 'put outside the camp.'"

Was Ofer being autobiographical? What had been the personal cost in terms of his relationship with his own family?

"Jesus came for the very least." he continued, "This is reflected in the new Messianic communities. They are full of the poor, needy, disturbed, and confused. Very few in the new Messianic communities come from the middle-classes. So this is not a popular movement. Also, even in a Messianic congregation the Israeli-born element is small, and therefore the Israeli segment feels even more outside of things. We need Patience, Love, Humility. The solution is to be filled with the Holy Spirit and to be a loving servant. If we come in the Spirit of Christ, which is humble and lowly in love, we will be effective. But if we come as something more, we will never touch the lives of those here."

"One positive thing in Israel is that *in Christ* Arab and Jew are really coming together. Nowhere else is there a real oneness. When we come into Christ we come into something else. We come into something new. This is the new possibility God creates. What is this possibility? It is a person, Jesus. When we come together in Jesus we never talk politics. Denominations in Israel have a very, very poor witness to the love of God. You know, Israeli police sometimes have to stop fistfights at the Church of the Holy Sepulchre between priests of the different denominations. What does that say to people? Will that bring Arabs and Jews to Jesus? Patience, Love, Lowliness, Grace, Humility, these are the power of God."

Ofer finished and we sat in silence.

"Any questions for Ofer?" David asked.

We had none. Partly because it had been a heavy morning of concentrated listening. But mostly because what Ofer said and how he said it lifted his talk onto a different level. We needed time to think. What Ofer had given us was existential theology. This was the real thing. This was meeting the real crisis of the human situation head on, but using spiritual means for spiritual ends.

The Armenian Quarter

At lunchtime James and I wandered round to the Zion Gate to buy bread and bananas. The shopkeeper was an Armenian, yet another George. And he was talkative.

"My friends, trade has been very slack for three months. In fact, even before that. Ever since Netanyahu came to power. We have no confidence in him. Armenians try to be neutral between the Jews and the Arabs, but we have no confidence in this government. The USA is unpredictable. Perhaps Europe can help us. Yitzak Rabin was good, honest, straight, but that is all over now. King Hussein is good. He is honest. He has a good plan for Jerusalem."

James asked, "George, do you worry for your family in the future?"

"Yes, of course I do. I worry for them. But we Armenians have always lived unsure of the future. This is our destiny!"

George told us about his family, of whom he was so proud. "My children at school learn five languages. We have good school for Armenian children. The very best."

James took George's photo and George thanked us for spending time with him. The people here are easy to talk to, and they readily respond if given half a chance. We walked back to Christ Church via the Jewish Quarter and the Souk.

THIS AFTERNOON DAVID TOOK us to visit various communities in and around the Old City. The theme for the whole of today has been 'My Brother' and we have been repeatedly confronted with the question: "How do I relate to this person, or to that community, as my brothers and sisters in the body of Christ?"

We walked up the slope from Christ Church, through the arched tunnel which leads into the Armenian Quarter. The posters about the Genocide which cover the walls of the tunnel can't be missed. When we reached the gateway to the Armenian Cathedral a brown-robed priest named Father Packrad met us and took us into the Armenian compound. He is in his early forties, powerfully built, but with the bearing and manner of a thinker and a leader.

Father Packrad explained that Armenians adopted Christianity in 301AD. Soon afterwards many of them flocked to the Holy Land, and to this south-western part of the Old City where the Armenian Quarter still exists. After settling, the priests and monks dedicated their lives to the Holy Places. In the fourth century they built a small chapel on the site where it was believed St. James was beheaded in 44AD. That James was James the brother of John the Evangelist, not James the step-brother of Jesus. But the chapel was destroyed in the Persian invasion and not rebuilt. Then, in the tenth century, the Cathedral of St. James was constructed, with its architectural mixture of Crusader and Armenian styles. Father Packrad said that St. James' head is still buried here, although, according to tradition, the rest of his body was thrown into the sea and washed up in Spain at a place now called Corpus Stella.

Tradition holds that James, the step-brother of Jesus, is also buried here after being beaten to death. He was originally buried in the Hinnom Valley, but in the sixth century the relics were transferred to the Armenian Quarter and lie under what is now the Altar of St. James. Once a year the Patriarch stands over his grave, as does any new Patriarch at his enthronement.

"My friends," said Father Packrad, "this where the real Via Dolorosa starts. The Via Dolorosa which all the tourist pilgrims walk along is not in the correct place. Let me explain. Now, do we agree that the Via Dolorosa is the route between where our Lord was sentenced to death by Pontius Pilate, and Calvary. Do you agree? Is that not so?"

"Yes."

"OK, the traditional tourist Via Dolorosa starts at Stephen's Gate where the Roman Antonia Fortress was. But Pilate would not live in the Antonia when he came to Jerusalem. He would live in luxurious accommodation beside Herod's Palace up in this area. What man would bring his wife to live in a soldier's barracks! Remember, when Jesus was brought before Pilate it was so early in the morning that it must have taken place at Pilate's residence. Remember also, Pilate's wife could get a message to him, and so must have been nearby. Herod, Caiaphas, and Pilate, all stayed near each other up here in the Upper City."

All of this tied in with what David Pileggi had told us about the rich part of the city in Jesus' day.

Father Packard continued. "In one of our courtyards you can see an olive tree which, by tradition, is the tree our Lord was tied to. It was there that our Lord was held before being interrogated by the High Priests. Archaeologists have discovered a first-century drainage system underneath the floor of the little church built on the spot. So Jesus was tried and sentenced up in this area of the city, not down by the Stephen Gate. And so the real Via Dolorosa is from here to the Church of the Holy Sepulchre."

Father Packrad's reasoning seemed impeccable! He went on to tell us that the Armenian Patriarchate was established in 638. Before that time all Christian communities were under the Greek Patriarchate, but they divided after the Arab invasion. When that split took place each community had to become self-reliant, which was only made possible by the many pilgrims who flocked to Jerusalem for Christmas and Easter bringing funds for their support. Each party also brought crosses to mark their pilgrimage, with the Armenian version quite distinctive. It consists of a large main cross with a smaller cross in each of the quadrants marked out by the arms of the main cross, and with the foot of the main cross broadening out into roots which fix in the earth. Father Packrad explained that this design is based on a legend that, after Jesus' resurrection, his cross became the tree of life, and this is why sometimes the smaller crosses in the quadrants are replaced by trees.

FATHER PACKRAD IS IMMENSELY proud of Armenians having an uninterrupted presence in Jerusalem though, over the centuries, the Armenian Patriarchate in Jerusalem has lived with chronic debt and lack of money

for its monastery. Fortunately, in the seventeenth century Gregory the
Benefactor bought land in the city which the community still benefits
from today. And in the eighteenth century another Gregory, known as
Gregory the Chain-Bearer, went to Armenia and collected money for the
Jerusalem community. Gregory the Chain-Bearer also donated a consid-
erable number of decorative works for the Cathedral.

"Father Packrad, why was he called the 'Chain-Bearer'?"

"His chains were worn as a mark of penance."

Remembrances of the great Armenian Genocide are never far away,
and we were not surprised when Father Packrad briefed us on the atroci-
ties. He told us that the Armenian people were deported by the Turks out
of their ancient lands into the desert. Massive killings took place in these
remote regions, and there are huge Armenian cemeteries in the deserts
of Syria. Father Packrad emphasized that 1915 was not the start of the
killings. For example, there was a massacre in 1895 in which 300,000
were killed in a single day. He told us that killings took place right from
1914 to 1918, with one of the blackest days being 24th April 1915, when
more than three hundred Armenian intellectuals were rounded up and
murdered in cold blood. In Father Packrad's view the Turks reasoned that
if they killed the intellectuals then the nation would be destroyed.

"But God be thanked! We are still a nation!" Then, in quieter tones,
and with a rueful smile, he said, "Until 1989 there was still a dream of
returning to Armenia, but the dream has faded."

We crossed the inner courtyard and an old man in a faded black
gown was sitting by the corner of a building, his face full of character
and experience. Although the sun blazed down he was bareheaded. I fell
behind the main group again, but soon caught up.

After making sure everyone was present, Father Packrad took us
into the Hostel building. The newest Hostel buildings were built in 1991
with first class facilities, a source of great pride to Father Packrad, who
told us that when the new building was completed the community came
alive again. Although the buildings are modern, the architect has kept
the feeling of a monastic building by having wide, well-lit, spacious corridors for walking and meditating in. We were amazed at the plush and
luxurious interior.

"We keep it looking poor on the outside quite deliberately," he explained. "A lot of earlier building took place in the 1850s and was the
responsibility of an Armenian family who were also commissioned by
the Sultans in Turkey to build for them. Incidentally, did you know that

Armenian tiles are on the Dome of the Rock?" Most of us nodded, this was something we had learned earlier. "Yes, King Hussein puts a high value on our workmanship."

THE ARMENIAN COMPOUND IS designed to be a self-sufficient village, protected from outside. That is why a walk through the Armenian Quarter reveals little of Armenian life. There are no side streets. There are few shops. And there are few houses to be seen. Nearly everything lies behind high walls. Their children learn six languages: Classical Armenian, Modern Armenian, English, French, Arabic, and Hebrew. There is a community school with both elementary and secondary education, plus a playground. The secluded nature of the school gives the children total security.

The whole Compound was at high risk during the 1948 Arab/Israeli War. During that conflict Armenians protected local Jews who had been their neighbors, and hid them in the convent until they were released by the Israeli Army. Because of this, Armenians are called Betrayers by some of the Arab communities. Father Packrad commented, "You know, we have lived many centuries in the Middle East, but in character we are Europeans."

"We have a community of monks here. A monk's life is an active life, not a passive one. Some people think that monks went into the desert to escape the temptations of the world. Not so. They saw the desert as a place of danger and demons, and so they were inviting temptation by going into the desert. They wanted to prove themselves and strengthen themselves. Our monks are busy. Each day there are several hours of prayer. Then there is work, which can be either physical work or intellectual work."

He explained that Armenians have two kinds of priest, celibate and non-celibate. If a candidate wishes to be a married priest, he must get married *first* and then become a priest. A celibate priest has to live in a monastery and is not involved in parish business, and only a celibate priest can have promotion to the office of Bishop. We were then taken to the church.

"My friends, when Jesus was arrested in Gethsemane the holy archangels Gabriel and Michael covered their faces with their wings because they were ashamed to see their Lord treated so. This is why our convent is called the Convent of St. Gabriel and St. Michael, and this convent is also the local parish church for the Armenian community. It is used for Baptisms, Weddings, and Funerals."

We entered the sanctuary, which was quiet and peaceful. Two Novices were lighting candles. Apart from ourselves there were only three other visitors. The Armenians do not keep tourists out of the church, but neither do they publicize its presence and so it retains a tranquil atmosphere. There are no seats or pews. Worshippers stand or sit on the floor. The whole interior is elaborately decorated. But it was a series of head and shoulders images over the altar which really captured our attention.

"My friends, these pictures relate to a third-century incident," explained the Father. "At that time there was a widespread persecution of Christians. Forty young Roman soldiers serving on the Armenian frontier of the Empire were Christians and they were condemned, tortured, and finally abandoned naked on an island on a frozen lake in the middle of winter. As they waited for death, their guard, who was watching from the lake shore, saw heaven opening up for them. This vision made him a believer, and he wanted to share their glory. So he ran across the frozen lake to join them. The faces above the altar are the faces of these forty martyrs plus the Roman guard who was converted at their death. We highly revere these Martyrs of Armenia."

We left the Compound encouraged by the tenacity of this Christian community. They are Christian folk, trying to be a people of faith in the midst of Jerusalem's polyglot environment. David Pileggi told us that the Armenian Patriarch would like some of the land that Christ Church has, and their determination to have it did not make for ideal relationships. We live in an imperfect world! With an imperfect church!

Gethsemane

From the Armenian Quarter David took us to the foot of the Mount of Olives. "Look Shoresh, the name 'Gethsemane' means 'the oil press', because it was the place where olives were pressed to obtain the oil. Now Pastors! There's a theme for a sermon! Because on the night of his betrayal Jesus' spirit was *pressed hard* as he wrestled in prayer."

We went into the chapel of the Cave of the Olive Press, and were met by a Franciscan monk who was expecting us. The monk had served most of his ministry in New York before applying to come to the Holy Land. He used to pastor two churches in the United States, working mostly with the black community, and immediately prior to coming to Israel he had worked as an evangelist. He greeted us warmly,

"Welcome folks! Now, what is a Franciscan doing in Jerusalem? Well, St. Francis came to Jerusalem to try to convert the Sultan. He was unsuccessful, but he established such friendly relationships with the Sultan that the Franciscans were given this site which had an early tradition as the place where Jesus prayed before His arrest. I understand that archaeologists favor this site more than the one along the road which is commemorated by the Church of All Nations. But, who knows!"

He chatted about his life, and the inevitable question of Jews and Arabs came up.

"I can't see peace between Jews and Arabs until Jesus returns. And you know, the Bible says that when He returns he'll walk from the Mount of Olives up through the Golden Gate. Well, I'm right here, right at the best place. So if the Lord spares me I'll walk in with Him through that Golden Gate! Yes, sir! I sure will!"

WE WALKED TO ANOTHER chapel which is revered as the Tomb of Mary, and which is kept by Armenian and Greek Orthodox monks who share the premises amicably. One tradition claims that, after Pentecost, Mary stayed the rest of her life in Jerusalem at the home of John Mark. If so, then it would be reasonable to conclude that when she died she would be laid to rest somewhere on the slopes of the Mount of Olives. But another tradition—quite a strong one—holds that Mary went to Ephesus in Asia Minor where she was looked after by the Apostle John.

Inside the chapel an aged Orthodox priest sat reading a small, leather-backed prayer book. Both Alison and I wanted a photo of him reading his book. He was delighted. Leaving the chapel, we wandered along to the Church of All Nations which is where most pilgrims go when looking for Gethsemane.

ARRIVING AT THE CHURCH, David had two more points he wanted to make. "Shoresh, this is important. Jesus' temptation to avoid the cross was very real when he came to Gethsemane. Look, where are we? We are at the foot of the Mount of Olives. Now, we know that the rule of law stopped at the top of the Mount of Olives. Beyond that was bandit-country. It was desert. It's like that today. The desert starts immediately. And in bandit-country Roman rule didn't really operate. You needed guarded convoys to go safely from one place to another. So, when Jesus wrestled with his destiny down here in Gethsemane he was well aware that a five-minute walk up the slope would enable him to slip out of the clutches of his enemies. That was a real possibility. It was within his grasp to do that. He could do it. Now, he did not. But the temptation to do so was real, and not just academic."

"Now, were any of these olive trees here in Jesus' day?" David pointed to the olives grove. "I don't think so. I agree that there are some pretty old olive trees. But, Shoresh, remember, Josephus tells us that when Titus besieged Jerusalem he cut down every living thing for miles around. So the probability that any of the Gethsemane olives survived Titus is really small."

Even at mid-day the Church of All Nations is gloomy and atmospheric. This afternoon, near sunset, it was even more so. As a Protestant I can sometimes fail to appreciate a wordless experience of the presence of God. But in this church, with its dark and brooding atmosphere, and lit only by a few lights, I stood and listened to a group of men from Germany singing the liturgy as they sat round the altar. Their deep voices rang throughout the building. As they sang, people passed by and knelt before the holy table. Awareness of such beauty of worship, with its sense of the presence of God, makes one want to do something: like lighting a candle, or making the sign of the cross, or even genuflecting. So I bowed as I crossed in front of the altar.

The King David Hotel

This evening we decided to have a night out at the King David Hotel. We couldn't afford to actually eat there, but calculated that we could stretch to a cup of coffee in Jerusalem's premier hotel. Consequently, after our meal at Christ Church we dressed in our very best and marched from the Old City to the King David. On arrival we caused quite a stir, partly because I was wearing the kilt.

The waiter came to our table, full of smiles. "Ah! Skirt! Scotsman!"

"My friend! Not a skirt! A kilt! What's your name my friend?"

"I am called Gabi, welcome to the King David Hotel."

Gabi plays in a Syrian Pipe Band and is a member of the Syrian Orthodox Church which is similar to the Maronite Church, although the Maronites are closer to Catholicism.

"After work, my friends and I meet and play Syrian bagpipes for hours and hours! I have been to your country."

"Oh! Where in Scotland?"

"Edinburgh. I went two times with a friend to get new bagpipes for our band. It was very wet, very cold."

"Did you get the bagpipes in the Royal Mile?"

"Royal Mile?"

"It's a street in the middle of Edinburgh. On a steep hill. And the roadway is cobbled. That's to say it has stones instead of tarmac. There are bagpipe makers there."

"Yes, that describes where we went."

"Wonderful! Gabi, tell me, has your band played in Scotland?"

"No, but we have played the bagpipes all over Scandinavia and we are coming to Scotland in 1997."

Gabi looked after us royally. Not only did we get our coffees at 10 shekels a cup, but Gabi and his friends provided free chocolates and biscuits for each of us. Jacques Chirac left the King David Hotel today, but it is doubtful if the President of France received better attention and consideration than we did. The waiter service was brilliant. The staff were charming. And Gabi made it special.

The Desert

— Day 17 — Qumran —

Thursday 24th October

"OK, SHORESH, TODAY WE go into the desert for a week." David was briefing us about the next stage of the tour. "Why are we sending you into the desert? Well, in the Bible, the desert is where God's people hear God's word. For Abraham, Moses, Paul, David, Elijah, John the Baptist, Jesus, the desert was the place where they were prepared for ministry. In the desert they learned total trust and total humility before God. To understand the Bible, you have to experience the desert."

Before departure an enormous bunch of flowers arrived for Sharon from Paul via Interflora. She rushed into the Souk to buy a large black pail, and then, fresh and watered, the flowers were brought onto the bus. Much of our luggage was left behind at Christ Church. Despite this, the minibus was jam-packed with baggage and people as we drove through the Jaffa Gate on our way south. The pail of flowers had its own seat of honor.

David Pileggi gave us a political commentary as we headed for Wadi Kelt and the Jordan Valley. The main highway now lies in the former Green Zone which used to separate East and West Jerusalem before the Six-Day War, and David commented on the situation.

"Israel has closed off the territories completely this week, because the news is that Hamas has more bus bombs planned. One of the problems in the Middle East is that only Turkey, Israel, and Egypt, have a sense of national identity. The other countries are simply creations made by Anglo/French lines on a map. Without a natural sense of nationhood, the allegiance of people in these countries is first to Islam, second to their tribe, and third to their family. These allegiances cross national frontiers, and they are far more important than any sense of nationality. So a country like Jordan, which Israel wants to be stable, has no natural coherence. King Hussein hangs on by his finger-nails. I fear that eventually Jordan as such could disappear and become a Palestinian State."

"How strong is King Hussein's position?" Tony asked.

"Well," replied David, "long before King Hussein's time, the Hashemite Dynasty was weakened when Jordan lost control of Mecca to Saudi Arabia. However, and importantly, he still controls the Holy Place of the Temple Mount in Jerusalem, but the Palestinians are trying to take that from him. If they succeed, then he will lose the allegiance of many Arab tribes. Israel therefore has a vested interest in making sure that does not happen; and so, however much it goes against the grain for the ultra-Orthodox, sensible Israelis know that King Hussein must not forfeit the prestige which goes with his Temple Mount custodianship."

HALFWAY DOWN SPECTACULAR WADI Kelt we stopped to photograph St. George's Monastery nestling in the gorge far below. This part of the Judaean wilderness is a desert of stones. The landscape is stark and immensely beautiful. But to live in it would be altogether different. We could see black Bedouin tents grouped together. Smoke from camp-fires drifted up into a cloudless sky. Travelling on, we came to the outskirts of Jericho and looked across at the ruined foundations of Herod's Winter Palace.

David thumbed through his notes. "Listen Shoresh, why did Herod have a Winter Palace here? Well, Jericho was the place the rich and famous in Jerusalem went to escape the bad winter weather. It was only twenty miles downhill from Jerusalem, but you went from winter cold to summer warmth. Jericho was the Palm Springs of Judaea!"

"Shoresh, in the story of the Good Samaritan, where was the priest coming from who passed by on the other side? What was his direction of travel? He was coming from Jerusalem going down to Jericho. Now, that direction of travel is important! He was a Sadducee looking for a break after doing his Temple duties. The Sadducees loved the trappings of wealth. And this Sadducee was looking forward to a luxury holiday down in Jericho! Jesus' hearers knew exactly what Jesus was getting at. Jesus was addressing more than one agenda in that parable. Sure, there was the issue of compassion, and there was the question, 'Who is my neighbor?' But there was also the issue of how a holy man might forget his vocation and sell his soul to what the world offers. Jesus' listeners knew exactly what he meant when he said that the priest and Levite were going to Jericho."

The Dead Sea Scrolls

Our first major stop today was Qumran. In the spring of 1947, in a remote cave close to the Dead Sea, a Bedouin shepherd accidentally discovered ancient Hebrew and Aramaic scrolls. These manuscripts had been deposited in several caves by members of the Qumran Essene community when the people of the area were being slaughtered by the Romans in the aftermath of the Jewish revolt of 70AD. The Qumran scripts have become pivotal in our whole understanding of the Old Testament, the inter-Testamental period, and the background to the New Testament. The heat was almost unbearable, but David found a shaded corner where he led a seminar on the relevance of Qumran.

"Right Shoresh, where do we start?" he began. "Remember, Shoresh, the desert was a place for mystics, bandits, holy men, murderers, and misfits. The Romans did not even try to control it. So the desert was the place to which people went if they rejected the prevailing culture and the prevailing society. Remember also, after Alexander the Great conquered the Middle East the great struggle in Israel was the battle to halt the spread of Hellenistic culture, philosophy, religion and morals. Now, the Maccabees defeated the Hellenists in the Maccabean revolt. But did they really win? You see, only a couple of generations later the Maccabees were looking and acting no different than the people they defeated. This brought confusion. To cut a long story short, one of the results of this confusion and disaffection was the emergence of groups like the Pharisees, the Essenes, and the Zealots, who had a common aim in making the nation 'pure' again. But they had totally different agendas as to how that would be accomplished."

"The Essene group went into the desert with a leader known as the Teacher of Righteousness. For them, everything in Jerusalem was wrong, and the Temple was polluted. Because the Temple was polluted they no longer went to it, and so they made a whole series of radical religious changes in order to emphasise their distance from what went on in Jerusalem."

"First, they changed the calendar. That seems nothing to us, but it was a revolution for them. You see, the popular theology of Judaism is carried by its festivals. Festivals proclaim and define the Faith. Judaism celebrates Passover, Pentecost, Sukkoth, and so on. The belief framework of Judaism hangs on its calendar. So, to change the calendar was a fundamental rejection of the accepted religious authorities."

"Second, the Essenes ceased facing Jerusalem when they prayed, and instead faced the rising sun. Third, they developed their own communal life. In fact, it is highly possible that the Early Church in the book of Acts got its idea of communal life and sharing possessions from the Essene concept. Fourth, they did not go to the Temple to make sacrifices. They did it themselves, and they saw themselves as a priestly class. Sincere believers, but taking an idea to an extreme. Yet, despite this extremism, their manuscripts still reflect enough of the debates in first-century Judaism to help us understand Jesus better."

David paused, and then made a big point.

"Remember though, the Essenes were not the mainstream. This is the mistake so many amateur scholars make in New Testament studies. Because we now have this wealth of documentation from Qumran, some scholars have exalted the importance of the Essenes too far. But the Essenes were not the mainstream. The Pharisees would eventually become the mainstream. The Essenes said that the Pharisees were making religion *easy* for the masses. Now, compare that to Jesus who said that the Pharisees were making religion far too *difficult* for the masses!"

"Essene standards were high. Their discipline was like the discipline of a military camp engaged in a war. And they believed that they were truly in a war. A war between the Sons of Light and the Sons of Darkness. They had two ritual baths a day, not just once a week as elsewhere! Shabbat was so strict that if an animal fell in a ditch they would not take it out. Again, contrast that with Jesus' teaching. Jesus specifically contradicted that example. And on Shabbat an Essene would go for hours without relieving himself because passing water was regarded as bodily work!"

"The historian Josephus liked the Essenes. He lived and studied with them for a while but never joined them. In fact, loads of people admired them. Qumran was the headquarters of the movement, and the really dedicated ones stayed here, calling themselves the 'Way.' Less committed Essenes lived all over Israel. So even a person like Jesus, brought up at the other end of the country, would be familiar with Essene ideas. Remember, the whole nation ate and drank Torah; and so views about the Essenes and other groups were discussed all over the country."

"Shoresh, here is something unusual. Qumran was a celibate community, which was extraordinary for Judaism. The equation 'Sex is Bad' was not natural to Judaism. It was more an idea in Greek thought, So, somewhere, there may have been a tie up between the thinking of Qumran and the Hellenistic thinking of Jews in the Diaspora who lived far from Israel in Alexandria or elsewhere, and who had absorbed some of these ideas. And it could also be that they refrained from sexual relations because they wanted to maintain a high level of purity—after all, they believed their community to be the replacement for the Temple in Jerusalem."

I interrupted. "But David, perhaps the Qumran celibacy came from the Old Testament idea of prohibition from sexual relationships while on a military campaign? That would especially be the case if they saw themselves as a spiritual military camp on full time military service in the war between the Sons of Light and the Sons of Darkness. Do you not think so?"

"Well, that could be the case," David replied. "But it would introduce a tension with the first command of the Torah which is '*to go forth and multiply.*'"

"I think," he added, "that Qumran had a strong philosophical link with the Diaspora. This comes out, not just in their attitude to celibacy, but in their theology of sacrifice. Consider this: Jews in the Diaspora, unable to visit Jerusalem or the Temple because it was too far away, dealt with the problem of not being able to sacrifice in the Temple by 'allegorising' religious duties. Now, Qumran also adopted that idea in order to legitimise their view that a Jew can have a full religious life without physically offering a sacrifice in the Temple. They said 'Our sacrifice will be the fruit of our lips.' To me, this was a theology of the Diaspora."

"David," said Tony, "Back home there are loads of publications which have the line that Jesus was simply another Essene."

"OK Shoresh. What about Jesus and the Essenes? It is possible that John the Baptist may have spent time here. And, certainly, Jesus was aware of this group, because they had other communities in Judaea, not just Qumran. And some ideas do dovetail with Jesus' ideas. But when you go deeper they are poles apart. For example, the Qumran sect were totally clannish and hated outsiders, whereas Jesus, in the Sermon on the Mount said '*love your enemies.*' In fact, some scholars think Jesus had the Essenes in mind when he said '*You have heard it said 'You shall hate your enemies'.*'"

"Similarly, consider the parable of the Unjust Steward. Now, we all know that this parable is hard to understand, especially Jesus' words: '*the sons of darkness are shrewder than the people of the light.*' But it may be that by the term 'people of the light' Jesus was making a mocking reference to the Qumran community's own description of itself as 'the sons of light', and in effect Jesus was saying: 'those who are *not* in that sect, are wiser than those in it, because, if you stay out of it you will have an opportunity to influence outsiders whom they do not bother with."'

"Here's another difference between Jesus and Qumran. If you had a physical defect you could not be a member of the Qumran community. But Jesus, on the other hand, in the parable of the Great Banquet, said that the Kingdom of God was for the poor, the crippled, the blind, and the lame. Also, there's Jesus direct contradiction of Essene teaching on not pulling an ox from a pit on the Sabbath (Luke 14:5). Now, these are sharp points of difference. Of course there are points of similarity. After all the Qumran community was trying to build itself on the Bible, so it had to get some things right. But Jesus was not an Essene!"

The heat was intense. There was no shade. There was no respite. There was no escape from the burning sun. To the east the Dead Sea shimmered in a haze. To the south we saw a road snaking along the foot of cliffs. These cliffs fall abruptly from the Judaean plateau to more than a thousand feet below sea level. After David's talk, we walked through the remains of the Qumran village, and looked over to famous Cave IV where many fragments of text were discovered. We could see why the scrolls remained undisturbed for so long. The caves were virtually inaccessible.

Having re-boarded the minibus, and motoring south from Qumran along the shores of the Dead Sea, David pointed out a large protruding rock near the side of the road, marked with red paint and the initials PEF, but more than two hundred yards from the water. "Shoresh, in 1913 the British Palestinian Exploratory Fund came and measured the Dead Sea. But since the 1930s the Dead Sea has been receding at about a yard every year. Its shrinking fast folks! Take your pictures now before the Dead Sea disappears!"

En Gedi

Killer-Hill lies several miles south of Qumran, but before the En Gedi oasis. On the Bike Rides of 1994 and 1995 the Thursday cycling took us from Almog, near Jericho, down the length of the Dead Sea, and we had to climb Killer Hill. The challenge was to cycle all the way to the top, without stopping, in the roasting heat of the mid-day sun. Even in the minibus the hill felt impressively steep and long, and Sharon and I congratulated ourselves on our achievements. A mile after Killer Hill there is a second, shorter climb. Then the payoff, a long downhill sweep into En

Gedi. Although I never had the nerve to lift my fingers from the brakes and let the bike really take off down this slope, many of the other Bike Riders raced downhill at terrific speed.

Today, lunch at En Gedi was where we lunched on the Bike Rides, near the foot of a huge gorge called Wadi David.

David had more to tell us. "Shoresh, the word 'En' or 'Ein' means a 'spring' and there are four springs of fresh water at En Gedi, with several large waterfalls in the gorges. En Gedi is where David fled to escape the jealous wrath of King Saul, and is mentioned several times in the Song of Solomon. 'Gedi' means 'a gazelle' and we will see ibex in and around the En Gedi gorges."

"Now ladies, something romantic. Mark Anthony once said to Cleopatra that she could have anything she wanted, anything in the whole Empire. What did she ask for? She asked for the Balsam groves of En Gedi, because the perfumes of En Gedi were more fragrant than any others in the world! In Roman times the En Gedi Balsam trees were legendary. En Gedi was known for the best dates, the best wine, and the best perfumes. That Balsam was different from what we know as Balsam today, and it grew in only two places in the entire Roman world, En Gedi and Jericho. When the Zealots were beaten south by the Romans in 66AD, the Zealots tried to cut down the Balsam trees but the Romans fought over every one. Enough trees were saved to continue sourcing the perfume for another three hundred years until it went out of fashion in the third and fourth centuries."

AFTER LUNCH WE MOTORED south a few miles more, before setting off on foot to hike back over the hill to the En Gedi gorge. David and his daughter had reconnoitred the route on Sunday, and we were warned to carry plenty of water. There was no vegetation apart from bushes or an occasional acacia tree. The sun beat down mercilessly. The sunlight reflected up from the dry limestone rocks and stones. The sheer brightness was blinding. I was stunned by how white the entire landscape was. On our right was the Dead Sea with Jordan's coastline and far mountains visible through the heat haze. Where we walked is part of the Great Rift Valley, that scar in the earth which starts in Lebanon and continues down into eastern Africa. The River Jordan, Sea of Galilee, Dead Sea, and Red Sea, all lie in this geological feature.

I was soon sweating heavily in the heat, and was glad when David stopped us for a rest beside the ruins of a Turkish flour mill. Then we climbed higher, reaching a small plantation of trees and bushes which had grown around a spring of water. All around was nothing but white stones and white rocks. The stones and rocks were rough and sharp, not at all weathered like the grey rocks of Scotland. After refilling our water bottles, we sat in the shade and David held another open air seminar, this time on the contrast between 'living water' and 'cistern water.'

"OK Shoresh, let's turn to Jeremiah chapter two verse thirteen."

He thumbed through his Bible. "OK, what does it say? *'My people (says the Lord) have committed two sins: they have forsaken me, the spring of living water, and they have dug their own cisterns, broken cisterns that cannot hold water.'* Now, Shoresh, Jeremiah's home village was on the edge of the desert, and awareness of the desert influenced all of Jeremiah's prophetic imagery. Here, in chapter two, Jeremiah makes a contrast between a forsaken spring and a broken cistern. It's no contest. Even a neglected spring still gives fresh water with a delicious taste. We've just tasted some. In contrast, even the best cistern water is 'yuk'! And it's worse than 'yuk' if it's been in the cistern for five to eight months in the dry season."

"Again, spring water is living, flowing water, not stagnant water as in a cistern. Liturgically, ritual baths had to be in living water; not water from a well, or from a cistern."

"Again, note that Jeremiah says the cistern is leaking. So, what was always a finite water supply at the best of times is in fact ebbing away even more. In contrast, even here at En Gedi, despite seasonal fluctuations, the springs lasts for ever. The only negative thing about spring water is that the further it is from the source, the more contaminated the water because it picks up dirt, salts, minerals and so on."

"Now Shoresh, what's the lesson? It's this: stick close to the Lord because he is living water. Who in his right mind would choose cistern water rather than living water? No rational person ever would. Jeremiah's point is that the people have rejected the living God and turned to stale, lifeless, idols. Jeremiah is saying that that is irrational behavior. There is no logic to it. Humanity is out of its mind. And this is exactly what Jeremiah concludes. See verse eleven: *'Has a nation ever changed its god? (Yet they are not gods at all). But my people have exchanged their Glory for worthless idols.'* What Jeremiah is saying is that the abandonment of discipleship is an act of irrationality. Now for us, we know that the reason people don't follow the Lord has rarely to do with logic or common sense. Rather, the reasons are spiritual. Evangelism is a spiritual battle. It's not simply discussing a problem in logic!"

We walked further in the blistering heat, scrambling up the stone covered slopes. A gecko lizard popped out from under a rock, and stayed motionless on a stone. Round a rocky bluff the path led to a flatter area beneath towering cliffs.

David stood in the center of a low-walled stone circle. He had something to say.

"Shoresh, in 3000BC. a Calcolithic Temple stood here. As you can see, the site of the altar is clearly marked. Archaeologists say that they worshipped the ibex. Look, Shoresh, when David fled from Saul why did he come to En Gedi? It was remote. It had caves to hide in. It had ravines where you could conceal yourself. But David also came here because he knew the area. En Gedi is shepherd's country. In the Middle East sheep are not put in fields as they are in Britain. Fields are solely for arable farming because that quality of agricultural land is too precious for sheep. So sheep did not graze on grass. Rather, sheep grazed on bushes and plants growing here and there in the desert. And a place like En Gedi with canyons, clefts in the rock, and shady damp places, was exactly the kind of place where bushes grew and flourished. And so David would probably bring his father's sheep here from Bethlehem for part of the year. The twenty-third psalm is based on a place like this. When we read that psalm we shouldn't picture a stream flowing through green fields! Read the psalm again with En Gedi type of countryside in your mind."

WE MOVED ON. THE afternoon sun was merciless. It was like being in a furnace. And our need to drink water was alarmingly strong. There is no sand at En Gedi, as in the deserts of a child's picture book, but it is a desert place all the same. A desert of rocks and stones, white and bright, dry and jagged. At the next halt David had more information.

"Shoresh, in the Bible the desert is seen as the place where God 'speaks.' For three reasons. First, in Hebrew alliteration 'davar' means 'word', and 'midbar' means 'desert', and the implication is: to *hear* God speak His Word (devar), you go to the *desert*, (midbar). Second, the Rabbis said that God chose the desert as the place to give his Word, because in these unclaimed regions the Word of God is owned by no nation, therefore addressed to all. Third, the desert is a place where there are few outside distractions, where one struggles to survive, and in such an atmosphere you are open to hearing God's voice. When you are busy and things are going well, you are far less attentive to God's direction and guidance. Cities are too morally corrupt and too concerned with commercial transactions. It's difficult to hear God's word in cities. And so the desert was really important in Judaism. God would renew His covenant with Israel *in the desert*. Luke emphasized that John the Baptist, the forerunner of the Messiah, had a ministry *in the desert*. Luke wrote, '*In the 15th year of Tiberius, the word of God came to John the son of Zechariah, in the desert*.'

EVENTUALLY WE ARRIVED AT a point where the path descended into the main En Gedi gorge. Several black birds with orange tips to their wings flew to and fro in the gorge. These are Tristram starlings and are the only birds named after an Anglican Bishop. Tristram are numerous at Masada and Grace and I had seen them there on previous visits. By this time the sun was lower in the sky, and the deeper reaches of the gorge were in shadow. In shade, the desert rocks which are so bright and white in sunlight look colorless and dead. They have no residual hues. The haze had also lifted from the Dead Sea and, on its far side, the Jordanian hills glowed pink in the early evening sunlight. The Dead Sea was as calm as a mill pond, with the colored mountains perfectly reflected in the water. We edged our way down to 'David's Pool,' and David Pileggi and Alison waded in its coolness.

Then a Park Ranger arrived.

"Would you please go back the way you came," he said. "It is too late in the afternoon to continue the descent." He told us that his task at this time of day was to survey the paths and ensure that no one was left in the gorge overnight. "There are still four leopards living at En Gedi," he added.

There was no option but to climb back up the cliff before cutting down to our lunch spot by a secondary path. But this route was precipitous, and Dee became extremely apprehensive. Eventually she sat on a rock, frightened and nervous. The path was especially steep at this point, but there was no alternative. We needed to edge our way around a jutting-out rock, despite a steep cliff-fall below.

"I just can't go on. I can't go on."

"It's all right Dee, we're here, we'll help you."

We persuaded Dee to stand up and face the rock-face. Then we helped her round the rock by keeping close and talking her through each step, one by one. While this was going on David Pileggi was answering his mobile phone which rang just as he negotiated a tricky section of the path. His secretary was calling to say that problems had come up about our overnight accommodation. We were due to stay at the En Gedi Youth Hostel, but it was now full up with High School kids. The Hostel had either double booked or, more likely, saw our small group as expendable when the school wanted to come with two hundred potential customers. We had already heard kids yelling to each other far below us, down in the lower part of the gorge. In fading daylight David manoeuvred his sizable frame around the En Gedi cliffs, holding his phone to his ear with one hand, while steadying himself with the other.

'Sodom and Gomorrah'

The phone conversation paid dividends, and alternative accommodation was arranged. Instead of En Gedi, we were now to stay at Masada Youth Hostel. Booking in at Masada was to be six o'clock, so to fill the time our bus-driver drove us down to the Spa resort of En Boqek, otherwise known as Sodom.

"Shoresh," commented David, "no one knows where the sinful cities of Sodom and Gomorrah were, but the popular theory is that they were situated on the southern shores of the Dead Sea. So, if you use your imaginations, you can claim to have 'lived it up in Sodom' when in fact you've had a quiet visit to En Boqek!"

The last touches of daylight disappeared as we were driving south, and a full moon was perfectly reflected in the still waters of the Dead Sea. Old maps show the Dead Sea as one expanse of water with a narrow waistline near its southern end. But, after the Dead Sea divided in 1976, the two parts are now separate. Its northern sector is by far the larger of the two and may be up to four hundred meters deep, whereas the southern sector is only two to five meters deep. The southern part has industrial mineral works which extract phosphates and other chemicals from the water. This is also where most of the tourist developments are, and an inevitable tension exists between tourism and industry.

"Shoresh, Dead Sea salts and Dead Sea mud have long been thought to have curative properties. In Roman times wounded soldiers and gladiators were brought here to aid their healing. Today, the German Health Service pays people to come for a fortnight at a time to bathe in the Dead Sea if they have skin diseases."

A water channel runs from the northern to the southern sector, and without this channel the southern part would disappear completely, disturbing the ecological balance of the whole area. Moreover, water is needed in the southern sector to keep the mineral extraction plants running, to say nothing of the tourist resorts. Ambitious plans to pipe water from either the Red Sea or the Mediterranean in order to raise the level of the Dead Sea have been mooted, but that would be immensely costly, and require enormous international cooperation. Moreover, the less concentrated saline water piped in would lie on the top of the existing Dead Sea, possibly creating more ecological problems although the salinity concentrations would eventually even themselves out.

AFTER A BRIEF VISIT to En Boqek we returned to the Masada Youth Hostel. Dee and Tony had paid a single room allowance when they booked the Study Course, but the hostel could not give them that accommodation, so Dee went in with Sharon and Rosie, and Tony joined James and myself. "I hope you don't think I was anti-social wanting a single room," said Tony. "I went for the single room option because once at a conference I was billeted with an impossible room-mate! The thought of a full month with a fellow like that was not to be contemplated!"

During the evening meal Bob Mullins arrived, and David Pileggi returned to Jerusalem. As our archaeologist in the field Bob will accompany us for our time in the desert, and his wife Kathy is to be with us for a few days as well.

I chatted with our bus-driver over the meal. "Hello, I'm Bruce, can I ask your name?"

"I am Toffiq, and I come from Nazareth."

"Are you married Toffiq?"

"For two months! I am missing my wife terribly because the bus driving keeps me away from home for whole weeks! I think about my wife all of the time. She is studying in Haifa to be a teacher and she has one more year of study to go."

After the meal Toffiq took us back to En Boqek, to a coffee and souvenirs shop. All Dead Sea resorts have loads of expensive perfumes and soaps made from the Dead Sea salts for sale, and bus-drivers who bring customers get free samples to take back to their wives. That is why Toffiq was so keen to show us En Boqek in the afternoon. He wanted to tempt us back in the evening to get some commission. We didn't mind. It was a nice night out. And we were able to write postcards home saying 'I had a night out in Sodom!!'

— Day 18 — Masada —

Friday 25th October

THIS MORNING, VERY EARLY, five of us set off to climb Masada by the snake-path. David, Alison, Sharon, Tony, and I started in cool temperatures, aiming to arrive at the top at the same time as the rest of our group who would take the first cable-car of the day. To our surprise there were hundreds of young people coming down as we climbed up. They had spent the night on the summit of Masada. As they passed we saw that some of their adult helpers were Rabbis.

"Last night," explained Tony, "Bob told me that groups often stay the night on the top. Apparently, about eight years ago an Australian couple slept overnight on the summit at one of the view-points. The girl shifted in her sleep and tumbled right over the cliffs to her death."

The heat from the sun soon became intense, and we were exposed to its full force as we made our way up the cliff. We halted frequently to drink water and to rest. Our shirts were soaking with perspiration long before the summit. On its eastern side Masada is 1300 feet above ground level, whilst on the western side, where the remains of the Roman ramp are, it is just 300 feet high. The height to be climbed is modest, but the tremendous heat increases the difficulty. After climbing for an hour we reached the cable-car upper station and waited for the others. More people were ascending the snake-path behind us, and we saw that one man was limping severely. When he reached us, he stopped and held his knee.

"Are you all right?" asked Alison.

"It's my knee-joint," he explained. "It has the habit of seizing up unpredictably. But it passes." After a while he felt better and went on.

There was no sign of the rest of the group. Yet the Youth Hostel was right at the foot of Masada, so they had no great distance to go after breakfast to reach the cable-cars. However, coaches full of tourists leave Jerusalem before dawn each day in order to arrive before the crowds, and so over a dozen coach parties were already in the cable-car queue before our group got there.

The Stronghold

Masada is in the mouth of a vast wadi which cuts down from the Judaean desert plateau to the shores of the Dead Sea. It rises as a massive rock in the middle of this wadi, with sharp, deep gorges separating it from the surrounding heights, and with cliffs over a thousand feet high. Herod the Great, who ruled under Roman patronage, chose Masada as a place of refuge from potential enemies. There he built fortifications and palaces, for himself and for his entourage. After Herod's death the Roman garrison continued to occupy Masada.

In 66AD, at the start of the Jewish Revolt against Rome, a group of Sicarii (Zealots) commanded by Menahem Ben-Yehuda of Galilee captured Masada. The Sicarii were a group of extremists determined to fight against the Romans till death, and took their name from the *sica*, which was a dagger they carried, similar to the *dirk* beloved of Scottish Highlanders. Masada then became a refuge for other zealots and their families, until over nine hundred people were based there. But, after the Romans had crushed the Jewish revolt in Jerusalem, Flavius Silva and his ten-thousand-strong army turned their attentions to Masada. As a matter of principle the Romans were determined to allow no outpost of Jewish power to remain. Masada had already been besieged by the Romans for three years, hoping to starve the 967 men, women, and children, into submission; but Herod's old grain stores and water cisterns were so full that the besieged never lacked food. So Flavius Silva ordered the construction of a siege ramp. After several months, when the ramp reached completion, the entire Zealot population committed suicide rather than be captured and humiliated by the Romans.

Ever since Masada was rediscovered scholars have argued whether or not the mass suicide really took place. When we visited Masada on the Bike Ride, our guide Chaim was sceptical. Bob, however, believes it to be eminently possible.

"Do Jewish soldiers take their oath of allegiance here?" Clive asked.

"No. Not any more."

"Why?"

"Well, for many years the Israeli Army did initiate new recruits by bringing them to Masada where they took the oath of allegiance to Israel with the words 'Masada shall not fall again!' However, not now, because the mass suicide has become regarded as an embarrassment in Jewish history, not an inspiration. Two factors. First, suicide as such is disapproved of in the Torah. Second, the Zealots of Masada did not in fact fight to the death, so, in a sense, they chickened out of the final conflict."

THE SUMMIT OF MASADA is a large, diamond-shaped plateau on which are the ruins of Herodian and Byzantine buildings. In sunlight the Masada rock is pink and bright and alive. In shade it is grey and lifeless. At the entrance from the cable-car and snake-path, there is an acacia tree growing beside a broken wall. Acacia trees are found in southern Israel, but no further north than Jericho. They are widespread in Africa where they grow much bigger than in Israel.

"According to the Old Testament acacia wood was used for the Ark of the Covenant," said Bob. "Although the land around Masada is now totally desert, pollen found here has been carbon-dated to the first century, indicating that cypress trees once grew near enough for the pollen to carry here."

"Was the climate completely different?"

"Not totally. But in the first century there was probably more rainfall at Masada than today. The cypress wood used by builders at Masada in Herod's time came from relatively near at hand: scores of miles nearer than any trees grow today."

Bob had been professionally involved in excavations on the site, and he outlined to us its strategic and political significance.

"Herod the Great was paranoid. That was why he killed so many people. That was why he murdered the wife he loved. That was why he slaughtered the Bethlehem children. So Herod developed a series of strongholds to protect his authority. The Herodian near Jerusalem. Marchelus in the Trans-Jordanian mountains where John the Baptist was executed. And Masada in the Judaean desert."

"Masada was already a stronghold with a palace on its western side, but Herod was so paranoid that he built a second palace, the northern palace, as a fortress within a fortress. So we have two stages of Herodian building, with the latter stage focussed on building an impregnable citadel at the northern end."

"After Herod the Great's time Masada declined in importance until the Sicarii got hold of it in 66AD and began making trouble for the Romans. Now, this Sicarii period reveals some really interesting archaeological features. For example, being strict Jews they had ritual baths. These baths had three containers. One for washing dirt from your body. One for the ritual bath itself. And a third to collect rainwater. Remember a ritual bath has to take place in *living* water, not *cistern* water. On Masada, living flowing water is rare, but the Rabbis taught that in extreme conditions it was permissible to put a few drops of 'living' water into a ritual bath filled mainly with cistern water, and that would 'purify' it."

"When these ritual baths were unearthed by archaeologists news was sent to Jerusalem, and Orthodox Rabbis rushed down to Masada. They walked up the snake-path dressed in their uniform of black coats and black, wide-brimmed hats despite the full mid-day heat, and at the top they did not even stop for refreshments but went straight to the ritual baths and measured them. The dimensions were the sufficient minimum size for Mikvah baths as determined by first-century Rabbinic Law. The Rabbis got really excited with that discovery."

ON MASADA'S FLAT SUMMIT we saw piles of round limestone boulders which, at the time of the Revolt, were used as projectiles by both besiegers and besieged. From time to time the Romans pulled a Jewish slave out of the mass of forced labourers constructing the ramp. The unfortunate would be tied to a boulder, and then fired by ballista-catapults against the cliff walls of Masada or onto the summit itself, showing the Jewish defenders that eventually all of them would die in agony like that man. In response the defenders threw boulders back down on top of the Romans. This retaliation became less effective as the Romans constructed defensive roofs.

"Most of the labourers were Jewish slaves," Bob pointed out. "And if the Jews above wanted to throw boulders onto Jewish slaves below, then the Romans were unconcerned."

The Romans ringed the base of Masada with a wall and a series of camps, totally controlling all coming and going. Another Roman camp to the south is perched on a high buff, higher than Masada itself, and from that dominating position the Romans could watch the Zealots and monitor all their actions. A vast quantity of cypress wood was used in the construction of the ramp, and pieces of the wood are still being discovered today. The ramp itself never rose to the level of the western gate of Masada, but the height of the ramp plus the height of a siege tower did. And when the ramp was completed the defenders knew their fate was sealed. It was all over.

At the foot of the staircase leading down to the central terrace of Herod's Northern Palace is a hole in the rock, which holds a piece of wood which was part of the original scaffolding which was used to help construct the terrace. We pushed our arms up this hole, and touched the tip of the wood with the tips of our fingers. It was an eerie sensation to feel something placed there before the time of Jesus.

We stayed for over four hours, absorbing all the information Bob was giving: more information than a *Journal* can record. From Masada we saw the surrounding desert, the cliffs of the Great Rift Valley, the two sections of the Dead Sea, the great canal between the northern and southern sections, the Jordanian mountains on the far side, and Mount Nebo from which Moses looked over to a land flowing with milk and honey, but which he was never to enter. Below us, ravens flew around the Masada cliffs. On the desert floor were the clear outlines of the Roman camps and the Roman wall which sealed off the besieged for three years. When time came to go down most of us decided to take the cable-car. It had been many hours since our early breakfast.

Crystals and Conversations

Swimming in the Dead Sea was the programme for the afternoon. Bob had planned to take us to the beach at En Gedi, but Toffiq was insistent that En Boqek was better. So we went there. The Dead Sea was a bright, bright turquoise, and although an occasional sulphurous whiff wafted across from time to time, the place was crowded with tourists enjoying the unique experience of floating in its waters. Clive and Marion, David and Anne, and Tony, all collected handfuls of Dead Sea crystals by ducking under the water and scooping them off the bottom. Marion and Clive have a son with skin problems and the crystals might help him.

While the others swam and bathed I wandered around En Boqek, took photos, bought postcards, met up with Bob and Kathy, and had coffee with them. We talked about the Study Course, and I told Bob how much we are benefitting from it, both in terms of academic input and spiritual experience. It gives such a distinctive view of the Holy Land and its peoples. I then asked Kathy about herself.

"I was brought up as a Roman Catholic," she replied, "but I went to a Protestant church when I was a student."

"Why the switch Kathy?"

"Well Bruce, I consider myself a Catholic. But I needed more teaching from the Bible, which I found in the Protestant Church. At the same time, I also need the sacraments, and so I have gone back to regular worship as a Catholic while still getting good substantial teaching from a variety of sources."

"Bob told us that you're in publishing."

"I have two jobs. I edit a Christian magazine in Israel which comes out quarterly. And I'm also an assistant to a professor who is heavily involved with Judeo-Christian contacts, exchanges with students, organising scholarships, things like that."

Bob talked again about the problems facing archaeology in Israel today. He had mentioned this before, and it was obviously a major frustration for him. "The ultra-Orthodox in Mea Shearim in Jerusalem are so inconsistent!" he said, shaking his head. "They object to archaeologists disturbing graves, and yet Mea Shearim itself is built on a cemetery which was blasted out with explosives to build the houses! In fact, in the cemetery—which has now become Mea Shearim—there was found the only crucified foot from Roman times with a nail hole through the foot bone. Now, the Romans rarely put the nail through the bone; normally it was through the ligaments. Anyway, even though this was obviously a burial place the ultra-Orthodox conveniently ignored the evidence. The ultra-Orthodox make their objections in order to have political leverage. The obvious inconsistencies don't matter to them."

Kathy was interested in how we saw the Holy Land. "What does the Holy Land mean to you Bruce? We've lived here for so long that it's home for us. But, from the viewpoint of a pilgrim, what so far has made the biggest impression on you?"

I thought for a while. "Well, Kathy, obviously Galilee is special. Galilee has real atmosphere. But the place that keeps drawing me back is the Church of the Holy Sepulchre."

Kathy was surprised. "That's unusual! The Church of the Holy Sepulchre usually puts people off because it's so noisy."

"Yes. But, you know, one of the great things about this Study Tour is the amount of time we have. We're not rushed from place to place like other groups are. Often I've returned to the church, sometimes very early when it's really quiet. And when it's quiet it does have a devotional quality. I like to sit in the courtyard, or just inside the main doorway, and watch people from all parts of the world coming and going. Some are there simply to look. Others come with real spiritual intent. That's humbling and lovely to see. Alongside the 'been there, seen it, got the T-shirt' tourists, you do see a simple, innocent, naive expectancy of faith which is really precious."

BACK IN THE YOUTH hostel Tony spread his bag of crystals on newspaper to dry overnight before packing them for the journey. After the evening meal I wandered up to a telephone kiosk near the cable-cars to phone home. However, there was no reply. It was Friday. Grace was probably out helping with the Girl Guides. As I waited, I looked at the black mass of Masada set against the starry sky. Then I turned and looked over at the dark waters of the Dead Sea shimmering in the moonlight. On this balmy, October evening, history was powerfully and intensely present.

— *Day 19 — Arad* —

Saturday 26th October

ROSIE LOOKED AT SHARON's flowers. "Sharon, you'd better dead-head some of these, though most of them are still looking good." Sharon agreed. So she and Rosie took out the wilted ones and rearranged the rest. Our minibus left Masada soon after breakfast, with Sharon's flowers, freshly watered, propped up in their plastic bucket on the back seat.

We motored south, through En Boqek and past the chemical and mineral factories until, at the extreme southern end of the Dead Sea, we left the main highway which continues to Eilat, took a road on the right, and then climbed uphill to the west. The road rose steeply out of the Rift Valley, following the course of a wadi, until it flattened out on the desert plateau. Toffiq stopped halfway up, and we disembarked to look at the view. From this vantage point we could see clearly that the southern sector of the Dead Sea has been artificially separated into sections for industrial purposes. At home in Crieff we have a satellite photograph showing these parallel lines, stretching from one side of the Dead Sea to the other. Closer at hand we saw the remains of a Crusader Castle, Mezad Zohar, in the wadi below us.

The skies darkened as we travelled in the direction of Arad. Black clouds matched by the black Bedouin tents of the desert. From the bus we noted numerous encampments by the roadside. The Negev is desert. But not a desert of golden sand or magnificent dunes; just a dusty, dark, bleak, stony, barren, rolling landscape.

"The topsoil is called 'loess,'" said Bob. "It blows over from Libya and settles here, forming a hard crust, impervious to water. So, when the early rains come, the water—instead of seeping uniformly into the

192

ground—becomes focused into narrow cracks through the loess, and the resultant heavy concentration of rain water in these cracks cuts deep channels in the fields which badly damage the crops. So the farmers have to break up the loess crust before this happens."

TENTS, SHANTY TOWNS, AND sprawling Bedouin settlements, were visible every few miles. Around them the crust of fertile soil had already been broken, raked and sown, ready for the rains which are not far off judging by the skies. We travelled along a major highway, on either side of which were huge and abandoned earth-moving machines, olive groves, and bare, rain-expectant earth. There was an unvarying background of bleak desert hills on which a few bushes grew. There was even an old, rusting, yellow combine-harvester, waiting incongruously for the desert to produce its harvest.

"Are there many Bedouin nowadays?" Tony asked.

"About thirty-thousand Bedouin live in the Greater Negev," replied Bob, "but many have left their tents for permanent accommodation under pressure from the government because the authorities in Jerusalem don't like them wandering all over the Negev. It wants to know where they are. When the Turks controlled Palestine they were extremely harsh on the Bedouin. The Bedouin used to attack pilgrims making the Haj to Mecca, and so the Turks established Be'er Sheva as a base to stop this. But the Turks were cruel, terribly cruel. This was why the Bedouin followed Lawrence of Arabia so readily."

"Do many still stay in tents?"

"Recently there has been the emergence of Bedouin towns, and several shift between tent-life and house-life. Many Bedouin are engaged in farming or making craft products. But it's a subsistence lifestyle."

"Does the government help much?"

"Oh yes. Give the government its due. The Israeli government has introduced medical clinics and schools staffed by Bedouin themselves."

Bob continued, "In this area there is hardly any rainfall, and the crops they grow are barley and tobacco. Now, the Bedouin have meat only on special occasions: so, if you visit a Bedouin family and are given meat, it is important to eat all that you're given, and express deep appreciation, because it involves real sacrifice for them."

David asked, "Are all Bedouin Muslim?"

"Well, Yes and No," replied Bob. "The word 'Bedouin' is the plural form of 'Bedou' which means 'man of the desert', and so although they are all followers of Islam, their isolated lifestyle means that they have built up idiosyncratic traditions. For example, many still sacrifice rams. Again, because the Bedouin are a nomadic people with traditionally no fixed base (although that is changing), if a Bedouin is asked 'where do you come from?' he will answer the name of his tribe and family, not a place."

Tel Arad

The bleak landscape continued all the way to Arad. Modern Arad developed in the 1950s with immigrants from Africa. These were extremely poor people with little education, and so Arad became an impoverished community. Recently it has improved considerably with new people coming to stay and the government ploughing more money into the town. We passed through modern Arad until, four miles to the west, we arrived at the remains of biblical Tel Arad. When we left the minibus the rain began, and a cold wind blew from the north. Sharon elected to stay in the bus and read a book. The rest of us dutifully followed Bob.

Ancient Arad has two main sections. Up on the hill are the extensive remains of a citadel from Solomon's time, within which are dwelling houses and a small temple-shrine which, on a miniature scale, had the same layout as Solomon's First Temple. The layout of the shrine deliberately resembled that of a typical domestic home, symbolizing that God dwells with his people. Further down the slope, and quite separate from the citadel, are the ruins of the Canaanite town of Tel Arad which existed long before Solomon's time. Canaanite Arad flourished from 3000BC until it was destroyed around 2700BC, and it was never rebuilt by succeeding peoples. Because of this, and because the remaining walls were never plundered for their materials, then the recently excavated ruins, covered for centuries by the desert, reveal a perfect example of a Canaanite settlement. The work was carried out between 1962 and 1967 under the direction of Ruth Amiran.

"The excavation work here has stalled," commented Bob, wistfully. "Ruth was the driving force. But she is unwell now, and unable to give leadership. However, the desert keeps protecting the site and someone will restart the work."

Bob unravelled the enigma of the abandoned town. "We have to ask the question: Why was a town with a population of over three thousand people built out here in the middle of nowhere? Any ideas?"

We shook our heads.

"Well, the answer lies in the trade-route between Canaan and Egypt. Olive trees did not grow in Egypt, but they grew all over these surrounding hills, and so Canaan exported great quantities of olive products from Arad. In addition, the Egyptians used asphalt and bitumen from the Dead Sea for coating their boats and the inside of coffins, and Arad became the center which controlled that trade as well. Added to this, the people of Arad were involved in mining copper to the south of here, and the copper was sold to the Egyptians."

"Was the trade two-way?"

"Yes. Gold from Africa was brought north by the caravans. So Arad was an extremely important place when trade with Egypt was good. However, around 2700BC something must have happened politically. At that point Egypt started trading directly with northern Canaan and the Lebanon. Arad was bypassed, went into eclipse, and the city was abandoned. Other southern Canaanite cities were affected as well. The ones near the coast were rebuilt, but Arad was too isolated to have any further significance."

We wandered along the streets of ancient Tel Arad, and Bob pointed out several family houses all of which have a common structure. Canaanite period houses were built around a courtyard, and extended families lived together. The houses had doors but no windows, with the doorway always facing east towards the rising sun. In similar fashion, the Bedouin have the door of their tent facing east, to greet the new day, and to have protection from the prevailing wind and rain which come from the west.

We returned to the minibus cold and wet. The skies were still filled with heavy grey cloud as we continued towards Tel Be'er Sheva. Toffiq loves driving fast along these big wide highways. He tends not to see junctions until the last minute and then stands on the brakes, hauling the minibus round in a screeching turn. He seems shy, and is reluctant to eat with us. Perhaps the bus company disapproves of drivers becoming over-familiar with guests.

Tel Be'er Sheva

After leaving Tel Arad we came to a major crossroads called Shoqed Junction. The signs at this intersection indicated Hebron to the north, Gaza to the west, Be'er Sheva to the south, and Arad—where we had come from—to the east. We turned south to Be'er Sheva, stopping for lunch outside the site of biblical Be'er Sheva, a few miles from the new town of Be'er Sheva which was built by the Turks as an administrative center. After parking the bus, we huddled together at a deserted open-air cafe to eat lunch. Then the lady who owned the nearby Bedouin craft-shop arrived, and invited us in to browse. It was filled with beautiful bright and black Bedouin clothes, trinkets, and crafts. I spoke to the lady, who was called Mazkarot Keider.

"Why are there so many objects of a triangular shape for sale?"

"All triangles guard against the evil-eye for the Bedouin. In the same way, the Bedouin of the desert will often dress male children up in girl's clothing to confuse the evil-eye."

When we came out of the shop Bob pointed to baskets piled up against the door. "Did you notice that baskets are all made from very light materials such as date-palm fronds? This is because the Bedouin have to transport their possessions everywhere, so the lighter a basket the better."

AFTER LUNCH WE ENTERED Tel Be'er Sheva, which was the Be'er Sheva of Abraham's day. The Be'er Sheva valley runs east-west, acting as a break between the southernmost Judaean hills to the north, and the Negev desert to the south. Bob commented on the topography.

"Folks, although nowadays we use the word Negev to describe the whole of the desert to the south of here, in the Bible the word Negev was only used of the Be'er Sheva valley itself. All the area to the south was simply known as The Wilderness. There were three wildernesses. The Wilderness of Zin. The Wilderness of Paran. And the Wilderness of Sinai. The Bible tells us that Abraham planted a tamarisk tree at Be'er Sheva. Now, the tamarisk has tubular leaves which are characteristic of desert plants, and it survives well in salty environments by pushing the salt onto its leaves and keeping the good water for its own use."

At the entrance to the Tel Be'er Sheva site is a reconstructed altar made of stones from the excavations. Within Tel Be'er Sheva itself there is a deep well opposite the city gate, which may be the well mentioned in the book of Genesis where Abraham and Isaac signed a pact with the Philistines. The oath which they took near this well gave the city its name, *'Wherefore he called that place Be'er Sheva, because there they swore, both of them.'* At a later stage stone houses were built, and, in the eleventh century BC, a new settlement was erected with houses connected to the city wall. During that time the settlement included some twenty homes and accommodated about one hundred people. The houses each had four rooms, typical of the period, with a courtyard probably serving as a pen for the livestock.

Bob shared more reflections on Be'er Sheva. "It was because the houses were shared with livestock that Jephthah in the book of Judges made his big mistake. Jephthah rashly vowed that he would sacrifice to the Lord the first creature that came out of his house. He watched, and expected to see the goats which always came out first in the morning, and he was totally shocked when his own daughter emerged."

The ruins at Tel Be'er Sheva are extensive, and come from several periods of Israel's history. There is little suitable stone for building purposes in the area, and so the walls were made of brick. However, if bricks are used at ground level then running rainwater in the streets erodes them. So the builders used whatever scarce stone they had at ground level, then bricks only above that. We were impressed by the thought that Abraham made this place his base. The area of the tel is so small, so local, so specific, and yet the figure revered in Judaism, Christianity, and Islam, settled here, lived here, and worshiped here. The whole biblical saga sprang from that.

In the twentieth century the long-abandoned tel had a further chapter added to its history. During the First World War modern Be'er Sheva served as a Turkish bridgehead for an attack on the Suez Canal. With the approach of the British Army from Egypt toward Palestine, Tel Be'er Sheva was fortified, and a Turkish cannon post was positioned on the mound. This was until the Anzac Division of the New Zealand and Australian cavalry unit conquered the tel on October 31st 1917.

The Joe Alon Museum

After Tel Be'er Sheva we were back on the highway, and Toffiq drove us to the Joe Alon Bedouin Museum. Joe Alon was one of the founders of the Israeli Air Force. He was born in Israel in 1929 but was taken by his family to Czechoslovakia, which had been the family home for generations. At the onset of World War II, Joe was smuggled into England where he was adopted by a family. After the war he returned to Czechoslovakia only to find that his family had all perished in the Holocaust. He then moved to Israel, and in 1948 joined the Israeli Air Force becoming one of its leading fighter pilots, both as an officer and a trainer. In 1970 he was appointed to the Israeli Embassy in Washington, where he regularly gave lectures to Jewish youth. But on July 1st 1973, only a few days before completing his tour of duty in the US, he was assassinated in front of his home in Washington. The case has never been solved. The Museum of Bedouin Culture was established in his honor.

One of the many fascinating exhibits concerns traditional medicine and religion in Bedouin belief. The display explains that there are four important figures in this area of traditional Bedouin life. First, there is the Exorcist or *Darwish*. The Darwish is a pious elder, whose attributes are hereditary, and the information board states that because the Darwish can heal many illnesses he is much loved and in great demand. Exorcism is performed in a special ceremony which is accompanied by constant drumming. Interestingly, the office of Darwish is hereditary. Might it be that something *learned* is not deemed to be supernatural, whereas something *inherited* retains its mystical origins? Second, there is the *Shabba*. He has the gift of detecting the source of the evil-eye. When he is called to a case the matriarch of the family heats three alum crystals over coals. The crystals change their form when heated, with the new shape suggesting the source of the evil-eye, and locating the source helps toward a cure. Third, there is the *Ziyara*, a holy man. A pilgrimage to the tomb of a Ziyara is believed to bring blessing, inspired by the conviction that he is the intermediary between the ordinary man and his God, and that he has the power to help. Fourth, there is the *Hawi*, healer of snake bites and poisons. This is a man whose healing powers were passed on to him in his infancy by a drop of saliva from another Hawi placed into his mouth. The healer rinses his mouth with salt water and sucks the poisoned blood from the site of the bite or sting, which he later massages gently with his hands.

We watched an audio-visual presentation of Bedouin life in the Negev and Sinai, and, when the lights went back on, Anne stood up and made an announcement. She was so happy. "I am delighted to announce that at six thirty this morning our daughter gave birth to little Matthew who is doing very well." We shared in the celebrations. All through the Study Course David and Anne have been contacting home anxiously for news of their daughter. This afternoon they heard the good news.

The Search

We left the Joe Alon Centre and motored south through modern Beʾer Sheva to try and find the Bedouin camp where we are to stay the night. Traveling by minibus is an ideal way to observe people as well as places. One of the things we have noticed is that all Israeli cars have mobile phones, and every driver appears to be on one. Most Israeli pedestrians also have mobile phones, and use them just as much as the car drivers. Even the Bedouin have mobile phones. Ironically, this modern technology helps to keep them free and independent, and able to maintain their traditional lifestyle.

Beʾer Sheva has grown rapidly in recent years, with a large population of Russian and Ethiopian Jewish immigrants settling there. This has changed the character of the town. It used to be a Bedouin town, with a famous thriving Bedouin market, but that now only takes place on a Thursday. On other market days people sell ordinary articles, and, even on a Thursday, there are fewer and fewer sheep being sold. South of Beʾer Sheva we saw a Bedouin camp, and next to it the massive high walls and towers of Beʾer Sheva prison. Immediately beyond the prison lay the Wilderness of Zin.

"It was into the Wilderness of Zin that Abraham cast out Hagar and Ishmael to fend for themselves," said Bob. "In effect, Abraham was sending them out to die. All because of Sarah's jealousy. Instead, the Lord rescued them and they settled farther south in the Wilderness of Paran."

MANY, MANY MILES SOUTH of Beʾer Sheva, Toffiq got lost. He was trying to locate our Bedouin camp. It was somewhere in the Negev, but finding it was becoming a hard task. The late afternoon light was failing, and the maps were of no help. We motored on. More slowly than normal. Then Toffiq turned west, towards the setting sun, but now at crawling speed.

Bob got on the mobile phone to David Pileggi in Jerusalem. "Hello, this is Bob calling with the Shoresh group. We can't find the Bedouin camp. Where do we go? Can you give us directions?"

The reception was poor and it took some time for Bob to get through to David and receive a reply. When he did, he asked Toffiq to turn round and go back the way we had come. Toffiq did this and started going east, very fast, then north, and then east again into the grounds of a kibbutz where he stopped the minibus. We waited, still and silent, as the sun sank below the horizon. Bob phoned again, and was waiting for a return phone call, which hopefully would give more directions, when two kibbutz members walked past. Bob wound down the window and spoke to them.

"Excuse me. We are trying to find a Bedouin camp which specializes in hosting tourist groups. Do you know where that might be?"

"Sorry, we don't know of one round here."

Apart from the lights of the kibbutz cabins nothing but the great, vast, dark, empty Negev was visible in any direction. While we waited Bob gave an impromptu talk. "In the early days of the State of Israel, David Ben Gurion tried to get more Israelis to settle in the Negev in order to make it a stronger buffer with Egypt. However, the settlements did not really take off. A few here and there succeeded, but not many."

Eventually, the phone call came. After detailed directions were written down we moved again. Soon we rejoined the main highway and started driving north again. Fast. Very fast. Toffiq was now more confident and showed this by driving very, very, very fast. Then, after some miles we again drew over to the side of the road and halted. Bob and Toffiq were on the phone again.

The last vestiges of diffused light, from a sun now well below the horizon, faded away. Vehicles passed, their headlights illuminating occasional clumps of thin, wispy, straggly trees. We could see the low sand walls constructed around these plantations to try and trap whatever rainwater there might be. The long term goal is the afforestation of stretches of the Negev, and what we were seeing is the beginning of the project.

More instructions came via the phone. The minibus was turned around. We hurtled south again. Bob was now permanently on the telephone, checking out each faintly seen landmark, junction, bridge, and barrier-gate, as we (hopefully) homed in on the elusive Bedouin. He almost missed the last landmark, but one more screeching U-turn and we arrived at the camp.

The Encampment

Our Bedouin tent is a large, spacious, traditional affair, set up for tourists and away from the Bedouin's main permanent site. A generator provides electricity for light, but that shuts down later in the evening. We tumbled out of the bus and the four Bedouin who met us were bemused by the sight of Sharon carrying her bucket of flowers. No local women were present. In Bedouin culture it is the men who welcome strangers. Inside the tent we sat on mats and watched as one of the men, Farhan, prepared coffee. It is traditional for Bedouin to give coffee to their guests, followed by tea. The bitter coffee is a reminder of the harshness of life in the desert. The sweet tea symbolizes the sweetness of hope in the future.

Bob whispered, "Traditionally a traveller in the desert would approach an encampment from the west and stand a short distance away until invited in. Then, when visitors arrive, the host prepares a fire using hot charcoal, and provides food for his guests."

Farhan pounded coffee beans in a bowl using a long-handled pounder. His pounding had a rhythmical repetitive beat: one, two, three; one, two three. Then a series of rapid beats. Then again one, two, three; one two three. We were anxious not to do or say anything which might be discourteous in Bedouin culture, so we just watched, in total silence. For the Bedouin it is an honor to have guests, and, in the era before radios, guests were prized as the only way to get news of the outside world.

Bob whispered again. "The culture of the Bedouin has much in common with the culture of Abraham's time, and yet there are significant changes. To begin with, these people are Muslim, Abraham was not. This is one area where the nineteenth-century Old Testament scholar Wellhausen made a lot of mistakes, because he assumed a one-to-one correspondence between the lifestyle of the modern Bedouin and that of Abraham."

"One of the Bedouin laws is that if you are accepted into a Bedouin tent, then your host is committed to defending you against any pursuer. You can stay for three days with no questions asked. After three days your host is permitted to ask who you are, where you have come from, and why you are here. The Bedouin speak a dialect of Arabic with an enriched vocabulary. For example, they have over a dozen different words which we translate by the one word 'camel.'"

THE ATMOSPHERE WAS EXTREMELY serious as we watched Farhan the coffee maker. This was until he spoke to Bob in Arabic, saying we could try on the costumes lying in the corner. The mood changed immediately. Solemn silence turned to fun and laughter as we dressed up and photographed each other. Eventually we were served coffee, which, thankfully, was in tiny cups because it was really strong and really bitter. After coffee came sweet tea served in glasses. Both cups and glasses had no handles as is the custom in the East. Then a Bedou entered with a stringed musical instrument. He played while another man sang, and Farhan kept time with the coffee pounder. Then Farhan played an Arabic 'violin' which had one string, a bow, and a sounding-board made of stretched goatskin. Bob supplied more background information,

"Folks, before this 'violin' became a Bedouin instrument it was Ethiopian and was called a Simsamea. Now, concerning the tent, the roof of a Bedouin tent is woven from *goat* hair, because when rain comes to the desert the goat hair fibres expand and make a total seal. The fibres contract when the sun comes out, allowing aeration. In the Old Testament the roof of the Holy Tabernacle was also made of goat hair. But the sides of a Bedouin tent are woven from *camel* hair which is not so expensive. The women do all the weaving of the tent, and it is also the women who erect the tents, and rear the children. The men deal with all the social and political obligations. This is why no women greeted us, only men."

Trays of food arrived, and we divided into groups of five, sitting on mats around a tray. All food was eaten either by hand or by using the bread as a spoon or bowl. Bedouin bread is unleavened, because unleavened bread lasts longer for a nomadic people on the move. The main course was chicken and rice.

TOFFIQ WAS IN HIS element. He chatted away happily to the Bedouin, and tried his hand at the instruments. Every so often he rushed out to check his bus which was parked beside the camel-pen. Despite his friendliness with our hosts, he was obviously worried that some of their cousins might remove the bus wheels or even the whole vehicle.

Bob's wife Kathy chatted to Toffiq about his family.

"I have six sisters and five brothers." Toffiq said.

"Hey, that's great," said Kathy. "I love big families. I came from one as well."

David Veness picked up the Bedouin harp and tried to get a tune out of it. His guitarist's technique did produce recognisable melodies.

We all slept in the same tent tonight. Traditionally, one side is for men and the other is for women and children. Sleeping bags were distributed and narrow mattresses were shared out. Rucksacks and other luggage doubled up as pillows.

After the meal the Bedouin left us alone. David washed his socks and stretched them over the coffee grinder to dry. "David, is that really culturally sensitive?" we teased him. A dog looked in under the tent flap, causing consternation. Would it come back in the night? Sharon's flowers looked bright and cheerful as ever. James suggested mischievously that the Bedouin had gone back to their houses to watch TV while we all roughed it, trying to imitate them! Meanwhile, we curled up in our sleeping bags waiting for the generator to stop and for the lights to go out. Outside, the camels snuffled and snorted.

— Day 20 — Be'er Sheva —

Sunday 27th October

THIS MORNING WE WENT camel-riding. The camels were fitted with double saddles, and two of us sat astride each animal for our trip into the desert. The seven camels were in two groups, one of three and one of four, each group led by a Bedouin on foot.

"Toffiq! Come and join us!"

"No, no. I will stay behind and wash my bus."

All through the night at the Bedouin camp Toffiq had been in and out of the tent, constantly worried in case anything happened to his bus.

The camel journey lasted two and a half hours, with stops where the guides explained how the Bedouin used the bare resources available to them in the wasteland. The desert was essentially stony, though with much more sand than the desert around Arad. Small scrub bushes dotted the landscape. Though the journey was comfortable, after an hour and a half our inside leg muscles were stretched and sore. The camels were placid, apart from the animal which James and I had. It consistently nipped the legs of the one in front. Camels are awkward creatures: awkward in shape, motion, and character. They have no trouble negotiating uneven stones, but are hopeless at spotting fence-wire which occasionally lay along the ground, and they stumbled whenever they tripped over the wire.

The Wilderness

Our first stop was at a well. This particular one was a cistern well, collecting water which washes off the desert hillsides during the rainy season. The other type of well is dug down to the water table. Our leading guide plucked some herbs and told us about their medicinal properties. Then he told us all about camels, with Bob translating from Arabic as he spoke.

"Camels weigh up to 300 pounds. Their nostrils can be closed to shut out sand in a sandstorm; and long hairs guard the entrance to their mouths, again to sieve out sand. They have broad, flat feet, and their knees have pads which protect them when they kneel down, with another pad on the under-belly. They can go without water for three days in the summer, or a full week in the winter. And they have two stomachs. A Bedouin without water, and in desperation, will push a pole down the camel's throat and the regurgitated liquid can be drunk! The average life-span of a camel is thirty-three years. The camel hair is shorn in springtime and is good for weaving. The camel has good 'homing' controls, and a Bedouin can trust his camel to take him home."

We had noticed that when our camel sweated, the perspiration was red.

"Bob, our camel seems to be sweating blood!"

"Yes, it's because the blood vessels are so close to the surface."

AT OUR SECOND STOP, deeper into the desert, we halted near two old field guns left by an artillery battalion. "Which war do these guns come from, Bob?" "I don't know, but I'll ask our guides." The guides shook their heads. They did not know either. So Bob listed the possibilities.

"The Egyptian advances against Israel in the Six-Day War and the Yom Kippur War did not reach as far north as this point, so it is unlikely that the guns are from these conflicts. Now, in World War I when the Anzacs liberated Be'er Sheva they passed this way: but the guns look more modern than that time. They might of course simply have been abandoned after a training exercise."

The leading guide then showed us how to make a desert rope. He broke a willowy branch off a bush, peeled back the bark so as to give him a couple of strips, each four to five feet long, and then, with the help of his partner, wove the strips together to make a tremendously strong cable. We had turns pulling it with all our might but it was never at risk of breaking. Bob suggested that when Samson was bound by the Philistines they probably used a rope like this.

Despite the barren landscape there were still signs of life. As well as scrub bushes, we saw huge, ugly, black beetles scuttling over the ground, large enough to be clearly visible despite us being perched high up on the camels. There were colonies of snails. Quail was plentiful. And we even came across a dead hedgehog. Overhead, we heard the drone of an aeroplane, and, when we looked up, it put out three bright flares which fell toward the desert. "Why did they do that, Bob?" "I don't know, but the whole of the Negev is used by the armed forces for training."

By now it was nearing mid-day, and we were wilting from the heat of the sun. It blazed down, and the stony ground again reflected the heat back up at us. The camels patiently lurched and padded through the desert. I was amazed at how the small, dry, dust covered bushes survived at all in such an inhospitable environment. We were really impressed by the guides who led our small camel caravan through the desert hills. They put themselves out to explain Bedouin life clearly, and make our experience interesting and informative.

The Town

After a picnic lunch we traveled north to Be'er Sheva itself, where Kathy left us to catch the regular bus back to Jerusalem. Bob was keen to visit the Be'er Sheva Archaeological Museum, but we had trouble finding it because there had been new building and new roads since Bob was last in the town. When we did find the museum—now located in a disused mosque—it had closed for the day. So we spent two hours walking around Be'er Sheva, which is one of the least attractive places we have come across anywhere in Israel. As a town, Be'er Sheva shows strong evidence of its Russian immigrants. There are numerous posters and signs in Russian, far more than in Hebrew or Arabic, and the bookshops and newsagents also specialize in Russian publications.

Tony went to the Bank to cash some Travellers' Cheques, and was detained in the office for ages, well beyond the stated closing time. James and I hung around outside, peering in through the windows. We saw that Tony was involved in lengthy discussions about his financial transactions. Eventually he emerged, having been charged over ten pounds for cashing a relatively small amount. Later, Bob told us that Be'er Sheva has a reputation for being unhelpful. He said that this, unfortunately, could be said of Israelis as a whole, but that it was particularly bad in the Be'er Sheva district. "The Arabs are much better, he said. "They are far more responsive, and want to help, whereas Israelis can be quite cussed!"

After Tony's banking, we were sitting at a pavement Cafe enjoying ice-creams when a young man approached.

"Excuse me, are you tourists?"

"Yes thank you."

We felt suspicious about the fellow and were reluctant to get involved in conversation.

"Excuse me, why do you come to Be'er Sheva?"

"Well, we have been to many towns in Israel in order to study, and Be'er Sheva is one of the places we wanted to see."

"Yes, but why Be'er Sheva? I mean, look around you, what is there to see here?"

The young man's insistence made us uneasy. And we definitely wanted to avoid saying anything negative about his home town. Eventually he moved off. Perhaps he was genuinely perplexed as to why any tourists would want to come to modern Be'er Sheva, which is a frontier-town dump of a place. Or perhaps he was curious about my kilt, which occasioned much pointing by the locals. In one street a man, who had been innocently drinking his coffee at a pavement cafe, dived into a bag at his feet and brought out a camera with a large telephoto lens. We never did find out if the image made the pages of the local newspaper!

Kibbutz Mashabei Sade

Our accommodation for the next three nights is to be at Kibbutz Mashabei Sade, which lies only a few miles from last night's Bedouin camp and is totally surrounded by the Negev desert. We were surprised that Shoresh had not arranged worship for us today. However, Alison and David Veness invited all of us into their chalet after the evening meal for worship and prayer. James had bought a *Jerusalem Post* in Be'er Sheva, and an interesting report caught our eye. On leaving Jerusalem last week David Pileggi told us that the Palestinians were trying to reduce Jordan's authority over the Islamic holy places in Jerusalem, and in today's newspaper we read:

Prime Minister Binyamin Netanyahu intervened in a Palestinian Authority bid to oust the Jordanian Wakf from the Temple Mount by phoning Yasser Arafat. King Hussein also phoned Arafat to complain. The incident upset the monarch in light of the fact that Hussein recently made a gesture to Arafat by visiting Jericho. There has been on-going friction between the Jordanian Wakf, which has been the custodian of the Temple Mount for decades, and the Palestinian Wakf which Arafat appointed after his arrival in Gaza in 1994.

The Palestinians eventually backed down, but they were clearly setting out markers for their long term goals. We remembered what David Pileggi had said: if King Hussein loses custodianship of the Temple Mount then his authority will weaken and his regime could collapse with consequences for the whole area.

I was tired today. Perhaps because I did not sleep or eat well at the Bedouin camp. Perhaps because it has been three weeks since I left home.

— Day 21 — Sde Boker —

Monday 28th October

THIS IS A NOISY kibbutz. Its regular permanent residents are extremely pleasant, but the kibbutz specializes in introducing Israeli teenagers to desert life in the Negev, and the two hundred teenagers who stay overnight, every night, are loud, generally undisciplined, and often disrespectful of others. The kibbutz knows this is a problem, and are planning to build accommodation which would move the teenagers away from the other tourist chalets, but as yet that is not finished. A lot of income comes from these High School groups, so the kibbutz cannot afford to lose them.

Kibbutz Sde Boker

This morning we travelled from Kibbutz Mashabei Sade to Kibbutz Sde Boker which had been the desert home of David Ben Gurion, the first Prime Minister of the State of Israel. 'Sde Boker' means 'Fields of the Morning', possibly referring to the rebirth of the Jewish nation.

Bob told us that the Greater Negev desert was 60 percent of Israel before the annexation of the West Bank. Ben Gurion foresaw problems with the Palestinians and he wanted Israelis to settle in the Negev, 'making the desert bloom.' But his vision never really took off. Some kibbutzim, such as Sde Boker and Mashabei Sade, try to fulfil that dream, but most Israelis want to live in more prosperous areas.

Bob commented, "For a Jew today, Moses is the significant figure in the Bible, leading his people into nationhood. Moses is as important to a Jew as Jesus is to us; and David Ben Gurion is seen as a new Moses, leading Jews into a new nationhood, and so his memory is revered."

BEN GURION'S DESERT HOME is a pale-green bungalow with a red roof. The books in his study have been left exactly they were the day he died. Intriguingly, the night he passed away he had been reading Hal Lindsay's book *The Late Great Planet Earth*, which looks at the future from the viewpoint of a Christian crisis-eschatology. When we arrived at his house a TV crew was setting up cameras and lights in the study, and an interviewer and interviewee were rehearsing their lines. Although the bungalow is small and modest, the study is impressively spacious and airy, and the books on the shelves show a wide variety of studies in Hebrew, English, French, Russian, and Polish. There are International Critical Commentaries on all the Old Testament books, volumes on the Talmud, books on the History of Art, the *American Jewish Yearbook*, an *Encyclopaedia of Islam*, books on the history of Zionism, a volume entitled *Suez: The Twice Fought War*, a *History of Mathematics*, the *Laws of Thought*, a *Greek New Testament*, plus hundreds of other volumes. These fill the bookcases and tables. One corner is heavy with military books.

"On military questions, Ben Gurion relied on the advice of men like Yitzhak Rabin," Bob pointed out. "But he was well able to understand the implications of their tactical advice. Unusually, Ben Gurion was head of the Jewish Defence Force and also the head of the Zionist political organization, hence he was in charge of both the military and political wings."

"It was Ben Gurion who made the official Declaration of the State of Israel in 1948. Now, when Palestine was partitioned in 1948, Israel had been preparing the infrastructure of a State for years, whereas the Arabs had refused to accept the idea that an Israeli State would ever come to be and so were totally unready for partition. Thus the Palestinian 'State' of the West Bank was unprepared and disorganized, and, when the Arab nations moved to try and snuff out Israel in 1948/49, Jordan simply annexed the West Bank."

"You mean Jordan wasn't meant to have the West Bank?"

"No. It was to be a Palestinian State. Jordan annexed it."

Bob smiled. "You don't hear about the Jordanian occupation. Everyone hears about the Israeli occupation. But, in a real sense, it was the Arab nations who first disenfranchized the Palestinians."

We wandered all through the bungalow, looking into its various rooms. Outside its back door was the air-raid bunker. Busloads of tourists were arriving, and so we made our way to the shop-cafe, and sat outside while Bob led us in a seminar on the concept of leadership in the Bible as represented by the principle of the Shepherd-King. We then visited the graves of David and Paula Ben Gurion on the outskirts of the kibbutz, at a spot with an extensive vista of the Negev desert. Reboarding the bus, we motored a few miles to the Great Canyon of Zin where Toffiq left us. He then took the bus by road to pick us up at the other end of the canyon after our hike.

Wadi Zin

The Great Canyon of Zin was formed over the course of many millennia by the action of a small stream eating its way down through chalky limestone. Geologically, this part of the Negev consists of two layers of chalky limestone and one layer of harder limestone. Flash floods find weak points where the water cuts into the rock, and eventually the water cuts through each layer until it reaches the hardest limestone. As we walked up the canyon from its lowest point, the steep, vertical, white canyon walls displayed layers and layers of rocky ridges which in successive eras have been the canyon's floor level.

I find that, within this *Journal,* I have to comment on the heat yet again. The temperature in the canyon was extreme. We found some shade for our lunch, but, outside of the shaded area, the concentrated heat was furnace-like. And, visually, the whiteness was almost too strong for our eyes. We saw a long yellow and green snake, stretched between two boulders. We saw ibex, with their rough, scimitar-shaped horns, appearing and disappearing. The canyon has two levels, and, deeper into it, we climbed to the upper level which is still well below the desert plateau. Here the stream has already reached hard limestone, but a fault in the limestone base, due to complicated rock movements involved in the formation of the Great Rift Valley twenty miles to the east, means that the two parts are offset at different heights.

Locally, the canyon is called Wadi Zin or Ein Avdat after the former nearby Nabatean city of Avdat. When we reached the upper canyon floor we saw caves even higher up in the canyon wall. These had been hollowed out by monks of the Byzantine period who wanted to live at a more remote place than Avdat. The Nabateans of the first century were traders from Arabia who controlled the trade-routes on the edges of the Roman Empire in Palestine. Later they become Christian.

BEFORE WE CLIMBED OUT of the canyon, Bob pointed to a grove of poplars which grew beside the stream. "Folks, these poplars are called

Euphrates poplars, and only grow where there is plenty of water, hence they are numerous in the valley of the Euphrates. Now, in the Bible this poplar is sometimes called the 'willow', and in Ezekiel we have a reference to this Euphrates willow."

Bob dug a Bible out of his pocket, and thumbed through the pages. "Folks, it concerns Nebuchadnezzar's campaign in 596BC, when he deposed the existing Israelite king and put his own man in power. Nebuchadnezzar thought that the new king was his ally, but it didn't turn out that way."

Bob found the chapter he was searching for. "Here we are. In chapter 17, Ezekiel writes: *A great Eagle with powerful wings, long feathers and full plumage of varied colors came to Lebanon. Taking hold of the top of a cedar, he broke off its topmost shoot and carried it away to a land of merchants, where he planted it in a city of traders.*' OK folks, these verses reflect Nebuchadnezzar's conquest of the nation and deposing the king. Then Ezekiel goes on to write, *'He took some of the seed of your land and put it in fertile soil. He planted it like a willow by abundant water, and it sprouted and became a low, spreading vine. Its branches turned towards him, but its roots remained under it. So it became a vine and produced branches and put out leafy boughs.'* Now folks, what Ezekiel is saying here is that Nebuchadnezzar's puppet king was meant to be like a willow (native to the Euphrates), but he became his own man, more like a vine (native to Judah)."

To climb the last part of the canyon wall we needed to scale a perpendicular section using steel rungs which are permanently fixed into the cliff face. Halfway up, a narrow ledge gave access to the Byzantine caves, which are simple habitations with door, window, and some niches in the cave wall. After the caves we continued further up the steel rungs until we reached the top. From there we looked over the canyon to the far side where, on an apparently vertical canyon wall, ibex danced their way from ridge to ridge.

The HaMakhtesh HaGadol Crater

Beyond the Canyon of Zin, we drove more miles into the desert to see one of several huge craters of the Negev. Unlike Meteor Crater in Arizona, these were not formed by meteor impact, but by the collapse of the desert floor due to erosion of soft rock below harder rock. The soft rock underneath was dissolved by water which had come through a narrow slit in the hard rock above, causing the heavier top rock to fall into the resultant gap. The crater we saw today is the middle-sized one. We are to see the largest one tomorrow at Mitzpe Ramon. The others are too far into the desert for us to reach.

On our way to the crater Toffiq really put the foot down, and the bus hurtled along the desert highway. He adores the desert roads and their miles and miles and miles of empty tarmac with no oncoming traffic. Toffiq hammered the bus over the undulating roads while we held on tight. We passed the development town of Yeroham, which is in the middle of nowhere, but which has been populated in the last two decades by Russians and Ethiopians. Its houses are two-storied white buildings with red tiled roofs. There are several blocks of these houses. But all around them is desert. They are like white monuments in a stony, limitless Negev.

Bob pointed over to the town. "As well as Russians and Ethiopians, a fringe religious group called the Black Hebrews live out here as well. These Black Hebrews claim to be the real descendants of Israel. They masqueraded as tourists several years ago, then stayed on as illegal immigrants. The Israeli government tried to remove them several times but failed. No one takes their claims seriously."

Eventually, after rocking and bouncing along a side road, Toffiq parked the bus. We then walked the short distance to the edge of the Ha-Makhtesh HaGadol crater. This natural wonder is three miles in diameter and two hundred feet deep. This is in an area little seen by tourists, but well known by the Children of Israel in the time of Moses as they wandered in the wilderness of Zin. All day we noticed a large white barrage-balloon high in the sky. Probably linked to the military.

The Desert Kibbutz

Back at Kibbutz Mashabei Sade we were joined by a young woman from reception. "Shalom! My name is Alisha. I am originally from Los Angeles, but I came to Israel fourteen years ago. I married a kibbutz member and now I am also a kibbutz member. My job on the kibbutz is to liaise with our visitors. May I apologise for the noise the high school kids made last night. We are really sorry about that."

We assured Alisha that it was not too bad, and that we had slept better than at the Bedouin camp. She then gave us a brief history of the kibbutz.

"In 1947, when it became obvious the British were leaving and the nation was to be divided, many Jewish Youth Movement members moved into peripheral areas of the country to help prepare for possible armed conflict. Twenty days before the declaration of the State of Israel, eleven settlements went up in the Negev, literally overnight. Each settlement consisted of fences and a tower. Our kibbutz came ten days later. Under the British Mandate Jewish settlements were illegal, and therefore they were set up as 'other things.' For example, one settlement, ten kilometers from us, was set up as a 'meteorological station'! But it never issued any weather forecasts!"

"The nearness of Egypt made that particular settlement very vulnerable, so other ones were set up by young people of sixteen and seventeen years old. These lines of untrained defenders pushed back the Egyptian army! We can still hardly believe it. It is seen as a miracle. Remember, there was no proper trained Israeli Army. During the two years of the war the Muslim Brotherhood took over a former British outpost and harassed food convoys, but eventually local Jews attacked and took it over, so these attacks ceased."

As Alisha talked, a crowd of teenagers gathered outside. We were occupying one of the public TV rooms and they obviously wanted to watch the TV. The door opened and they stood in the doorway talking loudly to each other. Alisha spoke to them sharply in Hebrew and they drifted off. She took up her talk again.

"Anyway, after the conflict stopped the people wanted a more settled life. But conditions were too hard down here in the desert, so some went north to Galilee. The problem down here of course is lack of water. That makes life amazingly difficult."

Alisha explained that deep under the Negev there is a huge lake of brackish water. This was drilled into and for some time this brackish water was the staple water diet. The children got so much used to it that when they were given fresh water to drink they spat it out. She emphasized that the land in this area is really harsh and when it rains the water is absorbed into the ground and it dries up quickly. If it rains harder there are flash floods, and it dries up again. Building dams does not work because they dry up as well.

"In 1955/56 after seven years, many kibbutz members said 'This is no good. We will have to abandon the place.'" Alisha told us. "So, to avoid this happening, the central government decided to supply all the kibbutzim in the Negev from a central pipe-line. This is our survival. However, for the last fifteen years a lot of research has taken place on how to use the brackish water. Cherries like it because the salt water helps the cherry to retain the sugar content more than normal. Other fruit flourish as well, and we have used the brackish water to create a fish farm."

We listened intently. Before coming to Israel some of us had been told that water used by kibbutzim in the desert had been taken from supplies normally used by Palestinian communities. Was that the case? Alisha assured us that was not so.

She continued. "We have had a major effort to try and become independent of water from the north. For example, there was a major drought six years ago, and we were faced with a choice: should we stop watering the grass which grows all over the kibbutz, or should we stop watering the orchards? The kibbutz decided to keep watering the grass because it means so much to us psychologically. We were determined not to live in a ghost town. Quality of life is so important. Green grass in the kibbutz was more important than the handsome commercial profits we get from the avocado orchards. We also use treated sewage water from Be'er Sheva and Tel Aviv for our orchards. The orchards are forty minutes away by truck, and in the old days the men stayed away at the fields all day for fourteen or fifteen hours."

Moving outside, Alisha explained that tourism is a major part of the kibbutz's economy. "When the Sinai returned to Egypt in 1982 the Israeli Army training relocated further north, up here in the Negev. The army is not meant to practice within two kilometers of the kibbutz, but, well, you know! Sometimes we hear booms and shooting day and night. Our hostel started as temporary accommodation for the army, and as time went by we realized that people had a desire to come and see the Negev. So today we have sixty-six chalets like the ones you are staying in, plus the hostel."

"To begin with all kibbutzim were based on agriculture. But some years ago the kibbutz decided we could not survive on agriculture alone and we entered the world of industry. We have a factory producing valves for the gas industry. We have a silk painting factory. A number of members work away from the kibbutz as doctors and so on, and their salaries come back to the kibbutz. Young people are encouraged to study what they want to study, but there is a limit how many astronomers or nuclear-physicists one kibbutz needs! Anyone who is a social worker or psychiatrist must work at another kibbutz outside of their area."

BY THIS TIME, WE had walked halfway round the kibbutz. Alisha pointed over to what used to be the children's quarters and explained the changing kibbutz philosophy towards children and family life. She explained that the original kibbutzim were started by people who had communist revolution ideals from Russia, and these pioneer kibbutz members rejected conventions such as marriage. This brought a lot of changing of partners. The problem came when children arrived.

"The women still wanted to be full workers in the kibbutz life." Alisha pointed out. "They still wanted to work in the fields and be totally involved members in every way. So nanny-rotas started. Eventually a system evolved where, at six weeks, babies left their parents and were placed in the nursery. When the children grew older they lived in their own sections, with the older children helping the younger ones. But the parents had to spend three hours' quality time each day with their children plus all day Saturday. That is much, much more than a modern western family."

"However, problems developed, especially with teenagers. The teenage sections became no-go areas for adults. And when drugs were introduced by delinquent youngsters who were being helped by the kibbutz, no parental control at all was possible over this major problem. Over the past ten years these units have been closed down, and children now live at home. But the tradition of making children take responsibility still shows dividends. For example, only two and a half percent of Israelis live on kibbutzim, but 37 percent of the Officers in the Air Force are former kibbutz kids."

According to Alisha the kibbutz was always first, second or third in the whole of Israel for milk. They have developed a circular cow-milking carousel which floats on water. The carousel takes twenty cows at a time, and slowly revolves as the cows are milked, with a computer detecting when a cow is finished and releasing it when the carousel next passes the exit gate. If the cow does not move off, a jet of water is squirted on its forehead between the eyes and that does the trick.

WE TOLD ALISHA ABOUT Kibbutz Malkiya, and asked if this kibbutz also had a synagogue. She shook her head. "No, there is no synagogue as such. But we are loosely affiliated to the Reform movement in Judaism. In fact, our silk printing factory produces a lot of religious work."

"But what about occasions such as Yom Kippur?"

"Yes, Yom Kippur is an unsettling day. How are we to spend it? Usually people spend it communally by reflecting on the past year, but quite a few members, including a lot of ladies, feel that a religious event would be good. A big problem is that two ladies on the kibbutz have become ultra-orthodox. One of them felt she was a great sinner! The other one, I don't know why. But they would like to control any religious activity."

"Has the kibbutz ever thought of building a synagogue?"

"Yes. In fact, the Ultra-Orthodox have offered to build a synagogue. But I and many others say 'No!' First, our kibbutz is affiliated to the Reform movement, not the Ultra-Orthodox one. Second, if a synagogue is to be erected then the people of the kibbutz will build it, not outsiders. Third, if we have a synagogue all kibbutz members, male and female, will be equal in it. The men and women will sit together. Women will lead prayers. The Ultra-Orthodox would stop all this."

The population of the kibbutz is varied. One or two of its families are from the Soviet Union and South America. One is from England. One is from New Zealand. Two are from Holland. Alisha looked at us and said, "The common denominator is that we are all Jews, and many of us started in the Jewish Youth Movement in our original countries. We have a tremendous commitment to Israel."

— Day 22—Avdat —

Tuesday 29th October

TOFFIQ IS WORRIED ABOUT his wife. On the telephone last night, she told him that she was feeling unwell, and was going to see the doctor today. He is going to phone again this evening to get more news. "Is she expecting?" wondered the ladies.

Last night the High School kids made so much noise. Alisha told us that the leaders of High School groups have absolutely no chance of keeping order or imposing a curfew. A raucous basketball game went on outdoors behind our chalets until at least 3.30 am, although later today we found out that the culprits were young soldiers. Under Israeli law every group of twelve children must be accompanied by someone with a gun, so older brothers and sisters who have served in the army come on school outings with rifles slung over their shoulder and ammunition round their waist. James was sure he had heard a gun going off accompanied by cheers.

The freedom given to Israeli children is, some say, due to the Holocaust experience. Hitler tried to eliminate new generations, and so children are seen as the most precious inheritance of Jewry and are allowed to be 'free.' But what kind of freedom is it to allow them to live without rules? The National Service years slap a degree of discipline on top of this unruliness, but it does not eliminate habits which develop through childhood.

Avdat

After breakfast we went south to the ruins of the Nabatean city of Avdat in the Wilderness of Zin. In Old Testament times this Wilderness was occupied by the Amalekites, and in New Testament times it was part of the vital trading route from Arabia. From 9BC to 40AD the sovereign of Avdat was King Aretas IV whom Paul mentions when describing his escape from Damascus after his conversion: *'In Damascus the governor under King Aretas had the city of Damascus guarded in order to arrest me. But I was lowered in a basket from a window in the wall and slipped through his hands.'* (II Corinthians 10:32). Aretas IV's daughter was Herod the Great's first wife, whom Herod subsequently divorced in favor of Herodias. In the early days of their marriage, Herod rebuilt the stronghold of Machaerus to the east of the Dead Sea and on the extreme borders of Judaea, close to Aretas' kingdom. Machaerus was a second Masada, another refuge fortress for the psychologically insecure Herod.

Bob explained that when Herod was scheming to divorce the daughter of Aretas, she begged to be sent to Machaerus. Once there, she escaped to one of her father's camps. King Aretas, like Herod, was a vassal of Rome, but, instead of appealing to his suzerain to right the wrong done to his daughter, Aretas prepared for war against Herod. Though the war came to nothing, Herod moved to Machaerus to confront Aretas. That was when he brought John the Baptist to its prison. As well as preparation for possible war, Herod moved John to Machaerus for two other reasons. First, he was fascinated by John as a preacher. Second, Machaerus was in Perea and John was not so well-known there as in Judaea, and John's isolation gave Herodias her chance to take revenge for John's outspoken, disapproving preaching against her lifestyle. It was as they waited in the stronghold of Machaerus for political events to unfold, that Salome entertained Herod with her dance, and Herodias took advantage of the entranced monarch, persuading him to have John beheaded.

WHOEVER CONTROLLED THE TRADE corridors controlled the customs taxes collected *en route*. Over the course of a journey from Saudi Arabia to the Mediterranean coast, taxes multiplied the cost of the articles seventyfold, becoming a lucrative source of income for the authorities. These caravans had up to two thousand camels, carrying myrrh, frankincense, gold, and a vast quantity of spices and perfumes. Each caravan took two and a half months to travel from Saudi Arabia to Petra. From there they crossed the Negev to Gaza on the coast.

The Nabateans controlled the trade-routes in the desert during the first century, with the Roman Empire stopping at the Israel border. There were sixty-five stations across the desert. Some were based at natural wells. Others had artificial reservoirs dug by the Nabateans. Then, from the Israel border to Gaza the King of Judaea benefited from the customs taxes, and this was Herod's primary source of income behind his building projects. The Nabateans were wealthy nomads for generations, at least until Rome could no longer resist the lure of these profitable spice trade-routes. Rome then took over the Nabatean's main livelihood. In 106AD the Nabatean Kingdom and Petra was annexed by the Romans. Much later, following the Islamic conquest of this region in the second half of the seventh century, the inhabitants of Avdat gradually deserted the city.

The museum at Avdat is a mine of information. It told us that in former centuries the people were particularly fond of frankincense and myrrh, which were used in the worship of the gods. These plants were grown mainly in what is known today as Yemen. On a hill-top we saw the remains of the ancient Avdat site, now decorated with life-size, bronze, silhouette figures illustrating features of the settlement. One line of figures depicts a trade caravan. Another depicts two figures talking. Another features someone pouring wine into a large jar, with an adjacent figure draining a cup of wine with his head flung back. "The Nabateans loved drinking wine," said Bob. "Strictly therefore, according to desert culture, they were not regarded as true nomads. In desert culture a man who drank wine ceased to be a nomad. Can you guess why?"

"Was alcohol against nomadic religious ideas?"

"No. Simpler. A true nomadic lifestyle precludes the growing and tending of vines, because vines need attention from a settled community. And if you stay at a place long enough to look after vines, you cannot not be a true nomad. So the difference was sociological rather than religious. By the way, do you know why grapes are trampled by bare feet!"

We shook our heads. Bob enlightened us.

"It avoids crushing the grape-seeds. Crushed grape-seeds make the wine really bitter. Any kind of footwear crushes the seeds."

"So sweet wine from sweaty feet is preferable to sour wine from clean feet!"

"Yep!"

In the fourth century the Nabateans became Christian, and, in the ruins of the Byzantine church, we saw a stone cross-shaped baptismal font. Bob told us that in Greek culture the word *baptidzo* was used both to describe washing hands before a meal and to describe baptism: there-fore, *baptidzo* did not always mean total immersion.

Mitzpe Ramon

Leaving Avdat we went south to Mitzpe Ramon which is on the edge of the Great Crater. On the way we passed another large prison with its high towers, high walls, barbed wire, and surrounded by desert. As we drew nearer Mitzpe Ramon, Bob remarked on the number of Bedouin camps in the area. "I may be mistaken, but there seem to be more Bedouin in this area than years ago. If so, I don't know why. Have they moved from the north as towns expand? Or is it due to polygamy? Or is it better health care? I don't know."

At Mitzpe Ramon we parked at the edge of the vast Makhtesh Ramon crater which marks the boundary between the Wilderness of Zin and the Wilderness of Paran. Technically, a 'makhtesh' is a valley surrounded by deep walls and drained by a single wadi. Like the crater we saw yesterday, this one was formed by the soft rock beneath the hard rock being eroded away and the upper layer collapsing into the space beneath. But such a description does no justice to the sheer scale. We had our picnic lunch sitting on the edge of the crater wall, sheltered from the wind. A cold wind was blowing in from the west over the Wilderness of Zin. Bob reminded us that we were two and a half thousand feet above sea level, and that a cold wind can blow for five months, from now until the end of March. When the Israelites wandered in this part of the desert they endured bleak and hostile conditions.

The Visitors' Centre has an excellent description of the complicated geological features, plus an audio-visual presentation of the wildlife of the crater floor. Bob gave us some Bible passages relating to Israel's experience in the wilderness, and each of us went to a quiet spot to reflect on them. I followed a path which went a short distance down the cliff of the crater wall, and sat there for a while thinking about the texts. Climbing back up I met a herd of ibex moving down from the outskirts of the town. Ibex are used to people, and I was able to photograph them from close range.

ON THE RETURN JOURNEY Toffiq was driving our bus along the desert highway at top speed, when he suddenly slammed on the brakes bringing us screeching to a halt. By the side of the road a herd of sheep and goats was following a shepherd. The shepherd's wife, clothed in full length black dress and wearing a black yashmak hung with gold and silver discs, walked at the rear of the flock leading their donkey. Earlier in the day we had said to Toffiq that we would like to photograph some herds of sheep and goats. He had remembered.

Back at the kibbutz, Toffiq telephoned Nazareth and was relieved to discover that his wife felt much better.

"So she's OK Toffiq?"

"Yes indeed. The doctor is happy with her. And I am so happy."

This evening we gathered in David and Alison's room for another of Bob's seminars.

— Day 23 — Eilat —

Wednesday 30th October

WHEN WE LEFT KIBBUTZ Mashabei Sade this morning, four other buses, each full of High School kids, left at the same time, giving the locals peace and quiet until a fresh detachment of chaotic youngsters arrived in the afternoon. Today we had to travel south, far south. To begin with, we passed places which had become familiar over the last few days: the Prison, Avdat, Mitzpe Ramon. Leaving the Wilderness of Zin, the road wound down cliffs to the floor of the Great Crater of the Negev crater, crossed its base for several miles past mining operations, before climbing out on the other side into the Wilderness of Paran.

This rugged landscape is immensely impressive. High cliffs and sharp ridges characterize the hills and mountains of Paran. There is very little vegetation. The road was quiet, apart from industrial lorries and an occasional car or jeep. Our destination was to be Eilat by the Red Sea, at the extreme southern point of Israel, and the journey would take several hours. Eventually our road across the Wilderness of Paran joined the main Jerusalem-Eilat highway at a junction far south of the Dead Sea. The plain between the southern tip of the Dead Sea and the northern point of the Red Sea is called the Arava. Across the Arava we saw the hills of Jordan.

Hai-Bar Yotvata

Our first major stop was the wildlife center at Hai-Bar Yotvata, a small nature reserve aiming to restore endangered animals to Israel's open spaces. At the center of the reserve is a tiny zoo featuring predators including wolves, hyenas, cheetahs, and vultures. Toffiq really enjoyed the zoo. He tapped with his keys on the glass barriers to attract the animals' attention, and was as happy as a schoolboy when they responded. The center also has a night-life exhibition hall which is in semi-darkness, illuminated only by low wattage bulbs. After a few minutes our eyes became accustomed to the gloom and we saw owls, bats, and night foxes, moving about in their enclosures.

The main part of the center is an open area which we toured on our bus. It was like a safari ride in Africa, though we went for ages without seeing anything other than a clutch of unattended ostrich eggs. Eventually, deep into the reserve, we came across ostriches, onagers, oryx, ibex, and donkeys. Toffiq loved every minute.

Timna Park

Leaving Hai-Bar we continued further south before striking over to the west to see the Timna Park Red Canyons, which is an extensive area of outstanding natural beauty surrounded by the Timna Mountains and rich in rocks sculpted into strange shapes by wind and sand. After an audio-visual presentation in a building at the entrance of Timna Park, we travelled several more miles to the old Copper mines, known as 'King Solomon's Mines.'

"There is no evidence that King Solomon ever used these mines," said Bob. "But the name has stuck."

Quarrying for copper at Timna began in 4000BC, and, in the fourteenth to twelfth centuries BC, the Egyptians established a huge complex for the mining and refining of copper, employing Midianites who lived in the northern part of Arabia. After a long interval, mining recommenced during the Roman occupation, and continued after the area came under Arab control. Some of the rocks have fantastic shapes. One, called 'The Mushroom', is shaped like an enormous, deep-red, sandstone fungus, and stands apart in splendid isolation. Nearby, the cliff-face has three massively high buttresses of sandstone called Solomon's Pillars.

Toffiq parked the bus near Solomon's Pillars, and Bob escorted us to the remains of a temple to the Egyptian goddess Hathor, who in Egyptian art was depicted with cow-like ears. We clambered up a series of steps cut in the cliff, and squeezed through a gap in the sandstone wall before descending on the other side. The Hathor temple is situated at the foot of a cliff and, some meters above ground-level, we could see a relief carved into the rock, depicting Pharaoh paying homage to the goddess. The carving was made when the Pharaohs controlled this area of southern Israel, and I was thrilled to see a relic from an era which has always fascinated me. The stylized relief in silhouette was so typically classical Egyptian.

Bob commented, "Folks, these stylized figures are what we normally expect Egyptian art to be. But, when Egypt turned briefly to monotheism the art-form changed, and for a short time Egyptian art was more realistic with three-dimensional representations of figures."

Eilat

After Timna Park we continued south to Eilat. Across the Arava the mountains of Jordan were clear and sharp, forming a solid barrier to the east. Far away, we could see lorries moving slowly up into these mountains on a modern road which follows the ancient King's Highway, which was the major route in Trans-Jordan in biblical times. We arrived in Eilat at about 4.00 pm, and Toffiq set us down at a public tourist beach just south of the main town where we could swim in the Red Sea.

EILAT IS BUSY AND modern. Towering gleaming white hotels, with balconies on every level, cluster along the sea front. Across the water is Aqaba in Jordan, but in Aqaba the buildings are smaller and more modest. Large transport ships stand at anchor. Luxurious tourist yachts sail up from the south. From the beach we could see four nations: Israel, Jordan, Saudi Arabia and, further down the coast, Egypt. The beach was deserted apart from ourselves and one heavily tanned middle-aged man, who was lying on the sand reading a book.

Rosie whispered, "That man is absolutely naked!"

"What!"

"Yes, I'm sure he is!"

She was right. In due course the man got up and went for a swim before returning to his book. In more modest fashion we used our towels to improvise changing facilities.

OUR ACCOMMODATION IS AT the Elot tourist kibbutz, two miles north of the main town. After settling in, James and I tuned in again to Jordanian TV. This time it was broadcasting Rowan Atkinson's '*Mr. Bean*' programmes. At the meal Toffiq showed us his wife's photograph which he keeps in his wallet. She is twenty-two, attractive, and from a large family. As well as a photo of his wife, Toffiq also has in his wallet a picture of the Madonna and child. We had noticed that his bus had several Bethlehem and St. George stickers.

"How old are *you* Toffiq?"

Toffiq tried to be coy, but was enjoying the attention.

"I am thirty. I want to learn German because nearly all the tourists are German."

This answer explained a lot. German and Filipino tourists tip extraordinarily well, and a bus-driver might receive money from each tourist each day if he is driving for Germans and Filipinos. Over the course of a ten-day tour of the Holy Land, that can accumulate considerably, between £500 and £1000. During the last two days we had become aware of tension between Toffiq and Bob, with Bob having to speak strongly to Toffiq. All their conversations are in Hebrew, but the strain is clear. We had assumed they were having a difference of opinion about the route, but tonight it became clear that Toffiq was unhappy being assigned to us. We could not give the huge tips he might get from other parties.

We asked Bob why so many Germans come to the Holy Land, given the history of the Holocaust. Are they not uncomfortable here?

"Well, perhaps, but in another way they are amazed by this people who survived the Holocaust. And, of course, they have the same pilgrimage reasons as the rest of us."

After supper Toffiq said he was going into Eilat to have coffee with other bus-drivers, and offered a lift to anyone who wanted to see the sights. He would pick us up again at nine o'clock.

It was a warm, balmy evening, and Eilat at night was even busier than Eilat by day. The airport is right next to the town-center and we were deafened regularly by the roar of aero-engines. At one point we looked up and saw an aeroplane only a few meters above the roof of a hotel. Passing directly over our heads, it landed on the runway which started no more than a few steps beyond the perimeter fence on the other side of the street.

Eilat is full of coffee-houses, shops, street traders, ice-cream sellers, and disco-music. It also has a carnival with Ferris-wheels and dodgems. Meeting Toffiq at nine did not give much time, so we hurried through the crowds, seeing as much as we could. Jewellery sellers were stationed on every corner, and Sharon, Rosie, and I were making our way back to the rendezvous-point when one of them called over to us.

"Are you folk from Scotland?"

"Yes, did you hear our accents?"

"Aye, I was in Scotland for a couple of years."

"Where about?"

"I stayed in Ayr."

"Ayr!" Sharon shouted, "that's where I come from!"

"What are you doing here?" he asked.

"We're on a Christian Study course," replied Sharon

"I went to the Baptist church in Ayr."

"That's my church!"

Sharon looked at him more closely. "Are you Larry?"

"Yes, I am."

"I'm Sharon McAuslane."

The conversation with Larry had to be brief because we needed to get back to the rendezvous-point. Larry invited us to come to his church fellowship tomorrow night, but we would be away by then. So we left him at his stall, selling jewellery.

Nine o'clock came and went. No Toffiq. Quarter past nine came and went. No Toffiq. Half past nine came and went. No Toffiq. Sharon, a compulsive communicator, spent the time phoning friends in Scotland. I still had three units left on my phone card so I also rang home, got through to younger daughter Alison, and, before the units ran out, was able to tell her we were in Eilat and could see the lights of Aqaba across the water. Quarter to ten came and went. No Toffiq. We gave him until ten o'clock. At ten o'clock, still no Toffiq and no bus. So we hailed taxis and returned to Elot

Interlude

— Day 24 — Journeying —

Thursday 31st October

ALISON CHALLENGED TOFFIQ ABOUT his non-appearance last night. He looked sheepish and guilty, muttering something about having been at the rendezvous point at nine o'clock and we weren't there. Toffiq was unconvincing, and we knew his claim was simply not true.

Today we travelled the two hundred miles from Eilat to Jerusalem. Bob made good use of the time, and, as we motored north up the Arava, looking out at the empty landscape, we had another of his minibus mini-seminars.

"Folks, two Red Sea ports are mentioned in the Old Testament, Eilat and Ezion-Geber, and both of them were well known in Solomon's time. Now, the location of Eilat is obvious, but where was Ezion-Geber? Ezion-Geber may have been where we swam yesterday, though no archaeological remains have been discovered there. However, five miles down the western side of the Gulf of Eilat is a coral island called Pharaoh's Island. On it are Crusader ruins. But there are also Phoenician Iron Age remains from Solomon's time. So, Pharaoh's Island is a possibility for the site of Ezion-Geber, because we know that Solomon had Phoenician influences."

Exodus

Tony asked a question. "Bob, what about the crossing of the Red Sea?" Bob nodded, flicked through his notes, and then began.

"OK, the question of the Red Sea. When the book of Exodus refers to the 'Red Sea', the Hebrew in fact says 'Yam SUF' which means 'The Reed Sea.' There is an outside chance that it could be 'Yam SOF', which means

'The Sea at the End', but this is unlikely. If Yam Suf meant the Reed Sea, and therefore had reeds growing in it, then it must have been a freshwater sea, or only slightly brackish at the most. If so, then we can identify Yam Suf with either the Bitter Lakes, or the artificial canal cut north-south by Pharaoh Seti the First. Seti's Canal was a man-made barrier constructed to stop Canaanites immigrating into Egypt. And to make it really effective it was filled with crocodiles! The Canal hypothesis would tie in with a late Exodus date."

"Now, the Bitter Lakes are natural shallow lagoons. But I feel that the Bitter Lakes scenario does not fit in with the flavour of the account in Exodus chapter 14, which gives the impression of Moses and the children of Israel meeting a very specific barrier to their progress. The canal, however, fits in with the picture painted in Exodus 14 of a definite barrier impeding the journey. Whichever stretch of water Exodus refers to, be in no doubt that a real miracle took place, because for the people to remain upright in a wind powerful enough to hold water back, God's intervention was necessary!"

"Are these the only possibilities?" queried Tony.

"These are the two main ones." replied Bob, "However, other scholars have the Exodus crossing at the Gulf of Eilat. Some even place the mountain of the Ten Commandments in Saudi Arabia. These scholars cite the text *'Yahweh coming out of Seir'*, and point out that Seir means Edom and Arabia. OK, that theory fits in with the Midianite setting of the wanderings, but it means that the wanderings did not take place in the Sinai. On the other hand, we have to take into account the fact that traditional Sinai is empty of relevant archaeological remains, whereas Arabia has lots and lots of pottery from that era!"

"So, what have archaeologists found in Saudi?"

"Not as much as they might! You see, the Saudi government blocks archaeological investigations because they fear Israeli claims for Arabia if any links are found with the Exodus wanderings! Basically though, the Mount Sinai of Exodus, has to be in today's Sinai Peninsula unless nomenclature changes are really radical. Speaking personally, I feel that archaeological evidence favors a late Exodus, and I support the canal theory. The line of the canal, parallel to the Suez Canal, can be seen from aerial photographs, and yet it was only rediscovered twenty to thirty years ago. It was mentioned in ancient writings, but people pooh-poohed the idea because no one knew where it was, at least until recently."

WE STOPPED FOR A mid-morning break at a scruffy roadside cafe. A wooden sign pointed the way to 'Rest Rooms' which James took advantage of. As he emerged he beckoned to us. "Hey! come and see this!" he shouted, "This place has luxurious toilets! Almost as good as those of the King David Hotel!" Few of us actually needed a comfort-stop, but, after hearing about these special loos in such an incongruous setting, we had to see for ourselves. The old man who sat by the doorway demanded two shekels for entry, but was prepared haggle the fee. The interior was spacious, gleaming, and high-tech. Well worth visiting even if not personally required.

Beside the cafe was a paddock with donkeys, sheep, and goats. On the other side of the road massive juggernauts lay parked while their drivers refreshed themselves.

Back in the bus, Toffiq pounded out the miles, overtaking vehicle after vehicle: lorries, cars, trucks, tank-transporters. Bob continued his instruction.

"You know folks; you get all kinds of weirdos coming to Israel. That's true even in the field of professional archaeology. You get so-called archaeologists coming who are determined to either prove or disprove the Bible, and their professional objectivity is forgotten."

"There's this guy whom I told some of you about before. He's the one who claims that Sodom and Gomorrah were situated on the Masada plain, and who says that the configurations in the desert at Masada are the foundations of these cities, whereas it's quite obvious that the formations were made by flood erosion. Well, this guy has a real following, and he makes a lot of money from his lectures because he claims to have 'proved the Bible' in all sorts of places. And of course, anyone who questions his evidence is labelled an 'unbeliever' and a 'liberal'. Well, I'm no liberal, but I think you have to be cautious about your claims. Look, this guy came to Jerusalem a few years ago, and he gave an illustrated lecture in a hall full of professional archaeologists and other academics. During his lecture he said that at the Adam fords, north of Jericho, he had discovered a piece of writing written by Adam."

"Well, at the question time I stood up, and I said to him, 'Sir, when you say 'Adam', do you mean Adam of Genesis chapter 1, the husband of Eve?' 'Yes I do,' he said. 'Well, Sir,' I said to him, 'this is most exciting, because if these writings are by Adam, they must be the oldest writings in the world.' 'Indeed they are,' he said. Well, Sir, do you have pictures of these writings? Could we see a copy?'"

"At this point he said there was a picture in one of his books, and his assistant would show me at the end. So, after the question time was over, I went to his assistant. But the assistant did not know where to look for the picture. We looked through all the books. There was no picture. The man simply wanted to shut me up. Yet this man makes a fortune in America giving lectures like this. He claims to have discovered the Ark of the Covenant, Sodom, Gomorrah, Adam's writings, and so on. He sells books and videos, and those of us who say 'Hey, wait, hold on', we're labelled as spiritually dead academics trying to undermine people's faith. It's real frustrating."

AFTER SEVERAL HOURS WE reached the Dead Sea. Alison wisely persuaded Toffiq to take a lunch break at En Gedi. We were getting concerned about his driving. But it was his last day with us and, after dropping us off in Jerusalem, he wanted to get home to his young wife in Nazareth. His speed was becoming alarming.

Dead Sea tourist boats are a recent innovation because the high concentration of salt in the water makes it difficult to maintain their engines. Nevertheless, a new company is trying to make a success of the idea. Bob is unsure about the venture. "Folks, I reckon that in a few years there will be disco boats on the Dead Sea as there are now on the Sea of Galilee!"

Leaving En Gedi we passed Qumran and Jericho, then up to Jerusalem. Dee was keen to film some of the Bedouin camps which lie on either side of the road, but Toffiq could not find a suitable place to park. He wanted home badly. In Jerusalem we picked up mail at Christ Church, then went out to Abu Ghosh where our extra luggage had already been taken. Toffiq dropped us off at the monastery, and then roared away in a cloud of dust. Bob had had a difficult time with him wanting more money and better tips from Shoresh. We liked Toffiq. And when he was in a good mood he was fun. It may well be that drivers, such as Toffiq, are poorly paid and depend on big tips to make a proper living. But we couldn't give him the level of tips he could get from richer tourists. With a young wife, and perhaps starting a family, Toffiq needed more.

Abu Ghosh Monastery

Two weeks ago, when David Pileggi took us on a quick visit to the Abu Ghosh Monastery it left a negative impression. But today, Sister Catherine, a cheery Irish nun, was there to welcome us, and when we went to our rooms we found that it was a truly beautiful and well-appointed center. This is going to be good. After we settled in, Sister Catherine gave us all a cup of coffee in the kitchen.

"Now then," she said, "Lord bless you! David Pileggi tells me you have been in the desert for a week. Well, you need a bit of comfort now. So welcome to our monastery, and we hope you will feel at home here. Now folks, what kind of food have you been having down there in the desert?"

"Chicken and rice, and rice and chicken, Sister."

"Lord bless you! Well now, we're going to have fish and chips tonight. And would you like a bottle of wine? Now then, if you do, there's wine in the fridge, and I think the price is on the fridge-door. Just come in here as often as you like."

This was paradise.

Sister Catherine told us that the monastery came to be as the result of a nun's dream. In her dream the nun believed she was being shown where the ark actually rested, and she organized the purchase of the property which is today the monastery. Today, it is set apart as a place for prayer, study, and contemplation. Sister Catherine also mentioned there had been recent excavations at the monastery which had uncovered remains of the Davidic era.

"We've been wanting to build more accommodation here for seven years, and it was a real struggle to get a permit. Then, two days after the permit was given, a team arrived from the Ministry of Antiquities. We had to postpone any building on the site until they had finished. More than that! We had to finance their excavations! They've filled in their discoveries with sand, but we have to leave a trapdoor for possible visitors in the future if the Antiquities people want to make it a public site. Lord bless us! Can you imagine a monastery of prayer and contemplation with a thousand visitors a day coming here! However, the excavations at least confirmed that we are on the original Tel. So this was indeed where the Ark of the Covenant rested."

Before dark, James, Rosie, and I wandered down into the village to buy picnic provisions from the local store. James and Rosie shopped, and I chatted to the old fellow behind the counter. I assumed he was the store owner because a large photograph of him was stuck to the wall behind his head. Also on the wall were photographs of Yitzhak Rabin, President Clinton, Yasser Arafat, and King Hussein of Jordan.

I introduced myself and said where we came from. He smiled in acknowledgment.

"My name is Abu Ghosh Hashim, and I am the owner of this shop. You are welcome in our village.

"Have you ever been to Scotland?"

"No, I was born in Abu Ghosh, but I have been to Britain."

"Oh, tell me more."

"Yes, my father served in the Palestinian Police in the British Army. In 1948 our whole family was based in Jordan when the Israeli War of Independence broke out. My father decided not to return at that time, so we were brought up and educated in Jordan. I trained as a Civil Engineer and I built roads and bridges all over Jordan, and Kuwait, and Saudi Arabia. I helped to plan and build the airport at Aqaba. Have you been to Aqaba?"

"Not yet, but I go to Aqaba next week. We came from Eilat today."

"Good. Well, my mother was eventually allowed to return to Abu Ghosh after the Six-Day War. In 1985 she made it possible for me to return as well. So I come home to my village. Abu Ghosh Hashim comes home! That is good, yes?"

"Yes! Of course! Very good!"

"But not so good for my mother."

"Oh. Why?"

"You see, my late father's estate is tied up in Jordan, and my mother is not allowed to transfer it from Jordan to Israel."

"So what are you going to do?"

"Well, if my mother goes to London and signs papers in London, the estate can be transferred from Jordan to London, and then from London to Abu Ghosh. But she does not want to go to London. 'It is too far,' she says. 'I am too old,' she says. But she will come with me. I know she will."

Yitzhak Rabin featured in several of the photographs behind Hashim. The non-Jewish people in Israel put so much faith in his leadership. We took our leave of this affable man who had spent most of his life in exile from his land of birth. Before returning to the monastery we visited the Crusader church which is built on a site believed by some to be the house at Emmaus mentioned in Luke chapter 24. It is a dark, cool, stone-built church, with a high-vaulted interior resembling the great hall of a Norman Castle. Apart from ourselves the church was empty, and we lingered in the semi-darkness. Rosie sang '*I am the Lord who healeth thee*,' and her clear voice filled the whole church. A special moment.

We then walked back up the hill to the monastery, and the sky in the west was a brilliant red, with the complete orb of the sun only a few degrees above the horizon. "Doesn't that symbolize modern Israel," commented James. "A fantastic sunset, silhouetting a telecommunications tower! The symbol on the Israeli flag should be a mobile phone!"

In some places minarets and church towers no longer dominate the landscape. Telecommunications buildings do. In Abu Ghosh the mosque is dwarfed by telephone relay-station pylons. Israel is a land of high-tech talk. Everyone has a mobile phone. All drivers seem to be on the phone as they drive. In the streets people stand, walk, and run with mobile phones stuck to their ears. There is a paradox in all this. Much talking but little understanding between communities. In a similar way, Jerusalem is a city whose streets and lanes have poster after poster declaring 'Peace-Shalom', but there is little real peace. Much talk. Much proclamation. Little progress.

James had bought the latest *Jerusalem Post* and found a couple of interesting articles. One referred to the Nafta Prison in the Negev, which we had passed several times: *"Police yesterday seized 30kg of marijuana after a chase involving trackers and a helicopter, that ended north of Mizpe Ramon."* Another article highlighted problems with the Israeli National Airline: *"El Al expects the company to end the year with a loss of about $100 million. The main reason for the loss is the drop in tourism. Other factors include the government's open-skies policy which allows almost completely unregulated competition."*

FISH AND CHIPS WAS delightful after having had chicken and rice every day for a week. We enjoyed the meal, and shared a bottle of wine. "Did you like it then?" enquired a beaming sister Catherine.

"Yes Sister! More of the same! Every day!" said Clive.

"Lord bless you! Oh no! We'll give you something different tomorrow."

"Are there many nuns here, Sister?"

"No, only a small community. But there's a young woman living here at the monastery who has chosen the life of a hermit. My goodness, she spends hours and hours in intercessory prayer. She comes from your neck of the woods in Scotland."

"Where in Scotland?"

"The island of Cumbrae."

"That's where the Fisherfolk have their community," said Sharon.

"Yes, she was with them. But they have another name too though, don't they?"

"The Fisherfolk was what they called the music group," explained Sharon. "I think their real name was the Community of Celebration."

"Lord bless you! Yes, indeed! Sure now, she was with them. She came here for eight months, and then went back home, sold up her property, and is now based here indefinitely. There's another woman here who does the same thing. They take turns of five hours each in the church, praying for Israel. Strong intercessory prayer. Wonderful people."

— *Day 25—Politicking* —

Friday 1st November

ABU GHOSH IS SEVEN miles outside Jerusalem, and, as David Pileggi had discussed with us previously, close to the reputed site of the New Testament village of Emmaus. From childhood I had imagined Jesus walking to Emmaus along a road in a broad valley similar to the wide river valleys in the Scottish Borders where I grew up. But the landscape in Israel is of an entirely different type. Israel had no Ice-Age, with glaciers creating smooth glens flanked by rounded hills, and so the topography is not the same. Judaean hills are the result of geological rock-movements rather than glacial-scraping, and so there are few natural through-routes as in Scotland. In Judaea, a traveller has to walk over irregular, undulating countryside. Travelling the highways and byways in Jesus' day involved hard effort.

The bus coming from Jerusalem to pick us up was delayed, giving us an opportunity to wander in the monastery grounds. We spoke to the gardener who turned out to be a Welshman, Eddie. Some time ago, Eddie's wife wanted to come and help at the monastery for a few months. She served the meal last night. Eddie had taken early retirement from the motor-industry, and for most of the year he and his wife tour Britain and the continent in their campervan.

When the bus finally arrived we had to detour to a retreat center called Yad Hashmona to pick up an American group which was also on a Shoresh course. Many years ago, Yad Hashmona was founded by Finnish Bible believers who wanted to settle among the Jews and help build the nation. They were given land on long-term lease from the Israeli government, which was no mean feat. Eventually, some of the original founders had to go back to Finland for National Service, and the ones who were left invited Messianic believers to come and join them, so now the community is essentially a Messianic Jewish community. The buildings are in Finnish style, with high peaked roofs, and constructed out of Finnish pine-wood, a sharp contrast to the concrete and limestone used everywhere else in Judaea.

Gabi Barkay and the Tombs of Jerusalem

Today is the first of November, All Saints' Day, and an appropriate day on which to have a lecture about the dead. Our morning seminar was entitled 'Tombs and Graves in the First and Second Temple Period,' and the lecturer was Dr. Gabi Barkay who teaches archaeology at the University of Tel Aviv. Our two Shoresh groups crowded into the Christ Church dining-room, and we listened as Gabi strode back and forth. He talks with the terrific energy and enthusiasm which is characteristic of Jewish people. They are like wound-up springs, bursting with vitality.

"Why study tombs? Why do we study tombs?"

Gabi looked around the room, casting his eye over all of us.

"I will tell you the answer. We study tombs in order to understand the living! You see, what tombs contain, and the manner of their construction, reveals the concepts held important by the living society. Tombs mirror their society. A utilitarian society reflects this with a lack of aesthetics in their tombs. A society which values family life, expresses it by having family tombs. Another point: tombs are not renovated by succeeding generations. For example, look at this room here where we are. Now, this room will be repainted, replastered, windows changed, perhaps a wall taken down, and so on. A building we live in, we renovate. But tombs are not renovated, thus they capture and preserve the time of their building."

Gabi explained that there are hundreds of tombs around Jerusalem, from different stages of the city's history. Moreover, because the tombs in the Jerusalem area are hewn out of the rock, they have not been robbed of stone blocks to build other structures. Consequently, they are relatively intact.

"South of the Temple Mount is the City of David, the ancient core of the city," Gabi continued. "There we have a cemetery from between the ninth and seventh centuries BC. This is the Siloam Arab village of today, and these Arab houses have remarkable antiquities built into them. Until recently no archaeologist dared enter the village. A century ago Charles Warren described Siloam as a concentration of the worst of the villains in Palestine! But, in the wake of the Six-Day War, when the Arab population was in shock following the routing of the Arab armies, a full archaeological survey took place. This was from 1968 to 1970. Every home was visited. Each householder was given five dollars for permission to enter their house. What was found was that fifty of the houses were simply extensions of burial caves from the early period. These had 'tent-shaped' ceilings, and were cut perfectly out of the rock. Unfortunately, sewage from Siloam village is penetrating the bedrock and spoiling the remains. By the way, we found that the measurements used in these tombs were multiples of the Egyptian cubit, roughly 52.5 centimeters. And we found many examples of headrests for the deceased cut out of the living rock."

Gabi told us that north of the Damascus Gate is another huge burial place from the First Temple period, now part of the Franciscan School of Archaeology. Also, all along the Hinnom Valley, on the western and southern sides of Old Testament Jerusalem, are more than forty graves from the First Temple Period.

Gabi's walking pace and talking speed increased in tandem as he went deeper into his subject. Information and analysis poured out of him. Graves. Ossuaries. Second Temple Period. The unlikelihood of the Garden Tomb being the Tomb of Jesus. The strength of the claims of the Church of the Holy Sepulchre. To everything he brought passion, humour, and intellectual analysis. He made the dead live.

"Consider now the Garden Tomb site," he said. Then he thought for a moment before continuing, and told us the story of how the Garden Tomb cave was first discovered by a Greek Orthodox peasant in 1867 who was trying to dig a cistern. Later, a scholar discussed the cave in a British journal. Later still, in 1881, General Gordon (of Khartoum) came to Jerusalem for religious meditation and stayed with the American Stafford family next to the Damascus Gate. One day the General looked out of his window at the hill opposite the house. To him, the two caves in the hillside looked like eye sockets in a skull. He remembered that Calvary was also called Golgotha, the Skull. So he went to the hill, found the cave of the Greek peasant, and the legend was born.

"But, what you must realize is that burial caves of the Second Temple (New Testament) period appear in their hundreds all around Jerusalem, but the Garden Tomb cave is totally different," pointed out Gabi. "Think about it. The tomb of Jesus has to be in the style of 30AD because the New

Testament states it was a new tomb, made for Joseph of Arimathea. And any tomb of that era would have places for ossuaries and so on. But the Garden Tomb cave has none of these. It is a First Temple period tomb, not a Second Temple one."

Gabi expanded on this further. "General Gordon's alternative Calvary was attractive for many people. You see, Westerners did not feel at home in the Church of the Holy Sepulchre. To begin with, often the church was crowded with Russian pilgrims. Then there were monks fighting with each other over who controlled this bit or that bit of the church. Some argue that the Crimean War started over a dispute in the Church of the Holy Sepulchre! Westerners just didn't feel a sense of God there, and so they looked elsewhere for that sense of holiness, and the Garden Tomb site was the perfect answer. In addition, the Anglican Church had come late to the Holy Land and owned none of the traditional 'holy places.' So again, General Gordon's claims were enthusiastically welcomed."

"In the 1970s I did an archaeological investigation of the Garden Tomb, and the Colonel at the Garden Tomb was open-minded when I told him my conclusions. He said, 'It doesn't matter. What matters is that Christ is risen.' This touched me deeply."

The Colonel in question was Colonel Orde Dobbie, later describe by David Pileggi as "A great man with Scottish ancestry." He was a member of Christ Church with his wife Flo while living in Jerusalem during the 1970s and 80s.

Gabi then discussed issues surrounding the Church of the Holy Sepulchre. Was the present site of the church inside or outside the walls of Jerusalem during the first-century? Gabi is convinced it was outside the walls, and backed up his argument with a little known detail. In the church, he told us, there is a neglected corner which belongs to the Syrian Orthodox Community: and, in this corner, there is a rock-hewn cave which is a perfect example of a Second Temple tomb of the first century. Gabi's point is that, by Jewish Law, there had to be fifty cubits between the last house of the city and the first tomb of any burial site. Therefore, that tomb was outside the city walls at that time. Therefore, the site now occupied by the Church of the Holy Sepulchre was outside the walls in Jesus' time. The city wall at that time was what we now call the Second Wall, as described by Flavius Josephus.

Gabi was quite definite. "Archaeologists have no objections to accepting the site of the Holy Sepulchre. Remember, the existence of ossuary niches in the Church of the Holy Sepulchre proves that it was outside the walls of the city."

IN THE AFTERNOON WE accompanied the American group to the Holy Land Hotel which has a massive model of first-century Jerusalem laid out in the hotel grounds. The bus was modern and luxurious, with TV and sophisticated air-conditioning. The driver had a necklace with an attached cross draped over his mirror. Beside him, near the bus door, was a small container of holy water.

When we returned to Abu Ghosh Sister Catherine was keenly interested in what we had been doing, and we told her about the lecture.

"Lord bless him! Oh yes! We know Gabi very well. He did the dig out here at the monastery when the antiquities people came. He is a lovely man. Archaeology is everything to him. But he is under a lot of pressure just now. Lord bless him! I was in his house once. It is a beautiful house, but there are no archaeological artefacts in it at all. Quite amazing considering that he eats, drinks, and lives archaeology all day long."

Oded Yinon and Middle East Politics

In the evening we joined with the American group, this time for a political lecture from Oded Yinon, a journalist from the *Jerusalem Post*. Oded lectures army units about the contemporary political outlook, and he pulled no punches as he outlined his belief that the situation is bleak becoming bleaker, that it always had been, and that it always will be. Oded lectured at a galloping pace. If Gabi Barkay was fast, Oded Yinon was supersonic.

"How does Israel survive?" This was his opening question. "We survive by evading the real issues. That is how we survive. Tomorrow is the second of November. It was the second of November when the British Empire decided to give the Jews a national home. Thank you very much!" He nodded to us—the British contingent—as if we had been personally responsible! Then he continued. "The Jews do not celebrate it. But the Arabs always remember it. They remember it with resentment and with hatred."

"Foreign aid gives a lot of wealth to Israel, but most Jews are unaware of the part non-Jews took in creating the nation. We are encouraged to believe that we did it all by ourselves. And this lack of awareness creates its own problems."

"Israel is a small country, but its problems are huge, and will remain so as long as the country lasts. Israel is 81 percent Jewish. It is the only Jewish country in the world, and therefore unique. Christians in the Middle East are a fading race. Islam and Judaism are the power religions. Christians have fled from Lebanon. Christians in Egypt are insignificant. Armenia is Christian, but there are only two million of them, and they have their own problems, huge problems. Therefore, Israel is the only non-Islamic enclave in the region. The prophets of modern Zionism never foresaw this problem."

"There exist many links between Judaism and Christianity, but none between Judaism and Islam. Islam is in trouble because its people are poor, very poor. Ninety-nine percent of Muslims are on the poverty line. David Ben Gurion understood that, whatever peace Israel may have with the Arab world, Israel must really look for stable relationships elsewhere."

"Israel is poor in natural resources. It has no oil. It has little fertile land. It has only eight and a half million people. And 70 percent of Israel is empty desert. The Middle East is the poorest region on earth apart from Africa, and yet it accounts for 50 percent of the world's arms sales."

"The USA is a pragmatic economy, and we cannot assume they will buy out of goodwill. The UK is friendly. France is uncertain. So Yitzak Rabin was looking for some sort of economic escape by making peace with the big four nations on Israel's borders. But Syria and Saudi Arabia are uneasy neighbors. And Jordan and Egypt are too poor to buy much from Israel. Therefore, in terms of contact with Muslim nations, the only economic path is to trade with the Far-East Islamic countries. This was the real economic goal of the Peace Process, the opening up of trade with the Far East. The biggest gain of the Peace Process is not Israel's relationships with its immediate neighbors, but with the Far East Islamic countries. You see, without the Peace Process these powers would not trade with Israel, because their first loyalty is to show solidarity with Islam."

Looking round, I saw varied reactions etched on the faces of Oded's listeners. Some were nodding. Some looked confused. Some looked anxious. Most were scribbling notes furiously, as I was myself. And Oded had much more to say.

"Israel needs a big economy to maintain a big army. But the USA will not give money for ever. We have to make money all the time in order to maintain our defence. We are a totally abnormal country because we have only six million available Jewish people to do all this."

"There are less than thirteen million Jews on earth, and it is a decreasing number. In the next century few Jews will live outside of Israel. Already 65 percent of all Jews are born in Israel. In Israel three children are born to each family, whereas in Jewish families in the USA the average is one child."

Oded was interrupted by one of the American ladies. "Hold on, in New York City there are as many Jews as in Israel!"

"No. You are wrong," replied Oded. "In the USA there are one million Orthodox Jews. Now, there are claimed to be five million Reform Jews in the USA, but more than 50 percent of Reform Jews in the USA assimilate into non-Jewish families. I have the facts here! The official figures!" Oded jabbed his forefinger at a pile of papers.

"I must tell you that Rabin and Netanyahu really follow the same policies. This is because policy is not determined by politicians or elections. Policy is determined by the Army. Existence and survival are the policy. Existence and survival. Just now Egypt and Syria are ready for war. For us, peace is a period between wars. Henry Kissinger once said, 'Israel is an abnormal people: when they go to war, they go to war from a state of war!' He was correct. Arafat, Mubarak, and Assad make Israel deploy its army all over the nation, wondering what is going to happen. Arafat controls everything just now. The fall of the USSR scared the Arab world. They were shocked by the possibility of powerful regimes being dethroned so quickly. But Arab Sheiks will never be dethroned."

Another American broke in. "But many Arab states are unstable with internal problems. They are falling apart."

Oded shook his head vigorously. "We fool ourselves! Look, an Israeli earns twenty-five times an Egyptian's salary: yet in Egypt the fundamentalists, who complain about many things, never have to complain about food. Mubarak ensures that food is supplied. Similarly, Saudis and Kuwaitis do not need to work: they are subsidized by rich oil Sheiks. Turkish citizens earn four thousand dollars a year, whereas Iranians earn only four hundred dollars, but Iranians do not rebel, and they do not rebel because they are an Islamic nation. The regimes are not helpful to their own people. And the regimes are always ready to go to war. But the people will never rebel. No popular rising will ever overthrow the power structures of Islamic nations. They have food for their daily needs. They have a cohesive religion. And they have a cohesive hatred of the evil enemy of Israel."

"Mubarak, Assad, and Arafat are popular because they speak of the possibility of war against Israel. The Islamic peoples profoundly hate Israel and the USA and so the regimes are secure. The Arab regimes cannot allow Americanization to happen as that would undermine them. So the Saudis keep the US forces far away from the native population, and they shoot US soldiers who mix with locals. Iran cuts out satellite TV channels and the Internet. Liberal people in the Arab world are killed. Fundamentalists support Arafat so long as he fights Israel. He knows that. And the moment he makes real peace with Israel he is finished."

I interrupted. "But there were food riots in Jordan earlier this year!"

"These riots were a blip. They were localized in Kerak. And they meant nothing. King Hussein altered the subsidy levels, but blame was diverted elsewhere, and the people now get plenty of bread. Saudis do not care that the USA saved them in 1991 in the Gulf War. In the Arab world the USA has no friends. The only friend it has in the Middle East is Israel, therefore the USA will continue to pour money into Israel."

"The Arabs believe that because they are so big they will win eventually. Israel has the smallest standing army in the region, but our whole nation is a shadow army. The problem is that no Intelligence Services on earth knows what the likes of Saddam or Assad have in mind, because they do not even tell their own generals. We saw this with Saddam's invasion of Kuwait. Now, let me tell you something: since August Assad has been moving his forces twenty-four hours a day. Why? No one knows."

Oded paused, looked at us, and smiled.

"Let me ask you a question. Why did Israel hand back the Sinai?"

"As a movement towards peace?"

"Rubbish! That's what Western liberals want to be the truth! No. Our former Prime Minister Menachin Begin gave Sinai back to Egypt simply because Israel could not afford to keep the Sinai! It had nothing to do with peace and goodwill. The Army told Begin that there were not enough soldiers to occupy the Sinai. In 1973 the cost of the War for Israel was not in human casualties, but in the economy. President Nixon saved Israel economically in 1973, and so Nixon is like a god in Israel. The USA makes up the difference that Israel cannot bridge with its own Gross National Product."

"Modern Israel has no ideology, just practicalities. David Ben Gurion killed ideology in 1948. What works wins! Practicalities mean that Israeli pilots are trained in Orlando. Practicalities mean that Israel no longer specializes in manufacturing tanks, planes, or guns. Following

President Reagan's advice, Israel has switched to high-tech industries. So Israel makes software for USA hardware, and US dollars enable Israel to survive."

Oded paused again. "Let me ask you another question. Why does the USA do this? Why does it support Israel?"

"Because of the powerful Jewish lobby?"

"Only partly. The reason is that, for the USA, Israel is a bulwark preventing a pan-Arab War which would be disastrous in terms of oil supplies for the rest of the world. If Israel collapses the Middle East will be like Afghanistan writ large. The surrounding countries will tear themselves apart over the spoils. And who would then emerge as the supreme power in the whole area? No one knows? USA AWACS reconnaissance planes guarded Israel in September during the time of the riots sparked off by the tunnel. For the Arabs, the USA is the worst evil on the face of the earth."

"King Hussein of Jordan has a country poor in natural resources. He also cannot survive without American money, and is vulnerable to American pressure, although in public he must always appear to be a man of independent mind."

"What pressures clinched the Peace Process? The USA said that if there were no peace treaties with neighboring countries Israel was on its own. Significantly, the peace treaties are counter-signed by the USA Congress, who have guaranteed to give help in the first twenty-four hours of a war. On the macro level, Jordan and the Palestinians gain little from the peace treaties. Jordan is nothing. The big military gain for Israel is that, under the terms of the peace treaties, Israel now has a corridor through Jordan to Iran or Iraq in the event of war. At present Jordan gives Israel a forty-eight-hour barrier with these nations. But the Sinai only gives a twenty-four-hour barrier with Egypt, and the Golan gives no buffer zone with Syria."

"Syria is a rough country, with a bad regime and a big army. In October 1973 the Israeli regular army could not withstand the weight of the Syrian army. They were outnumbered ten to one. Eventually Israel has to withdraw from the Golan. Everyone knows that."

Another of the Americans spoke up. "Surely the Peace Process can still be built on? Surely that is the way forward?"

Oded shrugged. "My friend, the Peace Process was effectually killed by the four bus bombs earlier this year. These bombs eliminated Shimon Peres as a politician. Let me tell you, Israel has started building a

Super-Highway from the north to the south of the country ready for war. Planes will be able to land on this Super-Highway. Troops can move at great speed up and down it. It is a vast project. Its purpose is to provide for the possibility of total war involving the whole populace. It will be a short war, but a total war. Then back to work!"

ODED PAUSED FOR A moment for a drink of water, and the room buzzed with talk as we turned to one another and tried to think through the implications of what he was arguing. If his analysis were true, then things are truly bleak. But then, he is a journalist! Oded restarted, focusing on the Palestinian issue.

"The Palestinians and the Jews hate each other. It is as simple as that. Yitzak Rabin did not make peace; he made total separation. Something had to be done with two and a half million Palestinians, but the peace treaties were going to provide them with only 5 percent of the territories. This has increased to 22 percent of the territories, but Arafat wants 100 percent of the territories."

"No Israeli government will ever grant a full Palestinian State. Why? Because a full State would have tanks, an army, and an air force. For that reason, the other Arab countries do not want a Palestinian State either. If Arafat had an airfield he would fly in arms and tanks, as the Israelis did in 1948 under their deal with Stalin. And so a real Palestinian State will never exist because Israel would never allow a Palestinian State with an army."

"Arafat wants his people to be either in the police or unemployed. If they are in his police, that gives him muscle power. If they are un-employed and poor, that gives him international political leverage. He has twenty-seven thousand police and 60 percent unemployment. A real Palestinian State would be very rich because Palestinians are clever and hardworking. But Arafat does not want stability. Stability means no more ambition. And other Arab states cannot afford to have a Palestinian State because it would be rich and they would have to reform to make their people the same. At the moment no one needs the Palestinians in Israel. There are plenty of Eastern Europeans and Filipinos to do work. So the Palestinians get poorer and poorer."

"In September Netanyahu gave the Palestinians and the Arabs an excuse to make a fuss when he opened the tunnel exit. Rabin and Peres would not have given them an excuse to riot. We have a saying 'If Netan-yahu can become Prime-Minister, anyone can be Prime-Minister.' Arabs do not want Israel to have one day of peace, because if Israel had real peace she could grow as a nation."

"Israelis are divided fifty-fifty on the Peace Process. There will be no more peace deals until the end of the century. The only real success of the Peace Process is that Arab Israelis are happy. But Arafat wants them to become unsettled, and so he will work towards that discontent. From our viewpoint it is good that Jordan wants Jerusalem, because King Hussein can struggle with Arafat. No one really cares about anyone else's 'rights.' 'Rights' are Western concepts from a Western philosophy. In the Middle East the significant word is 'Power.'"

"Assad of Syria has had three wars against Israel: 1967, 1973, and 1982. Each of them has been unsuccessful, and so Assad cannot make peace with Israel for the shame of it. Rationality is not the major factor in politics. Shame, loss of face, pride, are much more powerful. Arafat is sixty years old now, and he does not care what happens after him. Yet, if he dies, the internal strife within the PLO will make things even more difficult for Israel because of two factors. First, lack of central leadership creates splinter groups each with their own agenda. Second, aspiring Palestinian leaders would want to 'prove themselves' by conducting terrorist activities against Israel on a massive scale."

"Arafat does what he wants. Totally. He imprisons people. He tortures people. He keeps his people poverty stricken. Israel gives him millions of dollars a year for development, but where does it go? Any Palestinian who cooperates with Israel is eliminated. No one knows where the money goes that Arafat gets, but he has an enormous armed police force. You can answer the question yourself. Why does the USA prop up Israel? For justice? No! For sentimentality? No! Simply for economics. The USA wants Israel to be a pin-cushion to stop Arabs fighting each other, because if the Arab countries fought each other the oil would be cut off."

"The Golan as it stands just now is not a good buffer. It provides a border only twenty kilometers from populated areas. The Super-Highway will be finished in the year 2000 and Israel will hold on to the Golan until at least that date. But Assad knows that when the Super-Highway is finished then the Israeli nation is ready for war, because tanks can move at great pace from one end of the country to the other. That was why Hitler built the autobahns. Thus Assad has to strike before then. At the other end of the country the Sinai is simply to be a killing area in the event of war. Assad does not want to accept the Golan Heights back, because if he does then he has to make peace. If he accepts the Golan Heights back, he has no excuse for war and he has no grievance to air in the International Community. Benjamin Netanyahu did not understand this before he became Prime Minister."

"What kind of Israel will exist in the future? I do not know. Do Israelis have an identity? 80 percent of Jews are secular. 20 percent are religious. Jews are further divided by being Zionist, or Liberal, or Conservative. There is a real problem of Israeli identity."

"The Hebron problem is a big problem. In the Old Testament there were Jews in Hebron before there were Jews in Jerusalem and so Jewish roots in Hebron are very deep, therefore how can they give it away? But eventually they will have to, because that is what the Oslo agreements say. Half the Jews in Hebron are Americans, and most American Jews who come here are religious and extreme. They fly in from Brooklyn to make a statement by settling in Hebron, and open their windows in the morning and say, 'What are one hundred thousand Arabs doing here!'"

"In my view the blockades of the territories are stupid. They cause resentment. And they will never catch any real terrorist. Soldiers at checkpoints are stupid. Some are only eighteen years old and have no sense. Some checkpoint soldiers even turn back hospital cases and people die. The government is stupid and politically naive to have these closures. Islam regards itself as the last and true message. So Islam need not, must not, cannot, and will not listen to anyone. Islam must dominate."

Tony interrupted. "But the Kurds want to give up Islam. This creates opportunities for evangelism."

Oded replied. "You do not underestimate the impossibility of rebellion and revolt in the Islamic countries. No popular movements can survive. The only future is one in which power balances power, with war every so often."

ODED FINISHED HIS PRESENTATION, and a vigorous debate started, but we had to leave to get back to Abu Ghosh The minibus took half our party, and the rest of us started walking, enjoying the cooler night air. Three Alsatian dogs on the other side of the road started following and growling. We quickened our pace. David met us in the minibus, and a police-car hooted when he did a U-turn to pick us up. Was the future for Israel and the Middle East as dark as the heavens above us? Or did Oded's analysis leave out another factor: the wind of the Spirit?

— Day 26 — Celebrating —

Saturday 2nd November

TODAY WAS MY LAST day with the Study Group before joining the Bike Ride, and I am conscious of how unfit I've become, having not cycled for weeks. Hopefully, the hill-walking and road-cycling which I did earlier in the summer will see me through. This morning, the Study Tour continued, but David Pileggi rearranged the programme so that I miss as little of the course as possible. The others go on until next Thursday. Early morning, the bus took us into Jerusalem, and inside the Jaffa Gate were gatherings of young men standing around looking menacing. Most were drinking beer, and empty beer cans littered the area. David said that they were immigrant workers from Eastern Europe, many from Romania. On Shabbat they are at a loose end and can be a big problem.

Today we toured 'Holy Sites', but, instead of getting a tourist guide's account, David gave us his unique analyses. Our first stop was the Zion Gate on the south-western corner of the Old City walls. The stonework is pitted with bullet holes, made in 1948 during the War of Independence, and also in 1967 during the Six-Day War when Israeli soldiers led by Ofer Amitai's father stormed the Old City.

"Shoresh, the Zion Gate is so-called because it is on what is now called Mount Zion," David explained. "But this is not the Mount Zion of King David's day. The original Mount Zion is nearer Siloam village; but because this is the highest point of the area, the Byzantines thought it must be the real Mount Zion, and the misnomer has stuck!"

Nearby, we saw several significant buildings such as the Church of the Dormition, associated in Catholic tradition with the Virgin Mary. There is also the reputed site of the Upper Room, and the supposed site of King David's Tomb. But David allowed no mythologies: "Shoresh, re-member, Mount Zion is not the real Mount Zion. The Upper Room is not the real Upper Room: it is a later building built on or around where the original Upper Room must have been. The Tomb of David is not the real tomb of David: the real one is probably in the lower city. And the Church of the Dormition is not built where Mary died. However, these locations can be useful starting points for discussion."

The Upper Room

We made our way to the building commonly revered as the Upper Room where Jesus and the disciples had the Last Supper. The present site has a long, complicated history, and Christians since the Byzantine period have chosen this as the location where the Last Supper took place, where the Resurrection Appearances occurred, and where the Holy Spirit came in power at Pentecost. The room we entered was, in fact, built in the fourteenth century by Franciscans from Cyprus, after which it was briefly taken over by Muslims. Set into one wall is a prayer-niche directed towards Mecca.

Tony had a suggestion. "David, some people think that the events of Pentecost happened in the Temple Courtyard, and that was why so many outsiders saw what was happening?"

David thought about Tony's idea. "Well, that could be. But the book of Acts mentions 'the whole *house* in which they were sitting.' A *house* not a space. Again, remember that in Scripture we deal with compressed accounts, and so locations can change without us being told explicitly. Scripture is unclear as to whether the same location is being referred to for the events of the Last Supper, the Resurrection Appearances, and Pentecost. Personally, I think it reasonable to assume that the three events took place in the same setting, but perhaps not."

David then took us to a quiet corner of the Upper Room. "OK Shoresh, let's think about the Last Supper. OK, this room is not the origi-nal Upper Room, but it would be somewhere near here, in what was a wealthy, upper-class, closed compound in the time of Jesus. We know from the Gospels that Jesus had rich friends. Now, the Last Supper started out as a Jewish Passover. But a Jewish Passover was not a men's club, and so, at Jesus' Last Supper it is highly likely that as well as the disciples be-ing present, so were their families. It was a community event. When the bread was broken and the wine was shared, the whole fledgling believing community took part, not just the especially initiated."

"Now, move on to Pentecost and the giving of the Spirit. The Qumran Community taught that a full, sudden onslaught of the Spirit comes with the Messiah. But Jesus does not fully accept this idea. During Jesus' ministry the Spirit breaks in continually and progressively as the Divine voice. This happens at his Baptism, at the Transfiguration, and so on, although the complete coming of the Spirit is at Pentecost, after the Easter events."

"Now, when Luke comes to write his account of Pentecost he has parallels with the giving of the Law at Sinai in mind. In the Jewish calendar Pentecost is the birthday of the giving of the Law fifty days after the Israelites leave Egypt, fifty days therefore after Passover. According to Jewish Midrash, when God speaks from Sinai he speaks with one voice but in seventy languages. Seventy signifies completeness. Thus 'seventy languages' signifies that everyone on earth has heard. This is why Paul, in Romans chapter one, says that everyone is without excuse because all have 'heard' the Law. On the day of Pentecost, God visits His people and they speak out in the languages of the world, and three thousand are added to the Church. That mirrors the three thousand who were slain in the rebellion at Sinai. So, in the Pentecost narrative, Luke is giving an extended parallel with the Old Testament. This is the Rabbinic method."

David paused. "Shoresh, there's an important theological point not to miss. The giving of the Spirit introduces the concept of the Trinity into the New Testament. Now, for Jews, the doctrine of the Trinity is not only a problem of *logic*, but a problem of *attitude*. For a Jew, the doctrine appears to define God too much, and a characteristic of Jewish Midrash is that it always leaves loose ends without pushing logic all the way. This is the Jewish way. Things are *hinted-at,* they are not *defined.* Or, as Joseph Francovic would say, 'The timber is there but it is not always used to build.' This is why Jesus used parables. Parables draw a line beyond which rationalising stops, and loose ends are deliberately kept."

"But, Shoresh, don't make the mistake some Christians make of assuming that every Jewish practice they discover today puts them in touch with the customs of biblical times. Jews, like Christians, have picked up things along the way and have added these to their theology and practice. For example, various types of mysticism and magic have been incorporated into modern Judaism. Not everything Jewish is biblical."

WE MOVED DOWNSTAIRS FROM the Upper Room to the alleged Tomb of King David. Both Peter—in his sermon in Acts chapter 2—and Josephus mention David's Tomb as being in the City, but its exact location was only linked with this particular site in the tenth century AD. Contrary to normal practice, tombs of Kings were allowed to be inside the city walls as unique exceptions, and although most scholars suspect that this 'Tomb of David' is in fact the grave of a Muslim holy man, it *became* a holy place for Jews, and so we had to wear head-coverings. A man by the door handed out white paper kippurs.

Today being Shabbat, we saw several people engaged in Torah study, both in the ante-chamber and in the room containing the Tomb itself. In the ante-chamber a young man sat with his back to the window and a prayer-shawl over his head, fingering beads while reading his Hebrew scriptures. Beside the red velvet covered Tomb stood another man who gazed straight ahead, rocking as he recited his prayers. Another figure, a Hasidic Jew with a large flat fur hat, was seated at a table reading Hebrew texts.

The Calvary Tomb

Leaving the Upper Room buildings, we made our way through the Jewish Quarter to the Souk, and from there to the Church of the Holy Sepulchre, that ever-entrancing cornucopia of historical and theological delights. David's daughter was with us, and as we walked through the meat-market she averted her eyes from the severed sheep heads, and covered her nose to cut out the smell of blood and carcasses. After negotiating a labyrinth of lanes, David brought us onto the roof of the church, beside the cells of the Orthodox Ethiopian Coptic monks.

Nearly all scholars, Jewish and Christian, ecclesiastical and secular, agree that the Church of the Holy Sepulchre marks where Jesus was actually crucified. In the first century, crucifixion was a daily Jewish experience, and David reflected on Jesus' crucifixion as a deep identification with his people, sharing the fate suffered by so many. The Romans crucified people all over the Empire, not just in Israel, but Jews in Israel were especially aware of it because no other nation kept producing so many rebels, and malefactors and insurgents were crucified every day. The cross became so deeply identified with Jewish misery under the Romans, that it is deeply ironic that modern Jews now regard it as a sign of their suffering under Christian persecution rather than as a sign of solidarity with them.

In Galilee, in Roman times, the road from Sepphoris to Tiberias was lined with crosses. It was the same at Jerusalem. Where Jesus was crucified there would have been a line of crosses, though Scripture only mentions his cross and the ones directly on either side, to which two thieves were nailed. The uprights for crosses were permanently in position outside the city gate beside the highway, so what Jesus carried to Calvary would be the cross-beam of his cross. Crucifixion involved humiliation as well as agony. People were crucified naked. This was shameful to Jews. The only dilution of this shame was that women were crucified backwards."

"Jesus kept teaching right up until the last second of His life," David commented. "Luke tells us that the people who lined the route were weeping and wailing as Jesus stumbled past, and they cried out 'How long? How Long!' What Jesus said in reply was, 'Look, it's going to be much worse for you! If this is what happens when the wood is green, how much more when the wood is dry.' The grammatical structure used here is called a *kal va-chomer*, or a 'how much more.' Jesus was hinting at verses in Ezekiel which point to God bringing the hot fire of judgment, because in Ezekiel the green wood symbolizes the righteous, and the dry wood symbolizes the wicked."

FROM THE ROOF OF the church we entered the Ethiopian Chapel where a monk read the account of the Ethiopian Eunuch being converted. These monks are extremely poor and David encouraged us to contribute to their alms dish.

"Shoresh, the Ethiopian Church is remarkable. The Ethiopian commentaries on the Bible were passed on purely by oral tradition from the fourth century to the eighteenth century. At that point they were translated, written down, and made accessible by European missionaries. So, if you ever doubt the ability of oral tradition to preserve continuity, think again. By the way, these Ethiopian Christians incorporate a lot of Jewish things into their faith like circumcision."

WE MOVED DOWN TO the church courtyard, and into the Church of the Holy Sepulchre itself. David took us to the usual points of interest, and then to an isolated area behind the officially recognized tomb of Jesus. On the way we passed a long, silent, double-line of pilgrims waiting in the half-darkness to enter the sepulchre cave. One man, trying to light a candle, had set alight six large bundles of tapers, and was waving them in the air trying, ineffectually, to extinguish them. His wife came to the rescue. She was far more practical than her husband. She took the bundles from her panicking spouse and used the base of one bundle to smother the flames of the other five bundles and then stubbed the sixth out on the wall.

David took us to the spot Gabi Barkay told us about yesterday, the place where there are definite first-century tombs within the Church of the Holy Sepulchre. Once we had all arrived, David started his commentary.

"Shoresh, here we are. Now, to begin with, why are we so sure that this church is where Calvary was? Four reasons. First, Jewish Christians lived in Jerusalem right from the first century, and it was widely known—with no break in the chain of tradition—where Calvary was. Second, when Hadrian built pagan temples on Jewish holy sites he built a temple to Aphrodite here. Hadrian saw Judaism and Christianity as two sides of the same coin, and he knew this site was revered by believers, so he wanted to desecrate it. Third, when Christianity became legal and official in 313AD, Helena, the mother of Constantine, came to Jerusalem and all the local people told her this was the place. Fourth, there has never been any second site with a serious claim. So this is definitely the site of Calvary. But is it the site of the Empty Tomb? I am not so sure. OK, the Bible does say that the garden where Jesus was buried was close by, and we do have genuine first-century burial places here. But they are perhaps too near to the site of the crucifixion—only thirty or forty yards away—maybe too close. Anyway, this church is misnamed. It should not be called the Church of the Holy *Sepulchre*; it should be the Church of the *Resurrection!*"

We took turns going into the tomb. Inside was a space with two chambers. A small boy with a candle also came, lighting his candle in front of the burial chambers before entering reverently.

The Mount of Olives

After the Church of the Holy Sepulchre, we walked back to Christ Church and grabbed some lunch before meeting with Claire Pfann, who had talked to us on the theme 'Who is my Brother.' Claire gave another lecture, again at machine-gun speed. This one was on 'Angels in the Second Temple Period.' David Pileggi was cramming stuff in on my last day! The rest of the group will have a much lighter schedule in their last few days.

After Claire's artillery bombardment on the subject of Angels, David piled us into taxis and took us to the top of the Mount of Olives. There was confusion about the taxis. First we were directed to one. Then to another. Then the first taxi sped away with half the group and we were left behind. When we did get going, our driver stopped outside the New Gate in order to deliver stuff to his brother who works nearby. He dilly-dallied, so I told him that our friends would be waiting for us and that the afternoon daylight would fade soon. He shrugged his shoulders, but got back into the car and drove down to Gethsemane, then took the taxi up the narrow street that descends the Mount of Olives past Dominus Flevit Church. I had never seen a car in this narrow, high-walled street before, but our driver roared up the hill with his foot flat to the floor and pedestrians scattering in front of us. Some flung themselves against the wall! Others dived for the safety of the Jewish Cemetery! I was in the front of the taxi, all too aware that we were approaching each blind corner oblivious to what might be round it. Thankfully we shot out at the top without mishap, and bounced onto the roadway near where the others waited for us.

JERUSALEM FROM THE MOUNT of Olives is one of the scenic-wonders of the world. David pointed out significant buildings, reflecting on the political and religious history of the city. Below us, on the lower slopes of the Mount of Olives is a massive Jewish cemetery. The newspaper mogul Robert Maxwell is buried somewhere among its vast array of white, flat, limestone graves, each marked with white stones inscribed in Hebrew. Here and there we could see black boxes which store candles for those who want to light a flame for a loved one. When Robert Maxwell's son, Kevin, came back to find his father's grave last year, he struggled to find it because the place is enormous.

Day after day the sun shines down on this cemetery out of a blue sky. Because the stones are white and bright, and, because flat stones lying on the ground do not cast shadows like upright ones, the hillside is free of some of the morbid qualities which a Scottish graveyard, full of grey gravestones, and overarched by a grey sky, often has. But in Israel, white is the color of death.

We wandered down the hill. We visited the Church of Dominus Flevit. We had another look at the Garden of Gethsemane. David reminded us that Titus cut down every green and living thing for miles around Jerusalem when he besieged it forty years after Jesus' crucifixion, so there is little chance that any of the trees now growing in the Garden were there in Jesus' time. We then strolled back to Christ Church following the outside of the city wall, from where it was back to Abu Ghosh by bus.

Ben Yehuda Street

Tonight was our last evening together, so we all went to Ben Yehuda Street. David Pileggi overheard our plans so he made bus arrangements for us. David has been thoughtful all during the Study Tour, and tonight's provision of transport is another example of his helpfulness. He did not need to provide the bus, but he wanted to.

Ben Yehuda Street was crowded, noisy, and mobbed with people in happy, carnival mood. I had a cassette-tape of Scottish dance music, and we looked for a musician using a portable amplifier which might play the tape. The 'Sonny and Cher' duo were there again, with a huge crowd around them. Further up the street a man was playing his accordion, though with no one listening. He did have an amplifier, but it couldn't take a tape.

The accordionist spoke little English, but we explained to him that we wanted to do some Scottish dancing. We had dared ourselves to do this. So he struck up a lively Jewish tune, and we danced the Dashing White Sergeant in the middle of Ben Yehuda Street, as David Veness waved the Lion Rampant in the air. The crowds left 'Sonny and Cher' in hoards to see this new phenomenon! They clapped to the music. Some joined in, with dance steps becoming a hybrid between Scottish Country Dancing and Hebrew Folk Dance. Ben Yehuda Street has a marked slope, and the dance took toll of our energy. But there was no stopping until we had added the Gay Gordons to the Dashing White Sergeant.

AFTER THE DANCING WE found a pavement café, and Sharon treated us to bumper ice-creams and Knickerbocker Glories. After Sharon sorted out the payment, complicated by the fact that two different waitresses served us, we started to leave. Then a woman ran after us.

"Wait! Wait! Please wait!"

We stopped and paused till she caught up.

"Excuse me! Did you do the dancing?"

"Yes."

"We saw the crowd, and we asked people what it was and they said there were people from Scotland dancing."

The lady came from Ayrshire and was in the Holy Land studying at the Bethlehem Bible Institute. Then a young Jewish girl came up to us and said it was her friend's birthday and would we dance again. But we were on our way back to the bus, so she was happy with a photograph.

— Day 27 — Transferring —

Sunday 3rd November

THIS MORNING I LEFT the Study Group. Having spent four weeks with them, it was hard to say farewell. At breakfast we prayed together, and James laid his hands on my shoulders as he prayed. I was grateful to James for doing this. We all then travelled into Jerusalem and I got off at the Central Bus Station, carrying my large rucksack and holdall, plus camera case and golf club. James took my other rucksack, full of excess luggage not required during the Bike Ride week, with the plan of leaving it at Christ Church to be collected by me on my return from Jordan and Sinai. Although I got off the minibus directly opposite the Central Bus Station it took some time to cross the road because large safety-barriers blocked the way. In the end, heavily laden, I found a crossing point further down the hill.

The Central Bus Station was a clamour of noise and filled with masses of people. I pushed my way through the melee to the Enquiries Office where an apathetic assistant redirected me to the ticket office for Tiberias.

"Excuse me, how much is a ticket to Tiberias?"

"Thirty-four shekels, and a bus leaves in ten minutes."

Clutching my ticket, I shoved through the crowds and found the correct platform, where a long double-file of young Israeli soldiers, both men and women, were boarding the Tiberias bus. I joined the queue, but when I got onto the bus, the bus-driver, leaning lethargically on the steering wheel, stopped me.

"Your bags must go in the baggage hold."

"Where is that?"

"Underneath the bus."

I had to get off, go round to the side of the bus, open the hold, and push my rucksack and holdall inside. No one supervised this, which was extraordinary, given the bus bombs which exploded in Jerusalem earlier in the year. Here was a bus, full of Israeli soldiers, and anyone could push a rucksack, possibly containing a bomb, into the hold, timed to go off *en route*. The realization made me feel a bit vulnerable. This bus, and other buses, were prime targets for extremists. I thought about the elaborate security checks at Tel Aviv airport and on El Al airlines, contrasting it with a total lack of security for a vehicle carrying dozens of army personnel. It made no sense.

The West Bank

The bus moved off as soon as I took my seat, and, as we travelled through the Jerusalem streets, I looked at my fellow passengers. Apart from a handful of civilians all of them were young, dark-haired, tanned, uniformed men and women, who were rejoining their army units after a weekend and Shabbat in Jerusalem. Perhaps they had been in Ben Yehuda Street last night.

We traveled down the Jericho road, passing the 'Sea Level' notice on the way, skirting Jericho on the bypass, before travelling north through the West Bank, covering in reverse the route we cycled on the Bike Rides of 1994 and 1995. Every so often the bus stopped on remote stretches of road and one or two of the soldiers disembarked and made their way to isolated army guard bases. We passed the Peza'el Crocodile Farm, visited on the Bike Rides. Then we made a major detour from the main route deeper into West Bank territory, past more refugee villages, before rejoining the main highway further on.

A few miles short of Bet She'an the driver stopped the bus at a roadside cafe and everyone got off. I didn't buy anything because my supply of shekels was running low, though I could have done with something to drink because the heat was intense. No one gave a signal to reboard. The driver did not even bother to give a warning 'toot!' on the bus horn. He simply took his seat, started the engine, and off we went. Not all the soldiers were back on the bus, but the ones who had returned were unconcerned at the absence of their fellow travellers. Presumably those left behind meant to be left.

WE PASSED BET SHE'AN, and continued north towards the Sea of Galilee. Tomorrow I will be covering this section of the route on my bike on our southward journey, and have now travelled it so often that I am beginning to recognize individual fields and plantations. In one field a farmer carried a bundle of irrigation pipes on his shoulders. The sowing season has begun.

At Zemah Junction, where the road which circles the Sea of Galilee meets the main highway from the south, all the remaining soldiers got off and only a few passengers remained. Soon we were in Tiberias. White taxis were parked at the Bus Station, and I approached a driver.

"Excuse me. How much to take me to Kibbutz Ginnosar?"

"Thirty-five shekels, sir."

I looked at the change left in my wallet. The taxi fare for the five miles from Tiberias to Ginnosar was going to be more than the bus fare from Jerusalem to Tiberias.

"Look, I don't have enough shekels. Would twenty be enough?"

He said nothing, simply shrugged his shoulders, shook his head and turned away. I rummaged deeper in my wallet and found some British money.

"Will you take this five-pound-note as equivalent to twenty shekels? If you do, I have enough shekels to make up the rest."

The taxi driver shrugged his shoulders again, but this time followed it with a nod. Soon we were moving through the Tiberias traffic on the road to Ginnosar. When we turned into the kibbutz we saw loads of bikes leaning against buildings, and loads of people in yellow Bike Ride T-shirts. I got out, paid the driver, and made my way to reception.

The Bike Riders

Most of the Bike Riders were having lunch in the kibbutz dining-room, having arrived in Israel on the overnight flight from Heathrow. Most had not slept a wink for the past twenty-four hours. After lunch we set off in buses to see Capernaum and Tabgha before driving up to Nazareth to visit the hospital for which we are all raising money. At Capernaum we met Chaim who has been the chief Israeli cycling guide for the past three years, and I was taken aback to see him leaning on two crutches.

"What's happened Chaim?"

"Nothing really. I was with a group two weeks ago and fell over a rock, that's all."

"Will you be coming with us this year?"

"Only on the Israeli side."

Chaim then interpreted the Capernaum archaeological site for the group. As I listened, I saw that the effects of night-time flying with no sleep were taking their toll on the Bike Riders. Two slept as they stood, leaning against the wall of the ruined synagogue. Others tried hard to concentrate, but struggled to keep their eyes open. Chaim told us about the synagogue. He explained that it was not the one mentioned in the New Testament, because the synagogue which Jesus preached in was destroyed in the Jewish Revolt of the year 70AD. The one now visible was built in the same place about a hundred years later. We could see the essential features of a synagogue, including a place for the Torah and stone benches around the sides for people to sit on

I spotted big Dougie Sanderson in the crowd and made my way over to him. Dougie is a farmer from near Eyemouth in southern Scotland, and was on the 1994 and 1995 Bike Rides along with me and my wife Grace. Knowing I would not be with the group when they arrived this morning, I had asked Dougie, several months ago, to grab a good bike for me before they were all taken. He was with Mike Grant from Braemar, another Bike Ride regular.

"Did you get a bike for me Dougie?"

"Sure Bruce. A topper, a real topper!"

By the time we arrived in Nazareth it was late afternoon, and, as we walked up the hill to the hospital, the sun was low in the sky. Nazareth is a town of over sixty-thousand people, nearly all Arabic, and the Nazareth Hospital is the main hospital for the whole area. In 1861 the Edinburgh Medical Missionary Society (EMMS) sent Doctor Pacradooni Kaloost Vartan, an Armenian doctor who had trained in Edinburgh, to Palestine. He and his wife founded the first hospital, which to this day cares for the people of Galilee. That first structure was superseded by a new building in 1882, but, on the day it was completed, it was illegally confiscated by the Turkish administration. The people then had to start building yet another hospital. That became the current hospital on the hill, which has grown and expanded over the century.

In the reception area we were split up into groups and I was fortunate in being in the group led by Dr. Bashira. Dr. Bashira is a small, rotund, Arab Christian surgeon, whom we met on previous visits and who is endearingly delightful and charming. Last year, when the Bike Ride reached Jericho, Dr. Bashira was there to meet us with a huge smile, "Welcome to Palestine! Welcome to my homeland!"

We walked through the new medical wing, partly paid for by money raised by previous Bike Rides, and Dr. Bashira explained why the Israeli government does not fund capital building projects at hospitals.

"The problem is that Jewish hospitals are all supported by Jewish groups in different parts of the world. For example, the Hassada Hospital in Jerusalem is linked to Jews in Chicago. Therefore, when any Jewish hospital needs money for building projects the funds are provided by these support groups. Because of this the government passed a law saying that all hospitals must be funded privately for capital projects. But what about non-Jewish hospitals? How are they to be funded? They do not have rich foundations in America behind them. This is why the EMMS has had to find money from all over the world to build our new wing."

"We are a Christian Hospital," said Dr. Bashira, "but people work here who are from different parts of the community. Two years ago an incident occurred in Nazareth which became national news. An Israeli soldier was stabbed in Old Nazareth. Think about that! He was driven to a Christian Hospital, by an Arab taxi-driver, and he was operated on by a Muslim surgeon. We are here to heal divisions, as well as healing sickness are we not?"

"About ten years ago we realized that in order to continue to serve our community we had to expand, and we had to build a new wing with new equipment. This was called the 'Nazareth Project', and the Bike Rides and other agencies have made this possible. Today we are standing in the new wing, and this year the Bike Ride will be raising money for the Special Baby Care unit. The people of Galilee thank you so much, so very, very much."

FOLLOWING THE TOUR THERE was a service in the Hospital's Lecture Theatre, after which we were divided into groups of five or six to go to the home of a hospital staff member for the evening meal. Our group was taken to the house of a retired doctor called Samil. Thirty years ago Samil married Mary, an Irish girl, and their son, Chaffique, also works in the hospital as a physiotherapist. Samil told us how, during the 1948 War of Independence, the electricity supply to Nazareth was cut off; but the armies allowed the hospital to borrow generators from Tiberias and gave enough fuel to provide two hours' electricity for a major operation.

Samil and Mary's hospitality was wonderful. Even the tired travellers perked up. As Chaffique drove us back to the Nazareth Hospital he told us that he wanted to move on and do something different. Back in Ginnosar I met my room-mates, Paul and Andrew. Tomorrow the Bike Ride begins.

Over Jordan

—Day 28—Kfar Ruppin—

Monday 4th November

THE ALARM WENT OFF at five. We got up, dressed hurriedly, and made our way in darkness to the lakeside for a sunrise communion service by the water's edge. The service was led by David Cooper, Church of Scotland minister in Alloa. In dawn light, as the sun rose over the Golan heights, we broke bread and shared wine together as an act of worship and fellowship at the start of the Bike Ride. David's sister, Janet, had married Ian Wishart, the son of one of the families in our church in Crieff: tragically, both Ian and Janet were killed in a car accident six years ago. That was when I first met David, and was delighted that he and his wife Jill are both on the Bike Ride this year. One of their church members, Dr. Valerie Scott, who was on Bike Ride 1994, had come back for Bike Ride 1996. The ride this year is called *Over Jordan* because, after the first day, we are cycling east of the river, in the Kingdom of Jordan itself.

True to his word, Dougie had selected a good big bike for me, and the mechanic put additional grips on the handlebars. Each year the bikes provided by the organizing company have improved. This time they look very new, very robust, and in top condition. I replaced the bike's hard, narrow seat with my own padded seat which I brought with me. After a test-run around the kibbutz, I adjusted the seat and handle-bar height. All was set.

Setting Off

Following breakfast, our group of over one hundred cyclists, plus support personnel, cycled or walked the short distance to the pier, where boats were waiting for us. After all the bikes and people were loaded, we set off across the Lake to Ein Gev where we would start the day's serious cycling. Halfway across the Sea of Galilee we stopped. The boat's engines were cut. And David led us in worship. A film crew from the BBC are with us to film the Bike Ride and they asked us to sing the songs again in order to get a better recording. Today, while we cycled south, the film crew—both called Jennifer—spent most of their time filming at the Nazareth Hospital and interviewing people there. The plan is that, in conjunction with the EMMS annual Carol Service from the Usher Hall in Edinburgh, a programme about the hospital will be broadcast on the BBC on Christmas Eve. Dorothy McKenzie of the EMMS has been trying for years to persuade the BBC to profile the hospital. Now Dorothy's efforts are bearing fruit.

After landing at Ein Gev we collected our bikes, checked the gears and brakes, and then started the real business of hard cycling. In the hot morning sun, but full of eager energy, we raced the first few miles of the shores of the Lake before turning east along tracks through banana plantations. There we met Chaim who had come by jeep to give background information.

"Now, in one sense, what we see here is not Israeli." said Chaim, indicating the banana plants. "Bananas are not indigenous to this country. They are certainly not mentioned in the Bible. As you can see, banana plants have big leaves, open to the sun. This is not typical of vegetation in the Middle East which usually has small, closed up leaves. Big leaves are characteristic of tropical plants. But, where we are just now is a triangle of land between the River Yarmuk and the River Jordan, and this triangle is basically tropical in terms of temperature, though without the rainfall. Therefore, bananas can grow here as long as they have enough water. Now, in the real Tropics there would be a daily thunderstorm, but we do not have these in Israel. Therefore, we have to irrigate the plantations heavily. For bananas we use third class water which has been recycled."

Chaim peeled off the first layer of bark from a broken banana tree. Underneath the bark were thousands and thousands of cells full of water. "The banana is not a true tree, but a weed which happens to have fruit. Tell me, what is the difference between a tree and a large weed?"

Silence. Someone suggested, "A weed has no trunk?"

"Yes, that is part of the difference. The banana has no stem distinct from the leaves, the leaves are themselves the stem. All that is true. But the real difference is that the banana will grow bigger and bigger and bigger until it is either cut down or blown down. It has no natural height. That is characteristic of weeds. A tree will grow to its proper height and then stop, but not a weed."

"If all bananas grew then each flower would produce about seven hundred bananas, but each of them would be tiny. So, for commercial purposes the growers limit each bunch to about seventy. Even then, because the banana is essentially a weed it has no strong stem to support the weight of these clumps of bananas and so the plants have to be supported."

We noticed that the banana clumps were enclosed in plastic bags of different colors. Some were blue. Some were black. Some were white. Chaim was asked about this. He explained that because the banana is a weed it has no season as such, but each plant fruits at six month intervals. In a plantation such as the one we were in, there are plants at various stages, so banana clumps at the same stage are enclosed in bags of similar color which help the farmers to know which to harvest. The bags also protect the clumps from night frosts, because, for perhaps eight or nine nights of the year, the temperature drops to five or six degrees centigrade, even down in the Jordan Valley. Snakes are a problem for people who work on bananas in the summer, so they wear high boots for safety.

WE CYCLED AWAY FROM the plantation and joined the main Tiberias to Bet She'an highway. From my experiences of the Bike Rides in 1994 and 1995 I knew that the miles to Bet She'an are a hard, relentless grind. As the sun blazed down, so it proved to be. To add to the effort, the two miles immediately before Bet She'an are uphill, and we reached that tough section at mid-day with the sun at its height and the heat at its fiercest. By the time we arrived at the Bet She'an archaeological excavations we were in dire need of cooling. Outside the excavations an open channel carries water between gardens, and I plunged my hands and arms in it, allowing the cold, refreshing water to cool me down.

On the Bike Ride today there was no time for the riders to visit the main Bet She'an archaeological site, so we cycled to Sachne Springs for lunch and spent a glorious couple of hours relaxing, swimming, and eating, before cycling downhill to our kibbutz for the night, which is Kibbutz Kfar Ruppin. As we left Sachne a bride and her husband arrived for a photo shoot, and we clapped and cheered as we cycled past.

Kibbutz Kfar Ruppin

We had stayed at Kibbutz Kfar Ruppin both previous years, and, after cycling through fields of commercially grown sunflowers, we were welcomed at the gate by the kibbutz children on their own bikes. The children gave us fruit, sweets, and a cool drink, before accompanying us to the central gathering area where we were allocated our accommodation.

The senior member of this kibbutz is called Czecho, whom we had met before. Czecho is a veteran of years of conflict and, before darkness fell, he took us to a viewpoint near the perimeter of the kibbutz, showing us how close Kfar Ruppin is to the border with Jordan and why it has suffered so much over the years. Czecho transports himself around the kibbutz in an electric buggy, and carries a loud-hailer to make himself heard. During the Israeli War of Independence Czecho had been a commando, and we shuddered to think how many throats he had slit in the dark silence of the night. The two Jennifers, who had spent time in the Gaza Strip seeing the poverty of Palestinians, were uncomfortable with Czecho, despite him trying hard to be friendly.

When we first visited Kfar Ruppin two years ago in 1994 the accommodation was primitive, with the men crammed into rooms with inadequate facilities and broken down water supplies. This year we are astonished at the transformation which has taken place. The old chalets have been completely refurbished, with new beds, new showers, and pine-wood panelling. Outside our chalet, two kibbutz boys were playing football and, after showering and changing, we joined them for a game. The boys, Ophir and Cal, knew all about British football, and when I said that I came from Scotland they immediately responded, "England 2, Scotland 0" which was the score in Euro '96.

Before the evening meal we gathered in the kibbutz coffee lounge, where I wrote up some of my *Journal*. Valerie Scott was there and I told her about Ophir and Cal.

"You know Valerie; they knew all the scores from Euro '96."

"Bruce, you've been out here for a month. Have you heard what happened between Estonia and Scotland in their World Cup qualifier?"

I shook my head.

"So you didn't hear about the three-second-football-match?"

"The what?"

"Well, the day before the match, Craig Brown, the Scotland manager, wasn't happy with the standard of the Estonian floodlights, and he mentioned this to a FIFA official who changed the match to an afternoon kick-off. But the Estonians refused to turn up at the new time. So Scotland kicked off, the referee blew his whistle after three seconds, and the match was awarded to Scotland."

"So we got the three points?"

"Well, maybe. There's going to be a FIFA meeting about it next week."

Some young teenage girls came over to see what we were doing, and they giggled when I invited them to write their names in the diary. Eventually they did, transcribing their names into English characters, Tamar, Addas, Tal, Noga, and Ailsta.

IN THE TWO PREVIOUS years Czecho had his own session with the Bike Riders, recounting the kibbutz's history, and focusing on the bloodthirsty aspects of its past as it struggled for survival against the enemies of Israel. This year a different senior kibbutz member took the role, and gave a more temperate version.

"Prior to 1948 Jewish people owned some land here, and it was on that land that the kibbutz was founded. During the 1948 War of Independence we were very lucky because there was no heavy fighting here. Similarly, during the Six-Day War there was little action in this area. But, for the three years after 1967 we were bombed and shelled continually from Jordan. You must understand the terror we lived under, and we were not even in the disputed area of the West Bank. For three years the children slept in air-raid shelters *every* night. Every single night. Two people were killed and a few injured. We were lucky. In the Yom Kippur war there was no fighting here, but there was damage all around. Four of our kibbutz boys were killed in the Yom Kippur war. At the moment we have peace with our Jordanian neighbors, and hope it will continue."

Watching from the side, and listening to this presentation, was Czecho. I imagined he would want us to hear more about battles and raids over the border in the night. But this year's host had a different emphasis. For example, he explained to us that, from the start, the kibbutz had focussed on agriculture. It sells 800,000 carpets of grass a year. It grows dates. It has a dairy herd of three hundred cows, giving three million litres of milk a year. It has a poultry farm. It is involved in fish breeding especially carp, St. Peter's fish, and mullet. It sells goldfish overseas.

And it has a plastics industry, 50 percent of which is exported to the USA. At present the kibbutz has 170 full members and about 170 children.

Someone asked, "If you are born on a kibbutz do you automatically become a member?"

"No, someone born on the kibbutz does not automatically become a member. They have to *want* to be a member, and they have to be accepted by the general assembly of the kibbutz. About five hundred people live on the kibbutz. Not all are full members. For example, groups from the former Soviet Union come here for six month periods to learn Hebrew, and can stay on for longer. Two such families after two years became full members. Some army units also come here to do agriculture as part of their military training."

"Do many volunteers come to work on the kibbutz?"

"Not so many nowadays. We only have two just now. Interestingly, we find that volunteers come after wars have taken place. We think this is because times of danger give young people their strongest sense of wanting to take part in building and rebuilding our nation."

"What about education?"

"For our children, Primary School is at a kibbutz six miles away. Secondary School is at another kibbutz four miles away. Boys and girls born here are entitled to University study. At the end of their studies they give two years' service for each year they were supported by the kibbutz, or pay back the money instead. It is more difficult for young people to live on a kibbutz today than in 1948, because all of them have an awareness of the global village and exciting opportunities further afield. It is hard for them to stay on in a kibbutz with the limitations that means."

"When did the kibbutz concept start?"

"Good question. In Israel, the first kibbutz was founded south of the Sea of Galilee in 1911, by revolutionary pioneers from Russia after the revolution of 1905. They needed tight cooperation with each other in a difficult and hostile country. That is how the kibbutz ideal started. But everything changes, and kibbutzim must change. Nowadays, for example, we pay for our meals with electronic smart cards. Members get an allowance every month. But, very importantly, education and health are still in common for everyone. We also have received repayments from Germany in the wake of the Holocaust, but all these payments are made to the kibbutz, and not to individuals. Most members live in the kibbutz and work outside, but their salary goes automatically to the kibbutz."

"What would you say is the attraction of staying in a kibbutz?"

"The community. The strong bonds of community."

"What do you do with a lazy person who doesn't do their fair share of work?"

"You tell me! We would like to know the answer as well!"

Everyone laughed.

"Actually, this problem does not happen much, but if it gets too bad we try to persuade the person by reason. The laws of the State stop us simply expelling someone. But if the situation gets too severe the kibbutz might have to go to court to have the person removed. But that has not happened yet. Kibbutzim are not independent of the laws of the land, but they do add their own codes of discipline."

"Are there some communities where people can have private wealth?"

"You are thinking of the Mushavim. Yes, a member of the Mushavim has his own home and so on, but many things are still decided in community."

The Memorial

At the evening meal Czecho wandered round the tables being friendly with all the bikers. He carried his portable megaphone, and every so often he thought of something which he felt would interest the whole gathering, announcing this at full volume before clicking off and chatting to individuals. He spent a lot of time talking to the two Jennifers who found themselves in an awkward situation. Because of their Gaza experience it was difficult for them to warm to Czecho. Fatefully, as often happens in situations like this, Czecho fastened onto them in particular, recounting his deeds of valour in beating back the Arabs in the early years. Fortunately, the Jennifers saw the irony of the situation. Poor old Czecho. He had no idea of the tension he caused.

After the evening meal, the kibbutz held a ceremony to mark the first anniversary of the assassination of Yitzak Rabin. We joined the event and were profoundly moved, despite all of it being in Hebrew. We sat in a corner of the main dining hall. A large picture of Rabin was placed against a black background. An Israeli flag flanked it. On the floor was one large candle and many small candles. These flickered in the darkness. People arrived slowly, but eventually the whole area filled. Israeli music played over the PA system. Seven young people took their places, standing at the front, holding their scripts.

Though the proceedings were in Hebrew, the different sections of the memorial event were clear. A teenager read an introduction. A second teenager took over. The entire audience, of all ages, listened intently to the young voices. Here and there we heard the sound of stifled sobbing. Another teenage girl took up the tribute. All the young people were casually dressed, but totally serious in their purpose. A boy and a girl sang a duet which was solemn but strong and vital. A few voices in the audience joined in. Then the girl sang solo with tremendous power and passion. Her eyes were bright. Her bearing was confident. There was no clapping, just listening. A girl read. A boy read. Another girl read a poem. Then the young people sat on the floor as a film of Rabin was shown, showing his life from young man, to war hero, to politician, to the fateful night in Tel Aviv when he was shot. When the shooting was shown, the weeping was no longer hidden. People cried openly, and the sadness and despair was profound and deep. The film ended. The whole company stood to sing the Israeli national anthem. Then everyone slowly filed out.

We finished the day with an open air service outside the dining-hall. Old Czecho, despite his dark past, stayed with us all the time, not to check up on us, but simply to make us feel welcome. We appreciated that.

— Day 29 — Peace Bridge —

Tuesday 5th November

TODAY WE CROSSED OVER from Israel into Jordan. Old Czecho was keen to be a good host to the very end, waving us off when we cycled out of the kibbutz. From Kfar Ruppin to the border crossing at the King Hussein Bridge—Peace Bridge—is only a few miles, and we had visited it in 1994 on the Bike Ride when the crossing point was being rebuilt after years of closure. The slow, green, narrow waters of the Jordan flow below the bridge, and a large photo-poster of King Hussein with the words, 'Welcome to the Hashemite Kingdom of Jordan' met us as we entered another country. Leaving Israel was straightforward, but we had to wait for two hours on the Jordanian side for all our passports to be checked.

Over Jordan

On the Bike Ride our overnight luggage is transported each day by lorry, with Trevor Starr, a Bike Ride veteran, in charge. At the border crossing lorries were changed, and all the luggage had to be moved from an Israeli lorry with its crew, into a Jordanian lorry with its crew. Trevor had his work cut out maintaining his authority because all his helpers spoke Arabic and he did not. I had entrusted him with my golf club at Ginnosar, and, while we waited for passport verification, I went over to check its progress.

"Have you seen my golf club yet, Trevor?"

"I'm afraid not, Bruce, but I'll have a good look."

I could do nothing since the Jordanians were ensuring that no-one could interfere with the luggage transfer. So I left Trevor and went to the customs office to get some Jordanian money.

"May I have some Jordanian Dinars please?"

"In the Bank. Two doors along."

"Thank you."

But the bank officials were not helpful. I had assumed that, at a major international crossing point, there would be facilities to get cash using my Visa card, but not so.

"Not Visa. We cannot do Visa."

"But I need Dinars, I have none."

"The Bank in Amman, or the Bank in Aqaba, they do Visa."

"But I'm on a bicycle. I'm not going to Amman. And I won't be in Aqaba until Friday. I really need money now. I thought that at an international crossing point there would be facilities."

"You have Israeli shekels? We change them."

"No, I've run out of shekels. But I have a Visa card which is guaranteed. I want to buy things in your country."

"No. Very sorry. We have no facilities."

I gave up and left the Bank. Outside I met Fred Aitken who works for the Nazareth Hospital project and is an experienced traveller.

"What's wrong Bruce?"

"Fred, the Bank won't give me money on my Visa. In Israel there was no problem."

"Come with me."

Fred marched into the bank, and I followed in his wake. The tellers eyed him cautiously. On the wall of the Bank was a photograph of the King. Fred spoke to the teller, "My friend, your King is a very handsome man. He has done very good things for Jordan. You must be very proud of him."

The teller nodded.

"My friend here," continued Fred, "would like to see much of your country, and would like to spend money in your country, but he cannot because he has no money. His card is a Visa card. In fact, it is a debit card which is totally guaranteed. I am sure that you could help him."

"It is difficult. We must contact Amman."

Two of the tellers took the telephone and tried to get through to Amman. Fred turned round to me, smiled, and raised his eyebrows.

"We are sorry. We cannot get through to Amman."

"Look, you are an important man. You hold an important position in the bank. The credit card is guaranteed, and I am sure that you have authority to approve transactions."

DAY 29—PEACE BRIDGE   277

The teller sighed, reached under his desk and brought out a credit card slide-pad. He reached over for my card. "How many dinars do you want sir?"

"Fifty please."

"Do you have your passport with you?"

"Our passports are getting checked at the moment."

"When you get your passport back I will give the money."

As we left the bank I said to Fred, "Fred, that teller could have dealt with my Visa card all along! Why all the difficulty?"

"It's just their way Bruce."

When the passports were returned the bank teller was as good as his word, and, as we cycled out of the border control I had the cash in my money-bag. The baggage-lorry came alongside, and Trevor leaned out of the window: "We've got your golf-club Bruce! It was wedged between spars in the Israeli lorry, but now I've got it in the cab of this one!" The lorry roared past, and our one hundred, yellow-shirted cyclists moved onto the Jordanian roads.

The Peloton

In Jordan the traffic is much lighter than in Israel, with few private cars. There are lorries, buses, police vehicles, and military transport, but far fewer than in Israel. Another difference is that we are now permanently accompanied by a car full of policemen. These are the Tourist Police, who speed up and down our line of cyclists. Whether they are watching out for us, or watching over us, is hard to tell. Probably both.

Shepherds wearing red-checked keffiyeh tended their flocks of sheep and goats. One old Arab snarled at each Bike Rider, "Netanyahu, he no good." Spit. "Netanyahu, he no good." Spit. After each phrase the old man spat onto the ground, emphasising his point. He thought that since we came from Israel we must be Israelis, and the opportunity to make a political point was too good to miss. After a few miles, we left the main highway, taking a minor road which wound alongside the canal system. Like Israel, Jordan takes water from the River Jordan, and the canal system brings it to villages and plantations.

In Israel we had entered few towns, but in Jordan we passed through village after village. In each, schoolchildren rushed to the side of the road to cheer and wave as we passed by. Sometimes we saw them standing on the far bank of the canal, shouting, waving, and running, trying to keep up with us. Most of us have packets of sweets in our saddlebags, and, as we met groups of children, we handed them out. At one point I saw crowds of children on the opposite bank of the canal, so I halted my bike and threw over packets of polo-mints. Gideon, one of the Bike Ride cycling leaders, stopped beside me.

"A few years ago you wouldn't have done that."

"Oh, why?"

"Polo mints used to contain animal fats. So a good Muslim would not eat them."

Gideon comes from London, but for some years has lived on a kibbutz in Israel. All that he earns as a cycling guide goes back into the common funds of the kibbutz, and from it he gets his allowance. He was one of our cycling guides on the Bike Ride of 1994; in 1995 his wife was having a baby at the time of our trip.

WE CYCLED ON. In another village we heard more cheering, but no children were to be seen. Then we saw them. They were inside, pressed up against the windows of their school. They must have been standing on chairs and tables, because the whole window, from bottom to top, was filled with their faces.

The long wait at the border post meant we were well behind schedule, and soon it was midday although we had covered very few miles. Between sixty and seventy miles had to be cycled on this second day, and most of it was going to be in the afternoon sun. Worst of all, the wind was against us and, more than anything else, cyclists hate the wind. Even a hill is preferable to a wind. A hill is finite. And on the other side of a hill there is a bonus freewheel. But wind fights against the cyclist downhill as well as up: energy-sapping, frustrating, draining.

We saw workmen coming in from the fields. One man, riding his horse, was carrying a light wooden plough balanced behind the saddle. It is unbelievable how poor and undeveloped the economy is. Every hundred yards there is a photographic opportunity, but we were hurried along by Erich Reich, the main Bike Ride organizer. Erich was acutely aware that the timetable was totally awry. Today was to be hard work, pounding out the miles.

When we cycled through some of the larger towns, the local youths spat on us and threw small stones at our wheels. They too believed that we must be Israelis. We were glad of the Tourist Police who eventually became aware that harassment was taking place; so, in the towns, they started a policy of motoring up and down the main street, blaring commands through the car's loudspeaker. What they said was in Arabic, and, though we did not understand the words, we could see their effect. The crowds of youths moved quickly back, and stayed further away from us, but looking cowed and resentful.

In one town groups of schoolgirls were returning home after lessons, and we stopped to take their photograph. They were thrilled to be made a fuss of, smiling and waving enthusiastically for each cyclist who wanted to grab a shot. In their uniforms of blue skirts over blue trousers they were so smart, and their smiling, dusky-skinned complexions made them look so beautiful. All of them had straight black hair except one, whose hair was frizzy and ginger. To thank them for posing for us we offered sweets which they accepted, albeit hesitantly.

As the day wore on we continued to pound out the miles. Every so often one of our supporting vehicles waited beside the road with water for our water bottles. Halfway to the 'lunch' stop—which we eventually reached mid-afternoon—we had bananas, apples, dates, and oranges. In the back of the fruit van we saw chocolate bars and tins of Coca-Cola, but these were for sale, not for free distribution. This is new to us. In Israel the supporting vehicles do not carry chocolate or canned drinks, but the Jordanian company was taking the opportunity to run a commercial exercise beyond whatever fee they received for being our back-up team.

The villages are poor and dilapidated. The houses look like those of shanty towns, albeit with solid walls rather than cardboard ones. Crowds of men sit by the sidewalks. Whether they are simply meeting at siesta-time or whether they have no work, we do not know. Every so often we saw veiled women scurrying in or out of their houses. Small, barefoot children, with grubby shorts and T-shirts, jumped up and down waving at us going by. By the roadside we saw carcasses of animals. Dogs, the size of Labradors, lay dead with bloated bodies and legs stuck out rigidly in rigor mortis. Occasionally we passed a sheep's corpse. Regularly there were the remains of cats, mown down by the traffic.

After several hours travelling, one hundred cyclists become a long, extended line of wheels and yellow T-shirts. We started off as three groups, green, blue, and red, with the green group the fastest. Everyone, however, is free to cycle at his or her own speed, and, with a four mile per hour difference in speed between the fastest and the slowest, three hours cycling mean a twelve-mile stretch between the head and tail of the procession. From time to time, even as one of a hundred on the same road and going in the same direction, I saw no other cyclists in front or behind.

The women have been told to cycle together when going through the towns. Wearing cycling shorts, they are showing more female flesh than would normally be revealed in Jordanian culture. Jordan is an Islamic State and, though not extreme, its codes of public decency are different from those of the West. The girls are also told not to roll up the short sleeves of their T-shirts, or to alter the round-neck of the T-shirt into a V-neck. If possible, they are to ride through the towns in the company of some of the male cyclists. On the whole, the Jordanian people are happy to see us, and the warmth and exuberance of the children in the villages and towns is unforgettable.

After many, many miles, our lunch stop was reached. On the Bike Rides of the two previous years, we cycled down the Israeli side of the River Jordan, on a road parallel to that of today's. On these Bike Rides, through the West Bank, we passed a high, distinctive desert mountain just before the lunch stop, and, as we cycled ever farther south in Jordan itself, I kept looking across the Jordan valley, trying to spot the mountain in question. Eventually it came into view and, as I thought, soon after we passed it—albeit on the other side—we reached the lunch location.

Because of the late start from the border crossing, and because the battle against the wind sapped energy as well as time, we needed food badly. The benefits of breakfast at Kfar Ruppin had long gone. The Jordanian support crew had erected trestle tables and covered them with attractive red paper table-cloths. Delightful as these decorative touches were, what really drew our attention were the masses of large black flies over every bowl of food. But hunger overcame hygiene, and we refuelled with soup and salads. We also gave in to the commercial opportunities and bought Mars Bars and Coca Cola. Donald Walker and Robin Brodie, from Banchory, poured water over each other, luxuriating in its coolness after having felt nothing but heat, and more heat, for hour after hour. All morning the two Jennifers in the TV crew had motored up and down our line of perspiring cyclists, grabbing road-shots as well as pictures of Jordanian life. At lunch they filmed flies, food, and more flies.

The Dead Sea Rest House

After the lunch break we cycled further south, mile after mile, hour after hour. The villages became fewer in number. The road traffic even quieter. Occasionally a brightly painted truck, jammed full of people, passed us. These painted trucks resemble images I have seen of trucks in India and Pakistan, and the symbol of a love-heart is a prominent feature of their decorations.

Big Dougie came up behind me,

"Toyota seem to have corned the market here, Bruce."

"Aye, Dougie. Mercedes taxis in Israel. Toyota jeeps in Jordan."

But it was the lack of traffic which left the strongest impression. Eventually, after negotiating more tough, undulating, off-road tracks, we reached our stop for the night, the Dead Sea Rest House. The waters of the Dead Sea sparkled in the last rays of sunlight and some of the bikers went for a dip. I found my chalet and showered and changed.

AT THE REST HOUSE, we were received by Prince Mirad, a member of the Jordanian royal family and, as a symbol of friendship between the Nazareth Hospital and Jordan, a scanner was presented to the Prince from the hospital in Nazareth for the hospital in Amman. The Prince brought with him a troop of five, burly, ceremonially dressed soldiers who entertained us with vigorous traditional Jordanian dancing. As the evening wore on, the bikers joined in. Three musicians provided the accompaniment.

Prince Mirad is the son of King Hussein's cousin. After the official presentation he treated us to coffee and biscuits, and mingled with the Bike Riders. Paul, one of my room-mates, went over to him.

"I have a mountain bike." the Prince said to Paul, "But in the last two years I have not used it a lot. Perhaps I should join you!"

"Why not come with us tomorrow, Your Highness."

"Alas, I am busy. But where are you going tomorrow?"

"Along by the Dead Sea."

"Ah! When you cycle down beside the Dead Sea, you must look out for the magic tree."

"The magic tree?"

"Yes, it is so called by local people because it grows solitary on a sheer rock face with no ledge, just above the road."

At the evening meal I shared a table with one of the Jennifers, along with Katie and Amin who is one of the Arab members of the Israeli support team. Jennifer spoke about the situation endured by Palestinians in Gaza.

"When we were filming in Gaza we met a man who has a daughter in Bethlehem, and he has not seen her for a whole year because of the closed borders. That is inhumane!"

Amin spoke about the situation as seen from the Arab angle. He is so full of faith and we were uplifted and encouraged listening to him.

"What you say is true Jennifer." he said, sadly. "And there are many examples like that. The people in the West Bank are being driven further into poverty. For example, people outside the West Bank are seven or eight times richer than people inside the West Bank. The economic imbalance drives a huge wedge between them. Jennifer, I work at the Nazareth Hospital, and I am aware of the hardship of the people in our land. But, listen, I was on duty in Casualty Reception when the wounded Jewish soldier was brought in. And the cooperation seen that day is a ray of light for the future. I believe that if Clinton is re-elected he can put pressure on Netanyahu."

"But Netanyahu is a hard liner!" protested Jennifer.

"Look, before Netanyahu was elected he said, 'I will never shake hands with Arafat!' But he has shaken hands with Arafat! And Arafat is an old man. A tired old man. He only wants peace."

Remembering Oded Yinon's views I asked Amin, "Would Arafat ever be content with patches of autonomy here and there? Does he not want the whole West Bank?"

"Look, Arafat is old. He wants to be seen in history as a statesman. So he will not put off signing a final peace treaty."

After a pause, Amin continued, "The death of Yitzak Rabin was a great tragedy. Only God gives life, and only God has the right to take life away. The death of Rabin was not God's will. A man took Rabin's life, not God. But, remember, we believe in the Lord Jesus. In him we will have peace, a true peace. There are many good Arabs. There are many good Palestinians. And there are many good Jews. God will use them."

Coming from a man like Amin, his statement had a gentle yet firm authority. Jennifer squeezed his hand and smiled. "Thank you Amin. What you said tonight has really helped me."

Katie told us about an incident out on the road. "I stopped to have a rest and take a drink of water when a shepherd came over and indicated that he would like a drink. So I gave him my water bottle. But, instead of taking a sip, he put the whole bottle in his pocket and kept it. I didn't know what to do! Fortunately, a Bike Ride official arrived and sorted things out."

Our evening epilogue was held out on the terrace, overlooking the Dead Sea. When it ended some bikers went in to swim again. But, after a long day and long miles, I went to bed.

— Day 30 — Kerak —

Wednesday 6th November

WE LEFT THE DEAD Sea Rest House on a bright sunny morning, ready for another fifty miles down the eastern shores of the Dead Sea. Again the wind was against us, slowing our progress. But today we had the benefit of an early start, with no delays for boat-crossings or border controls, and that was a big advantage. Soon after we set off we crossed a bridge over one of the many wadis leading down to the shore, at the same time as a shepherd with his flock of sheep and goats passed underneath. He was taking the animals to the day's grazing which consisted of no more than a scattering of bushes growing out of the rocks and stones. These bushes were the 'green pastures' of the area.

The Jordanian Dead Sea road is much better than the Israeli equivalent, probably because it is *the* major highway in Jordan, going from Aqaba on the Red Sea to Amman. Even more than yesterday the road was quiet. Occasionally a truck met us, taking materials from a quarry or from a Dead Sea factory. Apart from these lorries traffic was virtually non-existent. On our left the high, jagged mountains of Jordan shimmered in the sunlight. On our right, the rocks by the shore were covered with thick encrustations of salt. The prevailing wind at the Dead Sea is from the west, meaning that the Jordanian shore is hit by larger waves than the Israeli side, with salt-saturated water splashing high up on the rocks, leaving saline deposits in a broad, three-meter-high band all the way along.

We passed through no villages until near lunchtime. And there were no more shepherds or flocks of sheep. This is because the road is cut deep into the flanks of mountains which plunge straight down into the sea with no possible space for pasture. The wind was strong, so we formed groups, taking turns at the front for two minutes at a time. Valerie Scott acted as time-keeper and took fiendish delight in prolonging the agony for people she knew well. Norman Wallace, from Charlotte Chapel in Edinburgh, gave an amusing running commentary on all things as we passed, and there was lots of laughter amidst the puffing and panting. Never before had we drank so much water. The heat, the wind, the gradients, made us swallow water by the gallon.

The Tourist Police raced up and down. At one place I stopped to photograph a soldier, but they appeared on the scene to forbid this. The soldier was pleased to have his picture taken, but our escorts would not allow it. Jordan is still getting used to tourism.

By lunchtime we were again tired. Really tired. I had already noticed at the end of each day's cycling that I was truly weary, whereas in 1994 and 1995, after a shower and change of clothes, I was fresh again. I think that the difference this year is my lack of cycling through October. The cycling muscles have lost fitness, though that is slowly coming back with each day's pedalling. The Bike Ride is hard work, but immensely enjoyable.

Up to Kerak

A mile before our lunch stop the road veered away from the Dead Sea, and ahead of us was a three-thousand-foot climb to Kerak on the Jordanian plateau. I had already decided not to try and be a hero. I would go in the support bus up this climb. But the decision was taken out of our hands. Because the wind had held everyone back, no one was allowed to attempt the climb because of time constraints. Even as we boarded the buses brilliant sunshine gave way to overcast skies, and rain poured down as we climbed the long, steep, winding road to Kerak. Erich told us he had climbed the road on his bike when surveying the route. If so, then either he was enormously fit, or he had not done three days tough cycling beforehand!

It was still raining when we arrived in Kerak, high in the Jordanian mountains. Kerak was famous in Lawrence of Arabia's time, and earlier this year was the scene of internationally reported civil unrest when bread prices rose overnight. Today, its sloping streets bustled with people wrapped up against the cold. We made our way to the Catholic convent, where we were met by the priest, the nuns, and some of the senior children, and we crammed into the hall with them for refreshments. They sang for us, with the priest leading and conducting, and we were impressed by the power of their young voices. We responded with some of our hymns of praise, '*Allelu, Alleluia*', and '*You shall go out with Joy*!' Everyone: children, Bike Riders, nuns, priest, support crew, held hands in fellowship as we prayed together. The atmosphere was terrific.

The priest told us the narrative behind the founding of the local church. In the nineteenth century the Sheik of Kerak was very ill and there was no hospital in the town, but he was told by an itinerant priest that he could get treatment in Bethlehem. The itinerant priest then travelled to Bethlehem and contacted the Bethlehem priest about the situation, who then came to Kerak to accompany the Sheik to Bethlehem for his treatment and accompanied him back again. The Sheik said to him, "If you promise to give us a priest like yourself, you can go home to Bethlehem, otherwise you must stay here with me!" Consequently, a priest was appointed for Kerak, and the Catholic community became established there.

Kerak has three Christian churches, Orthodox, Catholic, and Melkite, all of which, according to the priest, live in perfect harmony with no problems. One parish school serves all of the Christians and also all of Kerak's Muslims. "We have good harmony with the Muslim community," said the priest. "We thank the Lord for the harmony we are blessed with. The Crusaders were expelled from Kerak by the Muslims, but that history is in the past now."

The Catholic community in the town consists of the priest, three Sisters and ninety families. The Orthodox have one hundred and twenty-five families, and the Melkites have one hundred families. The warmth of welcome was outstanding. Because of the rain and the cold we did not see the ruins of Kerak's famed Crusader Castle, but we would not have exchanged our time in that crowded hall for a visit to yet another antiquities site, however impressive.

The Turkish Coffee House

Leaving Kerak, the buses started a three-hour journey in the darkness through the Jordanian desert to Petra where we were to stay for the night. Andrew, my other room-mate, and John McPhee, sang worship songs

from the Bike Ride song book. Some joined in the singing, adding har-
monies to the melodies. Others caught up on sleep. After two hours our
bus passed the first bus which had halted by the side of the road. Some
miles further on, somewhere in the desert, we stopped at a brightly lit
Turkish Coffee House. We were told by the Jordanians that the other bus
had mechanical problems and we were stopping to give it time to catch
up, and that we could wait in the Coffee House instead of on the bus.

Raoul, the Coffee House owner, welcomed us and showed us to our
tables. He brought a tray of coffee cups full of bitter coffee, and we drank
some sips out of politeness. John, Andrew, Mike Grant, and I sat together
at a table.

"Two of the Muslims at the front of our bus don't like us singing
hymns."

"What!"

"Yes, apparently they were able to make out some of the words. One
of them said 'If this was Saudi Arabia you would be arrested.' He didn't
look pleased."

"But this is Jordan, not Saudi. Anyway, most of the worship songs
we sang in the bus were taken from the Psalms and could be sung by
followers of any monotheistic religion."

"Apart from, 'When I survey the wondrous cross'."

"I suppose so. But, goodness me, the bus company knew what they
were taking on board when they got involved in the tourist industry.
However, we'd better be careful."

"Think of it. Last night we were received by Prince Mirad, a member
of the Jordanian Royal Family. He didn't mind us having an epilogue at
the Dead Sea Rest House. Maybe we should name-drop!"

As we looked round, we saw that the Coffee House was scruffy and
dilapidated. The clock on the wall had stopped at quarter past ten, probably some years ago. A grubby calendar with pull-off months hung on
one wall, and a picture of King Hussein hung on another. Near it was a
second calendar, this one featuring a Jordanian beauty dressed in a black
gown. The ubiquitous Coca-Cola dispenser stood in a corner. Smudged
glass-framed pictures of Swiss mountains hung crooked on either side of
the doorway.

The only women present were Bike Riders. Raoul and his staff were
presumably of Turkish extraction, and had dark, European style clothing. A cluster of Jordanian men, wearing their distinctive red and white
checked keffiyeh, sat at a central plastic table, and food was brought to

them from the kitchens. The keffiyeh were worn in a variety of styles. One man wore it as a scarf, wrapped twice around his neck. One had his kaffir folded on top of his head in the official style. Another had it as a head covering, with the ends draping down over his chest.

After forty minutes we wandered back to the bus, but the last two Bike Riders out of the Coffee House were hassled about payment for the coffee. We all genuinely thought that the coffee was provided by the bus company to compensate for the delay. None of us had ordered anything. After a difficult conversation we dug dinars out of our pockets and were handing over money when the bus-driver started up the bus, shouted at us to get on board, and roared off.

WHEN WE ARRIVED AT the Petra Hotel we found that the other bus was there already. At the meal Fred Aitken asked us about our incident at the Turkish Coffee House.

"Why did your bus-driver say he had to stop at the Coffee House?"

"He gave several reasons. First, that the other bus had broken down."

Fred shook his head, "We never broke down!"

"Second, that we needed a Tourist Police escort. Third, that we must travel in convoy. But when we left the Coffee House none of these factors seemed to matter."

"Something fishy is going on," said Fred. "The Coffee House owner has been raging at Erich."

"But Fred, after we realized that the coffees weren't free we started to get money out, but the bus-driver drove off before we could pay everything."

"Oh, it's not your fault. The bus-driver has been up to tricks for some reason. Don't worry, Erich will sort it out."

"So long as the EMMS doesn't get a bad name."

"Don't worry. It'll blow over."

Our concerns about the Coffee House incident faded away as we enjoyed a sumptuous meal at the Petra Hotel. Worryingly, some Bike Riders were absent due to stomach upsets. Tomorrow we are to visit the ruins of ancient Petra. During the evening we noticed that although Jordan is a Muslim country the hotel sells Amstel Beer.

— Day 31—Petra —

Thursday 7th November

IN THE LATE EIGHTEENTH century, an artist from Edinburgh called David Roberts came out to the Middle East to make lithographic drawings of the scenery. His images of Petra have become classics, and this morning we saw some of the stunning reality which he portrayed so well. At half-past eight we gathered outside the Petra Hotel, ready to walk into Petra through the half-mile long narrow canyon called the Siq. We heard the thunder of hooves down in the valley, where Arab horsemen were driving their horses to the Siq entrance, ready for any tourists who wanted to ride in. Thick clouds of dust rose into the air, and the noise of the horses, and the shouting of the men, created a thrilling atmosphere.

The 'Rose Red City'

Having cycled for three days nearly all of us elected to walk into Petra rather than ride. Walking path and horse path are separated by a low wall, and, after horse-riding tourists have been led sedately into Petra and left there, the horsemen mount their steeds and gallop back to the start at a manic pace. Some other tourists rode in one of the horse-drawn, twin-seated gigs which are also available.

Along the narrow canyon of the Siq are traces of the Nabatean civilization which first carved Petra from the solid rock. We saw ancient cave tombs, gigantic altars to long-forgotten gods, niches for religious statuettes, and an ancient water channel designed to divert the flash floods which are experienced in the winter. Over the centuries the water channel has deteriorated and in modern times no one bothered to repair it until, in the 1960s, several tourists were drowned in a flood which rushed through the Siq. After that tragedy the Jordanian government built a new water channel.

In David Roberts' time, Bedouin still lived in the old houses and caves of Petra, and this was still the case in the 1930s when H V Morton visited his 'Rose Red City, half as old as time.' Our official guide told us that his grandfather had been a Bedouin brought up in Petra. Nowadays the indigenous local people live in the new village of Petra outside the ancient city. The guide was good, but far too detailed and long-winded, so I decided to explore by myself rather than be limited by the slow progress he was making.

The Treasury building, Al Khazneh, is stunningly impressive. After walking through the dark, shadowy Siq, we turned a corner and there, in front of us, dominating and filling the frame made by the canyon walls, was the pillared Treasury, bathed in sunlight. It is not really a Treasury, rather a tomb built for King Aretas III, but the name has stuck. David Robert's drawings, and H V Morton's photographs, show one of the six pillars of its frontage broken. That pillar has now been repaired, but what has not been repaired is a stone urn high up at the apex of the Grecian style facade. British soldiers who visited Petra many years ago thought that the urn might contain jewels and precious stones, so they took pot shots until it shattered. It was of course empty.

In the square in front of Al Khazneh, Bedouin displayed their wares. Some offered brightly colored stones for sale. Another specialized in writing your name in sand inside a glass bottle. Another sold beautiful strings of beads made from camel bone. I bought three strings for six dinars, one for Grace, and one each for my two daughters. Camels and donkeys stood by their owners who smilingly invited passers-by to ride in comfort.

I walked deeper into Petra. On my right were massive buildings, which had been governmental structures in Nabatean times. The Romans left Petra alone until well into the first century, and signs of their occupation are visible at the far end where a paved Roman roadway is flanked by Roman columns. The Romans also constructed the one building in Petra which is free-standing and not hewn from the rock-face. Many of the Nabatean houses are very modest, amounting to no more than caves with elaborate frontages. But in these caves the Petran sandstone shows all its glory with different colored layers folding and curving over each other.

Alongside catering for the daily visitors, the Bedouin continue with everyday life. None are allowed to stay overnight in Petra, but it is still part of their living space. A woman riding on a donkey came past, with her donkey carrying water in tin cans on each flank. A line of camels came and went. Though photographic opportunities were endless, we still had cycling to do. So, reluctantly, we left the ancient city and made our way back up through the Siq, laden with beads, bottles of sand, painted stones, copies of David Robert's drawings, Arab head-dresses, and memories of one of the most remarkable places on Earth.

WHEN WE REGATHERED AT the buses it was obvious that many Bike Riders were unwell. For the last two days several have been complaining of stomach upsets. To begin with, the problem was thought to be no more than an expected reaction to being in a hot, foreign country and eating unusual food. But when the numbers affected by illness began rising it was realized that something more serious was abroad. The Bike Ride has a minibus which trundles along at the rear of the group, picking up stragglers and transporting any who feel unable to cycle that day. But today, even before cycling started, it was full of people who were ill. So the back-up from now on would be the Land-Rovers transporting the two Jennifers and their TV cameras.

Off-Road through the Mountains

The buses took us out of Petra to Dilagha where we saw the stunning bare mountains which surround the hidden city. Petra is the base from which the Nabateans controlled the trade-routes, and, until the Romans came, was impregnable. After the Roman period it lay unknown to Europeans for centuries until it was rediscovered in 1812 by the Swiss explorer, John Ludwig Burckhardt. The Petran mountains are pink, jagged, irregular masses of mountainous sandstone, creating a desert fastness for Nabatean kings.

When we restarted cycling it was through this harsh desert landscape. Joy upon joy, the first five miles were downhill, wind free, on a metalled road. The bikers pounded down the hills with gleeful abandon, and my words cannot convey the thrill of that desert ride. We passed Bedouin tents every few miles. The sun shone out of a deep blue sky. And an intoxicating spirit of freedom filled us.

One disconcerting fact was that the sun was throwing our shadows ahead of us, and therefore we were cycling north, whereas Aqaba, our ultimate destination, is to the south. Cycling north also explained why the wind was no longer in our faces. But this was remote country, well away from any main highway, and our route had to pick its way through the mountains where best it could. Erich discovered this cross-country route last year, and now we were being treated to the awesome terrain which it traversed.

The semi-metalled road was like a thin black ribbon in the desert, with bare, empty, rolling hills on either side. The road lasted as far as our lunch stop, and then it became a track in the sand. But before lunch we encountered a long steep hill, and over half of the Bike Riders had to dismount and walk because the hill went on, and on, and on. This hill was even more difficult than Killer Hill on the Israeli side of the Dead Sea, and we were glad when we saw, ahead of us and above us, the cluster of jeeps which marked our mid-day break. The location was spectacular. We looked directly across to the cliff-faces of the Petran mountains, with Petra itself hidden on the other side. Erich explained that our route to-day was essentially semi-circular, and that was why we started off cycling north for several miles.

Some bikers who had felt all right at breakfast now succumbed to the bug. Callum Henshaw, who has been on the last three bike rides, lay in the back of one of the Land-Rovers, too ill to move or care. Callum MacInnes was afflicted the same way, and sat cradling his head in his hands. But there was no easy way back from this point. They would have to be taken in the Land-Rovers over the route we were travelling, with all the bumping that went with it.

AT LUNCH-TIME THEO, ONE of the Israeli cycling guides, gave us an orientation talk. "When we started cycling today at Dilagha we were looking straight over at Prince Hassan's Winter Palace. King Hussein has his Winter Palace in Aqaba. Now, concerning Jordan, many of the problems are due to the British. My apologies for mentioning this!" Theo grinned at us.

"During World War I," he continued, "the desert Sheiks sided with the British to get rid of the Turks. But, after 1918, instead of rewarding King Feisal and the Arabs with their own land the British and French took over. 'Jordan' or 'Trans-Palestine' became a buffer zone between surrounding powerful Arab nations, and it was created with that purpose. King Feisal sent his four sons to different quarters of Arabia, and Abdullah became King of Jordan. He was very good and very popular, but he was shot dead at the El Aqsa Mosque in Jerusalem. Of Abdullah's two sons, one was not interested in politics, so the other took over, but he had to be removed from office because of ineptitude. So King Hussein came to the throne at the age of seventeen in the early 1950s, and he has been a wise ruler."

"Theo, Aqaba features in the film *Lawrence of Arabia*. Was it actually important?"

"Aqaba is Jordan's only sea-port," replied Theo. "But the Saudis also gave Jordan a few more miles of seaboard in exchange for some useless desert—although Jordanians joke that the Saudis are bound to find oil there!"

"The Bedouin have always been loyal to the Hashemite dynasty because the Hashemite family are descended from Fatima, Mohammed's daughter. It is Bedouin support which keeps King Hussein in power. When the PLO were using Jordan as their base for terrorist attacks, it was Bedouin support which enabled King Hussein to expel the PLO in September 1970, which the Palestinians call Black September. The reason Jordan did not condemn Iraq during the Gulf War was because another of Feisal's sons went to Iraq, and Jordanians have strong family ties with Iraqis."

AFTER LUNCH WE ENCOUNTERED seriously severe off-road conditions. The bikes sank a full two inches into the sand, and even going downhill it was impossible for us to ride them. This was where our amazing professional cycling guides showed their skill, and were able to keep their bicycles moving in sections where everyone else was sand-stuck. We made slow progress all afternoon. Though there were only twenty-six miles to be cycled, it took till dusk to complete the section.

But who wanted to race through this scenery? It was awesome. Never before had we been so remote. Never before had we seen such massive desert mountains and valleys. Never before had we had an experience like this. The TV Land-Rover bumped, and wobbled, and zig-zagged its way as the two Jennifers filmed, with one of them sitting on the knee of an Arab helper who in turn held her tightly around the waist in an attempt to get steady pictures.

Roberts' Rock

The sun had gone down. Only a faint, residual glow warmed the sky when we reached the Bedouin camp at Robert's Rock. This is where we are spending the night, beside Robert's Rock, named after the Edinburgh artist whose drawings opened the eyes of Europe to these lands. And this is where I need the sleeping-bag. As I prepared my place in the tent I gave a prayer of thanks for Paul's generosity in lending me his.

The lorry bringing food for the evening meal did not arrive for another two hours, and by then I was beginning to feel touches of the bug afflicting the others. I had already decided to limit my diet to soup (which had been boiled), bananas (which could be peeled), bread (which was pretty safe), and Coca Cola (which was in a tin). Dougie Sanderson and Mike Grant had some tins of Amstel Beer so I downed one of these as well. We noticed that the back-up lorry now stocked *bottled* water, whereas before it carried water in bulk-containers which perhaps had been filled from a suspect source, or at least with water which our stomachs could not cope with.

Twenty local men sat with us round the camp-fire. And, as the evening wore on, we experienced one of those thrilling times which come unexpectedly but are so precious. Douglas Renton and Gloria (one of the Americans) led evening worship. Gloria spoke of how she came to faith, and the American Mennonite Bike Riders formed a choir and sang 'Amazing Grace' in deep harmony. In the Jordanian wilderness, with its warm desert air, and with the silhouette of Robert's Rock picked out as a dark shape surrounded by stars, we listened, and worshipped, and prayed together. We sang 'Guide me O Thou great Jehovah,' and when we reached the line which speaks of treading 'the verge of Jordan' never before had it seemed so right. Here, in the heart of the desert, round a camp fire, and with dark Arab faces beside us, we felt something which was exceptionally powerful though intangible.

APART FROM THIS SPECIAL time of worship, we had fun, with Ismael, the chief Jordanian tour guide, challenging each of us to rise from a prone position with a glass of water balanced on our foreheads. Some succeeded. I failed. Ismael also explained keffiyeh cloths. "A Jordanian keffiyeh has red and white checks," he said, "whereas a Palestinian one has black and white checks; and a Saudi keffiyeh is pure white and made of silk so as to reflect the fierce sun they endure. Some Jordanians wear the Saudi style when it is very hot in our country."

After a while I went to my sleeping-bag, but continued to watch and listen as people sang, laughed, and rejoiced together. Some bikers tried smoking a Hookah. Another cyclist, Alastair, had brought his mouth-organ and the sound of 'The Northern Lights', 'Clementine', 'It's a long way to Tipperary', floated up into the darkness of the night.

The Bedouin tents were arranged in a square with the eastern side open, and with the men and the women in different sections. In every tent there were people feeling ill. So the medical back-up staff, plus any bikers who happened to be medics, went up and down the rows like latter day Florence Nightingales at a Crimean hospital after a bad day in the field. One of the Americans, Bruce Donaldson, lay next to me. Roger Nicols, an ENT specialist from the States came and gave him some pills. The same was happening all over the campsite.

Today has been hard, tough, and tiring. But it has also been one of the most exhilarating and spectacular days of my life. That may seem hyperbole, but it is exactly how I feel. Physically, today we drew on reserves of strength and will-power. Spiritually, we touched something primitive and essential. Perhaps the desert skies and the dusky faces round the camp-fire has turned our imaginations. Perhaps. Even if so, it is still true that the emotions and experiences of today have been overwhelming.

— Day 32—Aqaba —

Friday 8th November

VERY FEW PEOPLE RESTED well last night. For most of us sleep was broken and fitful. Illness and stomach discomfort kept people awake. The one bonus was that I saw the night sky of the desert in all its glory. The Milky Way shone brighter than I had ever seen it before, bringing home how immense was God's promise to Abraham that his descendants would be as numerous as the stars in the heavens. I was determined, if at all possible, to complete the Bike Ride, so I looked for Geoff Bird or Beris Bird, doctors from the Nazareth Hospital, who were our official medical team. I found Beris.

"Beris, can you give me something just to take away the symptoms?"

"Sure Bruce. Here, take these."

I swallowed the pills she handed to me, had a basic breakfast, and then saw big Dougie Sanderson standing in his cycling kit but looking far from well.

"Are you all right Dougie?"

"Not really Bruce, I was up twelve times last night!"

"You're not going to cycle today are you?"

"Well Bruce, I wasn't. But my head was in such a spin when I got up that I found I'd put my cycling stuff on instead of my other clothes. I just wasn't thinking straight. So I'll try and see how far I get. Mind you, it might be better cycling than sitting in the back of a Land Rover!"

This morning, the reality of the situation was that no room was available for any extra sick people in the back-up vehicles, and, unless someone was in dire need, everyone would have to cycle anyway. And yet, despite most of us being under the weather the mood was extraordinarily cheerful as we prepared for the last stage of our 250-mile journey to Aqaba. Roberts' rock was a hundred yards from the tents, and some of the bikers had climbed it. So I collected my golf-club from Trevor's lorry, dug into my rucksack for a golf ball, and hit a shot off the rock. David Cooper captured it on his video camera.

Like the Wind!

Erich assembled us for our start. "Cyclists!" he said, "I've got good news for you! The wind is from the north today, so it will be behind you all the way to Aqaba!" Cheered by this, we set off over the remaining two miles of desert track before rejoining the main highway of the Arava. We passed a shepherd boy giving water to his herd of sheep and goats. He let down his bucket into a well, then emptied its contents into troughs. Nearer the road, two other young Bedouin sat astride a donkey guarding their herd. They shepherded the flock by throwing stones to the right or left of the animals if they strayed.

The main highway was quiet, and we cycled into the sun with a strong wind at our back. What a difference that made. Upset stomachs, lack of sleep, tired muscles, all were forgotten as we indulged in an exuberance of pedal-power on the road south towards Aqaba. The miles sped past. On the right was the wide Arava, stretching far over into Israel and nothing but sand. On our left were the Jordanian mountains: huge jagged peaks appearing in grey silhouette through the haze. Here was real desert, with sand so fine that feet sank into it like a stone sinks into dust. Far over the desert plain, we saw a caravan of camels which could have time-travelled from Nabatean times. In the rocky foothills of the mountains, Bedouin women tended the flocks.

The founder of the Nazareth Hospital was Doctor Vartan of the EMMS, and this year his great-grandson, John Vartan, is on the Bike Ride. John is a stock-broker in London and is thrilled to be here. As with all the cyclists, the effort behind every bead of sweat, every muscle worked, and every hour in the saddle, has made the Bike Ride, the hospital, and its cause, something which is now part of him. It is now much more than simply another good cause. It has taken us over. It has wormed under our skin. And each mile seals it deeper.

Roger Nicolls, the ENT specialist, and who helped to look after some of the sick last night, is on his fourth Bike Ride. Always an individualist,

Roger rarely wears his regulation Bike Ride T-shirt, preferring his own colorful tops. Each year Roger brings with him a long plastic horn which he blows whenever arriving at a village, or mid-morning stop, or lunch break, or daily destination. Roger finds many other reasons for blowing it, and, over the course of the Bike Ride the sound of Roger's horn becomes a familiar and reassuring sound. In 1994 Roger was asked why he brought his trumpet. Roger replied, "I'm gonna blow my horn in Jericho to see if the walls fall down!" This year we were not going through Jericho, so Roger said, "I'm gonna blow a horn in Gilead, like it says in the Scriptures!" In Old Testament times Gilead was the region of Trans-Jordan in the north, Moab was the section immediately east of the Dead Sea, and Edom was the region south of Moab to Aqaba.

Jill Cooper and I cycled together for a while. Then I caught up with Big Dougie who was gamely cycling on, but far from well. The phlegmatic farmer was steadily pounding out the miles. His stoical cheeriness kept him going.

After lunch there was only a short distance to Aqaba. With the wind still blowing from the north, we knocked off the miles at record pace. We did not cycle into Aqaba itself, but turned off to the right and down to the Jordanian-Israeli crossing point where a lorry waited to transport the bikes back into Israel while we were bussed to the Miromar Hotel in Aqaba. Most of us had brought our own bicycle seats and, after unbolting them, bade farewell to the machines which had done sterling service.

Finale

At Aqaba those of us not confined to bed with queasy insides had a celebratory dinner. Frances, a deaconess from Ulster, and Tom and Mary, also from Ulster, shared a table with me. "You know," said Frances, "When we arrived in Aqaba this afternoon I wanted to go and have a swim in the Red Sea, but we weren't allowed on the hotel beach in swimming costumes."

"That was a shame not to be able to swim in the Red Sea."

"Oh, it didn't stop me! I just went in fully clothed!"

"Some of the bikers went out in boats," said Tom.

"Yes, so did I," added Frances. "It was great. I snorkelled from a boat, and it was wonderful, really wonderful."

"With all your clothes on!"

"No, I had my swimming costume for the boat. The boat owners didn't mind at all."

Tom and Mary had been on Bike Ride 1994 and I asked them how their fund raising went this time round. "Great Bruce, just great. But you know, to get to Heathrow to join up with the other riders we have to fly over from Ulster which is so expensive. So I wrote to British Airways and said what we were doing and that we were raising money for a charity. And, you know, they gave us free flights to and from Heathrow!"

AT DINNER I RESTRICTED myself to soup and wine. More bikers have been affected by the bug. Jill Cooper, full of energy all day, and who had cycled with real zest, suddenly succumbed as had others. My own stomach was on edge but a bitter lemon drink settled it a fraction. The hotel waiters were busy-busy, whipping away each plate the instant we stopped eating from them. The EMMS organizers made speeches. All of us received mementos of our *Over Jordan* expedition. Tomorrow the bulk of the group will be bussed back to Jerusalem, but about thirty of us are staying on to go to the Sinai. The final lap is approaching.

Beyond Aqaba

— *Day 33 — Wadi Rum* —

Saturday 9th November

THE CALL TO PRAYER from a local mosque, resounding all over the town, woke us up at 4.30 am. I was now sharing a room with Jim, who had brought with him several bags of clothes for poor Jewish Christians in Jerusalem. When the call sounded a second time Jim grabbed the bedside telephone.

"Hello, is that the manager? I want to speak to the manager!"

There was a pause. Someone spoke on the other end.

Jim was furious. "Are you the manager? What's that racket outside? We are very tired and cannot sleep with all that noise going on. Please tell them to stop. Some of us are feeling ill and that noise is unacceptable. I am a sick man! I can't get to sleep! How long will it go on for? Five more minutes? Thank you!"

I was dumbfounded. Obviously Jim had not travelled in the Middle East before. But surely even a first time visitor was aware of Islamic culture. We settled down again to sleep. Unfortunately, the call to prayer from different mosques is not synchronized, and, after ten minutes, two more mosques started up, with the mullahs' voices booming through the loudspeakers. Jim reached for the telephone, but I was ready for him this time and grabbed it first.

"No Jim! It's the call to prayer. You can't stop it. The manager can do nothing. This is a Muslim country, and this is what happens here."

Jim did not see why he should be subjected to this, but eventually accepted that complaint was futile and went back to sleep.

At breakfast it was clear that more Bike Riders were ill with the bug. Those in the main party, and who were due to travel all the way to Jerusalem today, faced a long uncomfortable journey from Aqaba to Eilat and all the way north. It would be a difficult drive for them, especially those who were unwell. Mid-morning, we waved off the main group. Our Sinai expedition did not leave Aqaba until tomorrow, and so some of us had signed up for an expedition to Wadi Rum. We gathered in the hotel foyer where Ismael met us.

"You will be taken in Four-Wheel Drive white jeeps into the desert to see Wadi Rum, and the cost will be thirty dinars."

Andrew tried to haggle with Ismael. "Look, opposite the hotel you can hire a jeep for twenty dinars, and drive it yourself. That means four of us could go for twenty dinars."

Ismael made no concessions. "But where would you go? Do you know Wadi Rum? I offer very good jeeps with experienced drivers. And they will give you a full tour of Wadi Rum and stay for the sunset."

Andrew tried to beat him down. "What about twenty dinars each?"

"No, I will not barter. I have arranged a tour for thirty dinars. If you want it, come with me. If you do not want it, you are free to make your own arrangements."

Andrew looked around for support, but none of us were with him. Although Ismael's tour was expensive we knew it would show us what we wanted to see. One organized by ourselves could be a big disappointment. We might never have the chance again, so we were prepared to pay more to see Wadi Rum properly. Ismael then talked to us about Wadi Rum, and introduced our guide for the day, who turned out to be a Glasgow girl called Deirdre. Deirdre is a geology graduate now making a living as a tour guide in Jordan, and specializing in hiking ventures in the Jordanian desert.

Ten of us went on the Wadi Rum expedition, occupying two white Jeeps driven by two extremely courteous and pleasant Jordanians. We raced out of Aqaba and climbed up into the desert, speeding past lorries and trucks. After many miles we stopped at a small settlement. There we bought bread which an old Arab gentleman was baking in an open kiln. We watched him for a while, re-boarded the jeeps, and then roared deeper into the desert.

Where Lawrence Went

Suddenly we saw the mountains which make Wadi Rum breath-taking. I kept wanting to ask our driver to stop so that I could photograph the scene, but managed to be patient and wait until he decided to halt at a viewpoint. I had imagined that Wadi Rum would be a single canyon, but it turns out to be a multitude of canyons, each separated from the other by two thousand feet high mountains of sandstone. It was awesome to see such spectacular beauty. Lawrence of Arabia describes his approach to Wadi Rum in words which have been quoted many times since he penned them in his book, *The Seven Pillars of Wisdom*, "Our little caravan grew self-conscious, and fell dead quiet, afraid and ashamed to flaunt its smallness in the presence of the stupendous hills." A perfect description.

Deirdre filled in the historical background. "From the thirteenth to the seventeenth century Wadi Rum was popular as the home of Bedouin tribes, especially the Howitat who came from Saudi Arabia. During the Arab Revolt the mass of the Bedouin moved here from Wadi Karam which is between Jordan and Saudi. King Feisal made Wadi Rum his base in 1917 and it was there that he met Lawrence."

"So it was Lawrence who persuaded the Arab tribes to rise against the Turks?"

"No. Lawrence did not start the Arab Revolt. Shariff Hussein Ben Ali started the revolt against the Turks in 1910."

"So, was Lawrence significant at all?"

"The Arabs are grateful to Lawrence," replied Deirdre. "But for them the real hero of the Arab Revolt is Glubb Pasha. Lawrence was a complex character. His father had four daughters by his wife in an unhappy marriage, but Lawrence was one of several sons to the 'governess' with whom his father lived. Lawrence read archaeology at Oxford and, prior to the First World War, studied Crusader castles in the Middle East. In 1914 he was drafted into the Intelligence Services because of his fluency in Semitic languages. Lawrence himself was genuinely sympathetic to the Arabs and acted as an interpreter for King Feisal at the Paris Peace Conference. He felt betrayed by the settlement in which the British and French carved up the Middle East between them. But he was not a professional soldier. He never commanded any regular British Army group. And his rank of Colonel was an honorary one."

"After the War Lawrence worked on Winston Churchill's staff for a while and then—under a pseudonym—he joined the RAF. None of the regular forces wanted Lawrence of Arabia. He was too well known. He was unpredictable. And he was not amenable to army rules. But he wanted to serve. His pseudonym was soon blown when he was recognized at social functions. As David Lean's film shows, he was killed on his motorcycle."

"Accident or suicide?"

"Probably an accident. As depicted in the film, he was trying to avoid two cyclists."

"Deirdre, how reliable is *Seven Pillars of Wisdom?*"

"Well, was Lawrence at Aqaba when the Arabs took it? Or did he just give them the idea? He lost the original draft, so how accurate was the second draft? We don't know."

OUR FIRST MAIN STOP was beside the famous Hajaz railway line which Lawrence and the Arabs blew up many times. On a cliff-face, above the railway, are ancient Nabatean rock drawings, and we climbed up to examine these. From this vantage point we saw a sandstorm blowing across the desert behind us. Our driver then adjusted the power to the front wheels of the jeep, enabling us to move off-road into the sand. The two jeeps criss-crossed as each driver sought firm ground. Speed created momentum. Momentum aided progress. Wherever possible the drivers accelerated the jeeps across the sand, up slopes and over dunes. A few times we had to reverse because the sand was too soft. But, each time without fail, our driver found solid ground and we continued. Scraggy bushes grew in clumps.

"When David Lean came to Wadi Rum to film 'Lawrence of Arabia,'" explained Deirdre, "he decided that it wasn't desert-like enough. So he hired several hundred Arabs to pull out the desert bushes. He wouldn't have got away with that nowadays, but in the early 1960s conservation issues didn't exist."

The sandstone cliffs are incredible. My best description is that Wadi Rum is a desert with canyons, and flanked by a hundred sandstone mountains, each standing up out of the desert like Buachaille Etive Mhor in Scotland at the entrance to Glencoe. Our drive through the heart of Wadi Rum was a series of routes through immense canyons, and past mountains of unbelievable rocky splendour.

"I often take groups out here for climbing, and camping, and trekking," said Deirdre.

"Is the sandstone not too brittle for rock-climbing?"

"In places. But if you know where to go it's all right. But the biggest danger isn't from the climbing."

"What's it from?"

"Well, after we've been out here a couple of days a jeep comes to take the group back to Aqaba, invariably driven by a ten or eleven-year-old boy. These kids are quite put out when I refuse to accept the transport. You have to be really firm. But it's fun. You have to argue and barter everything out here. It's fun!"

OUR INCREDIBLE AFTERNOON PASSED all too quickly. We saw the natural wonder of a Sandstone Bridge. We saw huge water trucks crossing the desert to remote Bedouin camps. We explored a narrow tunnel through the sandstone to examine more cliff carvings. These were truly astonishing, with representations of camels, ibex, human feet, Islamic writing, and human figures. One was of a woman giving birth to a child. "See that one of the woman giving birth." said Deirdre. "If you had an Arab guide they wouldn't show it to you."

The sun was low in the sky when our drivers took us to an elevated point to see the sunset. The rock was black volcanic material, in contrast to the warm red sandstone elsewhere in Wadi Rum. Our drivers gathered some twigs, started a campfire, and brewed tea as we prepared for the ending of the day. I sat down on one of the rocks and wrote in my notebook:

At this moment we are in the heart of Wadi Rum. The sun is going down. All around are the sharp, vertical, sandstone cut mountains of the wadi. Ahead of us, beyond the desert foreground, are rows and rows of sharp-edged mountain ranges. Where we are, is one of the black volcanic stone mounds which protrude every so often. Our two drivers are making tea on a fire, burning wood gathered on the way. One of them has been chanting an Arabic song. The 4x4s stand silent. Modern conquerors of the desert. But camel and desert may yet have the last word in centuries to come when the oil wells run dry.

A few minutes later the sun went below the horizon, and the sky filled with deep orange-red colors. Then our drivers made for home. We were now travelling the desert in darkness, but with easy skill they powered the jeeps through canyons, past mountains, through thin lines of bushes, and across the sand. When we neared the main road the wheel-drive was readjusted for tarmac. Then, joining the highway by coming up a one-way slip road in the wrong direction, we swept back to Aqaba.

Evening in Aqaba

The thermometer in the hotel foyer informed us that the hotel had been between twenty-four and twenty-five degrees Celsius all day. After refreshing myself with a shower and change of clothes, I went back down for a cool drink from the hotel bar. The Miromar is a pleasant, plush, well-appointed hotel, and very quiet. In a sitting area off the main foyer are symbols of Bedouin hospitality: a large rug, two long-handled coffee pounders, a brass Arabic tea-pot with exaggerated pointed spout, and a hookah. A young man stands at the lift doors hour after hour, waiting for residents needing his assistance. He stands like a motionless sentinel, never moving, and is always disappointed whenever a guest chooses to walk up the stairs rather than use the lift.

Following the evening meal, we went for a walk in the streets of Aqaba. Young men walked about in pairs or in larger groups, often holding hands. On meeting in the street kisses were exchanged. Occasionally I saw a husband and wife, but they never hold hands. Our all too brief time in Aqaba has shown it to be a pleasant, quiet town with a feeling of space. While we were at Wadi Rum some of the ladies went to the market. They were made welcome, given coffee, and allowed to look around without any hassle or pressure to buy. Street-traders in Jerusalem could learn much from the politeness of the people in Aqaba.

— *Day 34 — The Village* —

Sunday 10th November

DEIRDRE CAME TO SUPERVISE our departure from Hotel Miromar. She has had extensive experience of Jordanian baggage handlers and used her considerable authority to insist that our suitcases and rucksacks were not piled on top of the bus without strapping. The Jordanian bus-driver saw no need to take these precautions.

"They will not fall! I drive so carefully!"

"No, this is not good enough. Luggage must be secured!"

"I will drive slowly, very carefully, very, very carefully!"

"No! We need another bus to take the luggage inside!"

Deirdre put her foot down. She demanded an additional bus so that people could be in one, and luggage in another. The bus-driver shrugged his shoulders, shook his head, and folded his arms. Deirdre made the appropriate phone calls, and, after another half-hour, the extra bus arrived. The first driver, who had argued with Deirdre, and who had been throwing our luggage up onto the roof with gusto, now said that his back was sore: so we had to unload the luggage from the bus roof ourselves.

Safely aboard we motored to the Port of Aqaba, two miles to the south of the town. There we went through Jordanian passport control and boarded a Hydrofoil. The Hydrofoil was large and spacious, with only a few passengers, and the crossing to Sinai was made in comfort and at speed. After docking at the ramshackle port of Nuwaybi we were now in Egypt. It took a long time to get through Egyptian passport control because an International Economic Conference was taking place in Cairo and no black-listed person was being allowed into the country anywhere. Every passport was scrutinized by a gaggle of officials. Eventually we were given visas for the Mount Sinai, St. Catherine's Monastery, area, but not for the rest of Egypt. We boarded the transport for this leg of the adventure and met our new guide, a charming young man named Amgad. On the bus was also a Tourist Policeman, who, along with Amgad and the driver, comprised the official party.

The Sinai

The intention had been to climb Mount Sinai for today's sunset: but, as our journey into the Sinai mountains progressed, it became clear this was impossible. From Nuwaybi the road climbs steeply for seventeen kilometers up mountain ridges, before the vast plateau of the Wilderness of Sinai is revealed, dotted with rugged peaks. From the bus windows we marvelled at the lunar like landscape all around us. Moses and the people of Israel wandered amongst these jagged mountains, and, although we had already seen incredible scenery during the past week, we marveled at by the primitive grandeur of our surroundings.

Amgad was keen to tell us all about the Sinai. "The word Sinai comes from the root 'Sin' which means a 'Tooth', and refers to the shape of the mountains. As you can see, they are like sharp teeth."

By the side of the road we saw a Bedouin lady, totally enclosed in black apart from the eyes. Amgad pointed to her. "The women are not covered for religious reasons, but because the husbands are jealous for their wives. In the Sinai are one hundred thousand Bedouin who are all Muslims apart from twenty-five of them who are Christians. These twenty-five are the monks at St. Catherine's Monastery who are classified as Bedouin for registration purposes."

"This is inhospitable country Amgad, how do the Bedouin survive?"

"Unfortunately, many are involved in drug trafficking and arms trading. But they are also involved in tourism, and some do farming. If a tourist gives a Bedouin one dollar for the privilege of taking his photograph, that can be compared with an average monthly income of only two hundred and fifty dollars."

LIKE TOFFIQ, OUR BUS-DRIVER hammered along the desert roads. Suddenly, high on the Sinai plateau, as we shot over a crest, a camel was standing in the very middle of the road. The driver slammed on the brakes, and we shuddered, screeched, and slewed to a halt. The camel looked at us with unconcern, and ambled slowly to the side.

"Amgad, that camel has its feet tied together with rope."

"Yes, that stops it from wandering too far away."

As in Jordan, there were few other vehicles apart from an occasional lorry. On either side were mountains, standing out of the desert sand like miniatures of Wadi Rum. Here and there Bedouin encampments appeared as black dots in a sand covered panorama. There were no side-roads, because there was nowhere for roads to go.

After many, many miles we came to a junction whose signpost indicated St. Catherine's to the left, and the Suez Canal Tunnel to the right. A series of battered oil barrels filled with sand, and painted red and white, narrowed the road to little more than the width of our bus. In the middle of the roadway a small, plastic, traffic cone blocked our forward journey. The driver stopped the bus, and an armed soldier from the adjacent army post came aboard to check our papers. Because there was an Egyptian policeman from the Department of Tourism and Antiquities with us the soldier was content to take a copy of the passenger list, which Amgad had ready for him. Normally he would have looked at each passport, one by one. The oil barrels were so arranged that the bus had to weave and snake between them. There was no possibility of a vehicle being able to bypass this control point because the terrain off-road was impossible, so this simple army check-point had total control of the junction.

The soldier left the bus, bent down, removed the plastic traffic cone from our path, and we were able to move on.

"The other road goes to the Suez Canal," said Amgad. "We have a tunnel now to cross the canal. The tunnel started as a French-Egyptian project, but two years ago it was found to be leaking so we have changed to a German-Egyptian company. Before the tunnel was built it used to take hours queueing to cross the canal by ferry. It is much better now."

A LARGE PROPORTION OF the American contingent had decided to come on the Sinai extension. I first met H.A. Penner two years previously on Bike Ride 1994. Everyone knows him as H.A, and he is the chief coordinator in the USA for the Nazareth Hospital, succeeding year after year in persuading the US government to donate several hundred thousand dollars. If you say something to H.A, he takes time, thinks it over, repeats and rephrases what you have just said, and then, in his charming American drawl, gives his reply. After a series of these exchanges he then develops the conversation. It is such an empathetic approach in getting to know someone. People soon feel at ease with this big man.

"H.A, I'm Bruce. We met two years ago."

"Hi. Two years ago? Gee, two years. How'ya doing?"

"Fine H.A, I've been on Sabbatical Study leave in Israel."

"Sabbatical Study leave? In Israel? Bruce, ain't that great!"

"The Bike Ride's been pretty tough this year H.A."

"Yeah. Pretty tough Bruce. Pretty tough."

"You know Bruce, I've brought a little bottle of wine, and some bread from that hotel in Aqaba. When we get to the top of Mount Sinai we could celebrate communion? What d'ya think about that Bruce?"

"That would be wonderful."

H.A.'s warm, friendly, inclusive personality makes him an ideal travelling companion, although all our group of thirty-strong know each other pretty well by now.

The Desert Settlement

Late afternoon we reached our accommodation, deep in the vastness of the Sinai mountains. This is five thousand feet above sea level, with the mountain summits another two and half thousand feet above us. It was definitely too late to climb Mount Sinai for sunset, and so, after leaving our luggage at the chalets, the bus took us into St. Catherine's village for a look round.

The sun was now behind the mountains, and the whole village was in shadow. It is a small, dirty, unkept hamlet. A straggle of shops tries to cater for tourists, but few visitors come to the village. We parked by the edge of what is either a dried up wadi in the middle of the village or a large open drain. A 'tourist arcade' was across the overflow, and the village cemetery was ten yards to my right. I could see mounds of dry earth in the graveyard, like miniature ancient Neolithic long barrows, with stones marking the head and the feet. There are no markings on the stones. Neither are the stones fashioned in any way. They are as they were found, when first picked up from the hillside. No writing is needed. Everyone in the village knows the graveyard layout.

Bedouin women, dressed from top to toe in black, were bringing in herds of goats which had been nibbling bushes on the bare rock slopes which jut right into the village. Nearby were men, dressed in green, or white, or fawn colored gowns and wearing colored keffiyeh. They sat on the ground against a wall, talking to one another. Other men in the village wore jeans and denim jackets. A 4x4 jeep appeared from further down the valley, and rushed past. The call to prayer sounded out from the loudspeaker of the village mosque, but no one stopped what they were doing. No one knelt. No one faced Mecca. No one acknowledged the religious summons. Perhaps some did at home, in private, or in the mosque itself, but no one did so in public.

Amgad wanted us to leave at 1.30 am in order to be at the summit of Mount Sinai for sunrise. At the evening meal I took little apart from soup. The stomach bug was still working away, but, thankfully, not enough to make me really ill. Tonight, more than at any other time in the whole five weeks, I felt far from family; and so, although it cost ten pounds for a three-minute telephone call, I asked the man on reception to dial Crieff for me, and I put my watch on the desk to ensure I got my full three minutes. Alison was in, and though it was evening in Sinai it was still Sunday afternoon back home. It was good to talk with her. Then I went to bed, with the alarm set for 1.00 am.

— Day 35 — Mount Sinai —

Monday 11th November

IT WAS PITCH-BLACK WHEN the bedside alarm went off. Apart from removing shoes and socks I had not bothered to change for bed. So I rose quickly, put on footwear, picked up the golf club, and made for the reception area. Coffee was prepared for us, and after everyone arrived we set off. Unfortunately, Flora was too ill to come on this final leg and we had to leave her behind. The bus took us as far as St. Catherine's Monastery which was reached at 2.10 am. From there, in the darkness, we walked up a valley between two high mountains. The boundary between sky and mountains was marked by a change from starry darkness to pitch darkness. Torches were needed to pick our way up the path past rocks and boulders. In the mountain valley the air was warm and balmy, and we soon caught up with other groups who were also heading for the summit to experience sunrise over Sinai.

The Ascent

Helen Whittaker from Manchester, who has been on two Bike Rides, began to feel unwell, and some of us stayed beside her, walking slowly up the mountain as the rest marched on. Every so often we passed groups of camels sitting beside the path, whose owners touted for trade: "Camela! You ride Camela! Very good Camela! Up Jebel Moses!"

Local people name the mountain Jebel Moses rather than Mount Sinai, and the camel owners are ready for tourists each day, whatever time they arrive, be it in the darkness of midnight, or at noon. Some camel owners walked beside us for fifty or a hundred yards, entreating us to ride on their camels. Then they halted abruptly and went back, possibly because they had come to the limit of their beat.

After an hour it became clear that Helen was getting weaker. We held a conference.

"Helen, we think you should go on a camel."

"No, no, I'll be all right. I'll manage."

"No Helen. It's still a long way, and you're not well."

"But I don't have any money with me."

"We'll pay for it Helen, it's only ten dollars."

We spoke to one of the camel owners who had appeared beside us, as if by magic. Helen, looking pale and tired, got on the camel. The beast lurched to its feet and lumbered forward, following its owner up the mountain. It was still pitch-black darkness, and our torches were showing signs of battery power failing, but we wanted to keep track of where Helen was. Every so often we shone our torches on the path ahead to reassure ourselves that she was all right.

Paula, Rosemary, Valerie, H.A, and I walked steadily higher. On and on, upward and upward, in the darkness. Our torches showed the stones, the rocks, and the steps cut out of the mountainside. Above us, in the brilliant night sky, we saw Orion, the Seven Sisters, and the Plough whose 'handle' pointed directly to the earth. A million, million, other stars were stunningly bright, shining strong and sharp in the Sinai darkness. We continued on and on, upward and upward: Helen still ahead of us on the camel, the five of us following behind. Beyond and above, we could see other torchlights, in groups of six and seven. Some dots of lights moving right to left, others left to right, as the path zig-zagged up the mountain.

"What's that!"

"I don't believe it!"

Out of the inky blackness, a refreshments booth, complete with temporary electric lights, appeared. An enterprising Bedouin had constructed a shed halfway up the mountain selling soft drinks and chocolate bars. We laughed at the incongruity of the situation. We had come to find the past, but Coca Cola and Rowntree's Fruit Gums had taken over the present. But we were glad of the little booth, and halted for a rest and some refreshments.

THE CAMEL PATH CAME to an end a short distance after the shop, and beyond that point there was no assistance. Pilgrims had to climb the last one thousand feet on their own. We squeezed through the herd of camels which were sitting placidly all over the path, their owners waiting for tourists to come off the summit later on. Helen was waiting for us, and feeling much stronger. The camel ride had given her rest, and chocolate from the shop had helped as well.

"The camel owner wants paid," she said.

He was standing next to her, making sure she could not disappear. I went over to him.

"Twelve dollars for ride on Camela," he said.

"No, it should only be ten dollars."

"Twelve dollars for the Camela."

"No. Look, our guide, Amgad, comes here twice a week with tourist groups, and he told us that the rate was ten dollars and no more. So that's the price! Thank you very much for your help. Here you are." We handed over the ten dollars for Helen's ride, and the man seemed happy with the deal.

ROGER APPEARED BESIDE US. He also had found the going tough and had fallen behind the main group. We were delighted to see he had his horn with him. By now we were high on Mount Sinai, and the balmy air of the valley was exchanged for the chill air of the mountains. About a hundred yards beyond the camels, we passed through a v-shaped niche in the mountainside and turned left, then slightly downhill for a short distance, before climbing again. This, we found out later, is where an alternative route from the monastery joins the main route which we were on.

The seven of us plodded upward, conserving battery power by using torches in relays. We were determined to stay together, and so we rested frequently. Roger and H.A. were having a struggle, but Helen had a new lease of life. As we climbed, more of the star-filled night sky became visible above the mountain, indicating the summit was near. The path twisted round to the opposite side of the mountain, and, quite suddenly, there were steps, cut into the solid rock, which led us straight to the top. When we reached the summit we came on it almost by surprise, and made our way past the chapel to where the rest of our group were gathered in a sheltered corner. There was still an hour before sunrise, so we settled down to wait. It was now 5.00 am.

The Summit

In the east a straight, thin, red line marked the horizon, and an orange glow began to color the black sky. People huddled together to keep warm. Paula and Helen wrapped themselves in a blanket. A cold wind blew gently over the summit. At the extreme right-hand edge of the red line we saw the neighboring peak of Jebel Katherine silhouetted against the sky. From 5.30 am. to 5.45 am, the red line lengthened, the orange glow became larger, and the stars began to fade. I thought of how Moses must have seen that sight many times as he waited on the mountain summit to hear the Word of the Lord.

Other groups, of different nationalities, arrived and waited with us. Sunrise was not clear cut, because a narrow bank of cloud masked the sun as it rose. But the whole sky began to lighten, and streaks of sunshine started to pick out the highest summits of the Sinai range. We held a short service singing, 'Be still for the Presence of the Lord' and 'Guide me O Thou great Jehovah', before Valerie read the account of Moses being given the Ten Commandments. Then H.A. produced the bread and the wine, which we shared together in a eucharistic act of communion and fellowship.

As we completed our service of worship, the cloud in the east dissolved, and the full disc of the sun appeared. In sixty seconds everything changed. From being a faint red rim, the sun became a brilliant white globe, exploding sunlight into our faces. Every jagged peak was picked out in detail as the sun shone in unrestricted splendour. It was a magnificent experience. The low angled rays of sunshine made the Mount Sinai chapel glow with color. And, because the dawn sunlight was coming *up* at us, instead of shining *down* on us, then, as people looked towards the sun, their faces were bright and shadowless, radiant in the warm light of the morning. It made me think of how Moses' face glowed when he had been in the presence of God. The darkness changed to light. The cold changed to heat. And the dead mountains became living beacons to the glory of creation.

Russian pilgrims started to arrive. One of the priests from St. Catherine's Monastery tolled the bell of the chapel for Morning Prayer. As the sound of the bell rang out over the mountains, and as the sunlight streamed across the Wilderness of Sinai, the Russians began to sing in their deep, powerful, bass voices. No words of mine can adequately express the wonder and mystery of that morning on Sinai.

One more duty to be done. I dug into my pockets for the two golf balls I had brought from home, found a discarded bottle top to act as a tee, and drove two shots from the summit rock. They were not majestic drives: in fact, H.A. recovered one of the balls and brought it back for a better attempt. But the deed was done, and with lots of laughter we took photographs of ourselves before setting off down the mountain. Jebel Katherine, the mountain next to us, and actually higher than Mount Sinai, was now in full sunlight. Amgad urged us to leave quickly, because there was still much to do today.

The Descent

All the way down we met Russian pilgrims going up, and we were astonished at how elderly some of them were. One old woman was bent double over a rock, breathing heavily and gasping with the effort of the climb. An old man was being pulled up by two helpers, and pushed from behind by a third assistant. Aged women, in Russian peasant dress, steadfastly put one foot in front of the other in a determined attempt to ascend the holy mountain of Moses. Amgad told us that in Russian Orthodox piety a pilgrimage to the summit of Sinai is as holy as a pilgrimage to the Church of the Holy Sepulchre. There were dozens and dozens of pilgrims. Later we found out that over eight hundred had come from a ship which was their base for a tour of the Holy Places. These impoverished believers had saved up for years for this opportunity to make a pilgrimage.

Priests in Russian Orthodox robes, and priests in Greek Orthodox robes, climbed together. Men, in smart office-style pin-striped suits and white shirts, accompanied women with head-scarfs who were dressed as if for a day in the harvest fields of the Russian plains. The pilgrims were obviously wearing their very best clothes for such a holy event. Some of them had plastic carrier bags and were filling these bags with twigs of sage from the bushes which grew here and there near the summit. As well as Russians there were tourists from Japan, Korea, France, and Germany.

H.A. WENT DOWN THE mountain slowly, and Rosemary and I walked with him all the way. Every so often he stopped to look up behind us at the summit chapel, which now seemed so small and so far away above us. "Gee, were we really up there Bruce? That is some height!" We came to the fork where a steeper path went directly down to the monastery, but decided to stick to the camel path because that gave a more gradual descent and less jarring of ankle and knee joints. We saw Andrew and

Paula going down the direct route, and Roger followed them. Rosemary, H.A. and I took the other path, chatting all the way.

"How did you become a Christian, Bruce?"

"I was brought up on a farm, H.A, and when I was about sixteen a new minister came to the church in the town. I went along to the Youth Fellowship for two years and argued black was white against religion. Then I came to believe. And one Christmas, I gave my life to the Lord."

"Gee, that's great Bruce. I was brought up on a farm as well. At seventeen years old I was only five feet two inches! A little runt! I was academically minded, but my folks wanted me to get out there and do farm work instead of wasting time reading books. I think they wanted me to grow bigger. Well, I'm six foot four now! But eventually I went to college, after giving my life to the Lord when I was about ten years old or so."

WE PASSED BEDOUIN WOMEN, dressed traditionally in brightly colored silk clothing, who were tending sheep and goats. On Sinai I saw absolutely nothing to give the animals nourishment. Nevertheless, somehow, somewhere, they found something to eat amongst the scree of rocks, boulders, and stones. These women were less coy about being photographed and smiled at the pilgrims. H.A. looked over at them. "You know Bruce, there is an anomaly somewhere in the Bedouin attitude to women's dress. On the one hand they are fully covered in order to be modest and avert the eyes of other men; but on the other hand they are so beautifully dressed that they attract attention."

We met up with an Orthodox priest.

"Christos Anesti! Christ is risen!" I said.

He jerked round, and replied with the Easter greeting of the Orthodox Church. For the first time I had found New Testament Greek useful in ordinary conversation.

"Are you with the pilgrim group?" we asked.

"Yes, our ship is at Port Said, and we have visited Bethlehem, Jerusalem, and the Sinai. Sinai is very, very important. It is where the holy Moses received the law. Our people have paid seven hundred dollars each for this pilgrimage."

He looked at me again. "What is that in your hand?"

"This? Oh, it's a golf club." I was reluctant to tell him that I had hit two golf balls from the top of such a holy mountain. For him it might have been as inappropriate as playing bowls in the aisle of a cathedral.

Some camel owners were resting by the side of the path. One had his cloak covering him like a tent. Others lay in the sunshine and snoozed. One young Bedouin came up to me with his camel and pointed to the golf club. He offered to give a free camel ride to the foot of 'Jebel Moses' if I gave it to him. But I declined. The club was going to be a memento back home. And then, as we neared the foot of Mount Sinai, we looked round to have one last look at the immense and awesome peaks around us.

"What d'ya think of the mountains Bruce?"

"Well, H.A, mixed feelings."

"In what way?"

"Well, these mountains are far more spectacular than our hills. No doubt about that. But yet, standing here, I realize how much I love our green Scottish hills."

"Now, that's interesting Bruce, why do you feel like that?"

"Well, I suppose our hills are greener, and have lovely streams, and have different colors and wildlife. I suppose part of it is that they are the familiar hills of home. But, you know H.A, I think that a big factor is that I can name our hills, whereas these peaks are anonymous. They look so confusing and jumbled. Awesome, but nameless."

St. Catherine's Monastery

When we reached the walls of the monastery we found Amgad, who was looking anxious. We were the last group down because the others had taken the short cut. All the rest were back at the chalets. So Amgad chartered a taxi-jeep to take us there, and we had a quick breakfast before packing our luggage into the bus which then took us back to the monastery for a proper visit.

Amgad was well versed in what we needed to know.

"My friends, St. Catherine was born 'Dorothea' in Alexandria in 294AD. She was well educated, beautiful, and part of a rich family. A Syrian monk taught her about Jesus Christ, and when she was converted to Christianity she was baptized as Catherine. During the savage persecution of Christians in the early fourth century she professed her faith and publicly accused the Emperor of sacrificing to idols. Under torture she succeeded in converting members of the Emperor's family, and after her execution her body vanished. According to tradition, angels transported it to the peak of the highest Mount in the Sinai, which now bears her name, Jebel Katherine."

"So the monastery was founded after that?"

"Yes. But, my friends, something very remarkable happened. About three centuries later, guided by a dream, monks of the monastery found her body, brought it down from the mountain and placed it in a golden casket in the church. They say that her body has remained intact and unperished, and the sweet fragrance of her remains is today a continuous miracle!"

"However," continued Amgad, "there were monastic communities in the Sinai long before the time of St. Catherine. So to say that the monastery was specifically founded in her honor is not exactly correct."

"Amgad, was this where Moses received the Ten Commandments?"

"My friends, long before the time of St. Catherine the mountain was revered as the mountain on which Moses received the Ten Commandments. So the tradition that this was the true place is deeply rooted in history. And, another point: Jebel Moses is not the highest mountain in the area, so there must have been strong reasons for it to be identified as the one."

THE MONASTERY OF ST. Catherine is surrounded by high, sand-colored walls, with rounded, castellated corner towers, giving it the appearance of a desert fort from *Beau-Geste*. We almost expected to see the French Foreign Legion riding out of its gates. Amgad told us that the monastery had been secure all through history, having been given a written promise from Mohammed, the founder of Islam, that it would be protected. Subsequently, Arab Caliphs, Turkish Sultans, and Napoleon, have all taken the monastery under their protection, preserving it from pillage. It has never, in its long history, been conquered or destroyed. Though the German scholar Tischendorff visited the monastery in the nineteenth century and discovered the *Codex Sinaiticus* which he smuggled out. Tischendorff's justification was that the monks were using ancient manuscripts as fuel for the fire!

The monastery was heaving with tourists when we arrived, packed with all the Russian pilgrims who had come down from Mount Sinai. We went first to the Charnel House and looked through a metal grille at the hundreds of bones and skulls collected there. When a monk of the monastery dies, his body is laid to rest. Then, after a year, when all the flesh has dried and decayed, his bones are collected and placed in the Charnel

House. Skulls are placed in one section, thigh bones in another, and so on. The skeleton of one of the early chief monks, Bishop Stephanos, sits clothed in his chair.

The main church is adorned with magnificent carvings and icons, and over its door is a painted frieze representing Moses, Elijah, and Jesus. Russian Orthodox pilgrims are allowed direct access to the Chapel of the Burning Bush, but others, including ourselves, have to be content with a squint through a narrow window from an outside courtyard. Most of us saw nothing through the window, as it was so dark inside the chapel. Amgad told us about the tradition which claims that the bush grew on the summit of Mount Sinai, but was brought down to the monastery for protection, and has grown there ever since. Though it is doubtful, to say the least, if the bush is the same one that Moses saw three thousand years ago, Russian pilgrims revere it as a sacred and holy relic. Nearby, we saw the letter of protection signed by Mohammed, now encased in a glass frame.

One of the twenty-five monks of St. Catherine's is from England, and Janice sought him out and gave him a bookmark which has a biblical text of encouragement. The site is only open to the public until noon. After that time the monks close its doors. At 4.00 am. and at twelve noon the monks go to the summit of Sinai to pray, every day of the year.

Heading North

We had to leave. Three of our group had to catch a plane at Eilat by half-past four. After that, the rest of us had still to get to Jerusalem. The journey was going to be long, starting in the depths of Sinai, through the Taba border crossing, past Eilat, and all the way north. As the bus sped across the Sinai plateau I looked again at the massive, naked, mountains. The terrain was primitive, primeval, and beautiful. Every so often we passed an Egyptian Army post. After a couple of hours, the driver stopped for a rest. We had had no opportunity to buy food, but we shared anything left in our rucksacks, and there was a great atmosphere of friendship and fellowship. The bus itself was cool and pleasant, but when we got out to stretch our legs, we were hit by the full force of the heat bouncing up from the tarmac.

At the Taba border crossing the three who had to catch a plane rushed through first and we last saw them hailing a taxi. It was already three o'clock, and it took a long time for the rest of us to be cleared. In the

Israeli section of the border-control I noticed that the person operating the X-Ray scanner was a trainee, and that the official training her was stopping suitcases in the machine and describing to the trainee how to interpret the picture showing on the screen. All my photographic film was in my rucksack and there was no way it could survive thirty seconds exposure to X-Rays. So I fished out the films, and asked the attendant to do a manual inspection.

"Sorry, all articles must go through the X-Ray."

"But these are just films. Look, you can see that."

"Sorry, all articles must go through the X-Ray."

I put them in the tray for miscellaneous items and hoped that the operator would not stop the tray in the machine. Fortunately, the films passed through without being halted, but, as anticipated, my main rucksack was stopped for instruction purposes. Having passed through immigration control procedure, I then discovered that my money belt, which contains passport and air-tickets home as well as cash, had disappeared. In a panic I raced back to the X-Ray machine and told the assistant. She looked around, and found it under the machine. It had slipped down between the rollers of the conveyor section.

WE WALKED OUT OF Taba border-control into Israel. Waiting for us was a minibus which was far too small to hold everyone plus luggage. Yet somehow, we pushed everything in, though, if three of the group had not gone ahead, it would, without exaggeration, have been impossible. The rest of the day was taken up with the long, long journey to Jerusalem. Hour after hour of travelling. Darkness fell half way between Eilat and the Dead Sea. We stopped at En Boqek for some food. Late at night we came over the Mount of Olives into Jerusalem itself.

We were all meant to be staying at the Beit Schmuel hostel, apart from Bruce Donaldson, the American who had been beside me in the Bedouin tent. Bruce was booked into the King David Hotel. Beit Schmuel was totally unprepared for us. The girl at the desk simply put her hands in the air, and invited us to find space in rooms already occupied by bikers who had come to Jerusalem with the main party on Saturday, and who were staying on for a few days. Twenty-one hours after we rose, ready to climb Mount Sinai, we clambered into our bunks in Jerusalem.

Postscript

Ending

On the Tuesday morning I transferred my belongings to St. Andrews's Hospice where I was going to stay until flying home on Thursday. Then I collected the luggage which James had taken to Christ Church when I left the Shoresh Group. After returning to St. Andrew's, I had a shower and a shave before setting out, determined that my last few days in Jerusalem would not be wasted. At the Bible Lands Museum, I joined up with an elderly group who were being taken round by a guide. But after an hour I realized that I was far too tired to take anything in. So I bought a copy of the guide book, resolved to study it later, and went back by bus to St. Andrew's.

The visit was not totally fruitless. At the museum the Israeli Ministry of the Environment were having an International Conference, and I persuaded the lady at the desk (who was the Minister of the Environment's personal secretary) to send copies of their report on Green Issues to Joe Leckie of my congregation who had asked me to keep my eyes open for anything to do with renewable energy and conservation in Israel. The only other information I had found for Joe were leaflets at Sde Boker about solar energy in the Negev. Back at St. Andrew's I went to bed and slept all afternoon. After the evening meal, I sat in the lounge and read a novel which I found on the bookshelf.

Wednesday

Wednesday was for photography, and the whole morning and afternoon was spent in the Old City, wandering between the Jaffa Gate, the Church of the Holy Sepulchre, the Damascus Gate, the Western Wall, and the Souk. Any map drawn of my peregrinations would have represented a tangled ball of string. There was no plan in mind, except going where the next idea suggested.

On Wednesday evening Jim McIlwraith of California, a local man from the Bible Society, gave a presentation in the St. Andrew's Lounge. He showed a video about the history of the Bible Society in Israel, explaining that in some of the Gulf States the Bible Society was not allowed to have an official office.

"Our Israel branch is part of the United Bible Societies European Section. But we are not yet independent financially, with about one-third of our budget subsidized. We produce Arabic, Hebrew and Ampari Bibles."

"Jim, are you allowed to publish in Israel?"

"Oh yes. The Israel Bible Society is a translating and a publishing Bible Society and we are proud of that, because not all national Bible Societies publish. In 1983 the Hebrew translation got an Israeli national award for its literary excellence. It was amazing to get an award for something which included the New Testament."

The Bible Society movement in the Middle East started in the nineteenth century when colporters came from Norway selling Bibles. The Palestine Bible Society was established in 1860, and a Bible Shop was opened in 1905 inside the Jaffa Gate. In 1923 the Bible Society purchased land in the city, but in 1948 had to leave Jerusalem and relocate in Haifa because of the War of Independence. Then, in 1979, it repurchased land in the Old City.

I asked a question. "Jim, I hope you don't mind being asked this, but do you find that you relate more to the Jewish or the Arab population?"

"Bruce, there are really two Bible Societies in Israel. One is Arab. The other Israeli. But we work together really well because we have found our real identity in our relationship with Jesus Christ."

"One of the exciting things recently is the use of video. We took the 'Jesus' film to two hundred Chinese workers near Be'er Sheva. These are people from rural China who come for one or two years' work in Israel, and they stay in a compound with nowhere to go and nothing to do when off-duty. Well, two hundred of them crammed into this hall, and we video-projected the film onto a big screen. Their response was amazing. At the trial and crucifixion scenes they became real verbal, shouting at the injustice, and expressing outrage! They really took it in. Hopefully the seed of the gospel will find fertile ground in their hearts."

Homeward

On Thursday morning I made sure all my luggage was packed, booked a Cheroot taxi-bus to take me to Ben Gurion Airport in good time for checking in, then spent the remaining hours in the Old City. At the Western Wall several Bar-Mitzvah celebrations were taking place.

At Ben Gurion, booking in was straightforward, though I was taken aside and asked a long series of questions; not surprising since I was on my own and had been travelling in Israel, Jordan, and Egypt. As the aeroplane took off into the night sky above Tel Aviv, I put on head-phones, selected an audio-channel of country and western music, closed my eyes, and settled back into the seat for the long flight home. In five weeks I had seen so much. I had heard so many voices. I had been challenged by big questions. I was leaving to return to my home: safe, secure, peaceful. Back there, down there, Arab and Jew, Christian and Muslim, what did the future hold?

As the mountains are round about Jerusalem,
So the Lord is round about His people,
From this time forth and for evermore.

Lightning Source UK Ltd.
Milton Keynes UK
UKHW021523011021
391503UK00007B/159